D0558445

GUATEMALA

TYRANNY
ON TRIAL

GUATEMALA
TYRANNY ON TRIAL

Testimony of the Permanent People's Tribunal

Preface by George Wald

Introduction by Marlene Dixon and Susanne Jonas

Edited and translated by
Susanne Jonas, Ed McCaughan
and Elizabeth Sutherland Martínez

Synthesis Publications   *San Francisco*

Copyright © 1984 by Synthesis Publications
All rights reserved. No portion of this book may be reproduced, by any process or technique, without the express written consent of the publisher.

Library of Congress Cataloging in Publication Data

Permanent People's Tribunal of the International League
   for the Rights and Liberation of Peoples.
   Guatemala—tyranny on trial.

   Hearings held in Madrid, January 27-31, 1983.
   Includes index.
   1. Civil rights—Guatemala—Addresses, essays, lectures.
2. Terrorism—Guatemala—Addresses, essays, lectures.
I. Jonas, Susanne Leilani. II. McCaughan, Ed, 1950-
III. Martinez, Elizabeth Sutherland, 1925-
IV. Title.
JC599.G8P47   1984   323.4'9'097281   84-17359
ISBN 0-89935-032-1
ISBN 0-89935-024-0

Published by Synthesis Publications
2703 Folsom Street, San Francisco, CA 94110

Printed in the United States of America
10 9 8 7 6 5 4 3 2 1

The editors wish to recognize the unique contribution of Marlene Dixon, Research Director of the Institute for the Study of Labor and Economic Crisis and editor of its journal, Contemporary Marxism. *It was she who immediately initiated and arranged for an English edition of the proceedings of the Permanent People's Tribunal session on Guatemala, when she attended it in Madrid. Without her energetic dedication to breaking the wall of silence about Guatemala in the United States, as a step toward changing U.S. policy on Central America, this book would not exist. That dedication is informed by a worldview expressed in the Introduction which she co-authored: a worldview that understands why the fate of Central America is crucial to bringing peace and self-determination not only in the region but to all the world's peoples.*

ACKNOWLEDGMENTS

The editors wish to thank the following people for their contribution to this book. Their work not only made it possible to complete a project of considerable magnitude; it is also an important contribution to public understanding of events in Guatemala, the Americas, and the world at large.

María del Carmen Victory of the Institute for Political Studies of Latin America and Africa (IEPALA), Madrid, the sponsoring institution of the Tribunal on Guatemala, who was Coordinator of the session, and Gianni Tognoni, Secretary General of the Permanent People's Tribunal, for their encouragement and assistance. In particular, we thank them for facilitating permission to publish this English edition of the proceedings.

Professor Richard Falk of Princeton University for his painstaking care in checking the English version of the Tribunal's lengthy Judgment for accuracy in its legal terminology and references.

Staff members and colleagues of the Institute for the Study of Labor and Economic Crisis, in particular Suzanne Dod, Magally Huggins, Ana María Marini, Esther Madriz, and Rebecca Schwaner for their work on the translation—a massive and challenging task.

Richard Schauffler, Janja Stanich, and Jean Taylor for editorial assistance. Chris Engemann, Laura Ingram, and David Westerhold for assistance in transcribing the English translation from tapes. Jane Armbruster, Colin Bonnycastle, Tom Cooper, Kathryn Davenport, Richard Geitzen, Bob Gould, and Don Hickerson for their work on indexing the book.

The Guatemalan Human Rights Commission, USA, and Reginald Norton of the Washington Office on Latin America for assistance in clarifying terminology and historical details. Steve Richardson for providing tapes of some of the proceedings. The Guatemala Relief Project for graphic assistance.

Cover photo: Courtesy of IEPALA

Design: Vanda Sendzimir

A Note to the Reader

The proceedings of the Permanent People's Tribunal on Guatemala followed a careful and thorough format in which expert witnesses gave overview presentations on various topics, followed by eyewitness testimony by individuals that corroborated and amplified the presentations. Expert witnesses usually submitted two versions of their material, one long and one short, sometimes with additional evidence; other written material was also submitted. All in all, the Tribunal proceedings were voluminous.

With the goal of reaching as broad an audience as possible—particularly in the United States—and at a price that most readers could afford, the editors have sometimes abbreviated or synopsized the text. Also, the presentations included in this volume are almost always the shorter, not the longer, version of what was submitted to the Tribunal. The order of the proceedings has been rearranged somewhat, for clarity and accessibility of information.

The full program of the Tribunal's proceedings may be found in the Appendix of this volume. The complete proceedings, including the longer versions of presentations, have been published in Spanish by IEPALA of Madrid under the title *Tribunal Permanente de los Pueblos: Sesión Guatemala*, in 1984.

MEXICO

BELIZE

EL PETEN

HONDURAS

EL SALVADOR

ALTA
VERAPAZ

IZABAL

HUEHUETENANGO

EL QUICHE

TOTONICAPAN

BAJA
VERAPAZ

SAN
MARCOS

SOLOLA

ZACAPA

EL
PROGRESO

JALAPA

CHIQUIMULA

SANTA
ROSA

JUTIAPA

RETALHULEU
QUEZALTENANGO
SUCHITEPEQUEZ

ESCUINTLA

CHIMALTENANGO
SACATEPEQUEZ
GUATEMALA

GUATEMALA

Contents

Intellectual Life

U.S. Complicity

On International Law and Guatemala

III THE TRIBUNAL'S JUDGMENT

APPENDIX

Preface
by George Wald

What is going on in Guatemala holds a mirror up before the American people, our history, and our government. There is no dearth of such mirrors; but Guatemala will do.

The U.S. government constantly talks democracy without ever defining what it means. In present parlance, democracy is equated with periodically holding elections. They need not involve any meaningful choice. The ritual exercise of letting—even making—people vote is enough. Guatemala offers an exemplary instance.

The U.S. government is leading what it calls the free world. That now includes the largest collection of military dictatorships ever assembled. By now our government clearly prefers complaisant military dictatorship in the Third World to any other form of government. It supports such dictatorships when offered, and otherwise produces them. Guatemala offers a fine example.

For democracy is in its very essence unreliable. It has built-in mechanisms for change. The government requires a popular base and must respond to its needs. The government must to some degree serve its own people in preference to a foreign sponsor. That is much less desirable than delivering its people for foreign exploitation. And that is what military dictatorship is about. The business is not to serve, but to control its people. At a price the foreign sponsor is glad to pay.

Our government takes some trouble to get the controlled and exploited to like these arrangements. It wants to win their hearts and minds. So in these Third World countries—though not at home—it is for land reform, a particular structure of land reform whose slogan is "land to the tiller" and whose guru has been Roy Prosterman, Professor at the University of Washington in Seattle.

It has been tried in Vietnam, the Philippines, and El Salvador, in all three places accompanied from the start by a program of repression and assassination, the point of which is to exterminate all peasant leadership ("dissolve the rural infrastructure") and block all attempts at peasant organization. In Vietnam this was the job of the Phoenix program, which killed some 20,000 persons; in Marcos's Philippines it was martial law; in El Salvador it was the "state of siege." To the public it is called land reform, by the governments involved it is called rural pacification.

Guatemala once tried land reform without an accompanying terror (under President Arbenz, in 1952); but our government quickly stopped that, as we shall see. It has not been attempted since. Its last dictator but one, Ríos Montt, who ruled during our Tribunal, instituted terror without land. In his three years of special officer training in the U.S., he had absorbed well the lessons of Vietnam. He set out to turn Guatemala into a pattern of strategic hamlets under army command and free-fire zones. The slogan was "Beans and Guns." Families that turned themselves in to the army, leaving their homes, fields and villages, were promised protection (from the army!) and beans; others were fair game. What that meant, as our witnesses who had survived army attacks told us, was almost indescribably brutal.

Coming out of a previous Permanent People's Tribunal, on El Salvador, I had a question about the terror—a question to which I found the painful answer in testimony given before the Tribunal on Guatemala. That question was: how does one—that is, how do these governments—get peasants in uniform to do things to peasants out of uniform that essentially deny their own humanity? How can we explain the phenomenon of indigenous peasant-soldiers in Guatemala forcing an entire village to watch them tear apart, often literally, a dozen peasants who have been identified as "guerrillas" or "guerrilla sympathizers"? Witnesses at the Guatemala Tribunal gave us the key: from the moment they are impressed into service, these indigenous peasants are systematically destroyed as Indians and as peasants, and reconstituted as new, zombie-like creatures, capable of such dehumanizing actions.

The Tribunal made it impossible for me, as an American, not to confront the sad realization that our government speaks in the name of democracy but in fact prefers military dictatorship to all other forms of government in the Third World, no matter the human cost. And if military dictatorship is not the spontaneous outcome, the U.S. government will destroy democracies—as it did the Arbenz government in Guatemala—in order to create such dictatorships. This is the reality that we, as Americans, must fight to change. There is no more powerful example than Guatemala.

Cambridge, Massachusetts
June 1984

Introduction
by Marlene Dixon and Susanne Jonas

In January 1983 in Madrid, Spain, the Permanent People's Tribunal held a three-day session on Guatemala, whose proceedings are presented here in English. As the U.S. editors of this book, we have two purposes. First, and most obvious, we feel the urgency of making available to American and other English-language readers the testimony of the Guatemalan people. Specifically our main objective is to expose the harsh truths about the Guatemalan military dictatorship originally imposed and continuously supported by the U.S. government. At this stage of the crisis in Central America and in Guatemala, it is essential that citizens of the United States be informed about the human consequences of 30 years of U.S. interventionism in Guatemala. Thus we hope to break the wall of silence in the U.S. press and the U.S. Congress concerning the U.S. role in the brutalities of the Guatemalan dictatorship. It is our desire in this way to contribute to the struggle against U.S. intervention that is central to the struggle for the sovereignty of the Guatemalan people.

In regard to the struggle for popular sovereignty, the contribution of the Permanent People's Tribunal is unique. Going beyond violations of the rights of individuals, it directly addresses violations of the most fundamental rights of entire peoples, in this case the violation of the right of the Guatemalan people to self-determination, which is largely a consequence of U.S. intervention in its various forms.

Our second concern, which we shall address in this Introduction, forms part of the theoretical framework within which we understand the significance of the Tribunal. The rise of the revolutionary movements and the struggles for popular sovereignty in

Guatemala (and in the rest of Central America) are occurring simultaneously with the global decline of American power. Indeed, it is one of the most striking realities of the contemporary world that the U.S. government, armed to the teeth, has been unable to retain its imperial hegemonic control through indirect means, political or military, in the underdeveloped countries of Central America. Today U.S. hegemony, established at the time of the Monroe Doctrine, is being fundamentally challenged, even within the Western Hemisphere, and the U.S. stands to lose the last bastion of its empire in Central America. This reality has profound implications for the peoples of the U.S. and the entire hemisphere, and gives much broader importance to the struggles in Central America today.

Within this context, as we shall see, the phenomenal statistics on repression and exploitation in Guatemala can be understood more fully. For they represent not simply the wanton, brutal actions of the Guatemalan security forces; they are the violent, desperate thrashings of an entire system of U.S. imperialism in decline.

I. THE PERMANENT PEOPLE'S TRIBUNAL AND THE STRUGGLE FOR POPULAR SOVEREIGNTY

The Permanent People's Tribunal, as is explained in the first selection of this book, is an international "public opinion tribunal" that has taken its place in the tradition of similar initiatives in the Western world, beginning with the International Military Tribunal of Nuremburg. Founded in 1979 as the successor to the Bertrand Russell Tribunal on Latin America, the Permanent People's tribunal is a permanent body that organizes sessions on particular countries. It is organized around the concerns established by the Russell Tribunal: "The systematic violation of the fundamental freedoms of entire peoples—the right of every people to self-determination, to their culture, and to the exploitation of their own natural resources...principles which have been impressed on the international conscience over recent decades thanks to the anti-colonialist and national liberation struggles of the third world."

In its 1983 proceedings on Guatemala, the Tribunal provided, at one level, an international forum—one of the first in recent times—for a public hearing about the realities of the war in Guatemala. This war was set into motion by the United States 30 years ago when it intervened directly, militarily, to overthrow the democratically elected, reformist, and nationalist government of Jacobo Arbenz, and to install a permanent counterrevolutionary military dictatorship. The realities of this war, which has raged year in, year out, virtually since 1954, were graphically exposed in the Tribunal proceedings, which brought together 19 witnesses from Guatemala, 13 witnesses presenting "expert testimony," and 15 leading intellectuals, parliamentarians, theologians, and international legal experts who were on the Tribunal jury.

Guatemalans from all walks of life—peasants, labor leaders and organizers, revolutionary priests, former army personnel, university professors, writers, refugees—all spoke eloquently and convincingly about their direct experiences of terror, repression, and resistance. The picture they painted in the three days of testimony at the Tribunal stands as a profound indictment of the successive Guatemalan military regimes. What became clear from the testimony is that we are witnessing today the consequences of the 1954 U.S. intervention in Guatemala. The incessant bloodshed unleashed by that violent interruption of a democratic process, the permanent polarization of forces, are unparalleled anywhere in Latin America. Indeed, now that Washington is seeking a Guatemalan equivalent of Christian Democrat José Napoleón Duarte in El Salvador, as a cosmetic facade to hide the sordid truth of Guatemala, such a person is extremely difficult to find—very literally because there is no "middle ground." Nearly all moderate opposition leaders have been killed in cold blood, one by one, over the years. The same is true of all areas of civilian life. Among trade unions, as Uruguayan writer (and Guatemala Tribunal juror) Eduardo Galeano asked rhetorically, "Would Lech Walesa be alive if he were a union leader in Guatemala?"

Further, in a country where more than half of the population is Indian, increasingly the reign of terror has taken the form of genocide in the strict sense of the word, i.e., "actions perpetrated against members of a group with the intention of totally or partially destroying a national, ethnic, racial or religious group as such." These policies involve a view of the indigenous population which reduces them to subhuman. The charge of genocide was made at the Tribunal by revolutionary priest Ricardo Falla, taking as his example the San Francisco massacre, where village members were killed not simply for being guerrilla sympathizers, but for being Indian—including children below the age of reason.

Over all, by the calculations of numerous observers and human rights organizations, more than 100,000 civilians have been assassinated by government and right-wing forces from 1954 to the present. With slight variations, the statistics on "disappearances," assassinations, torture, etc., have remained constant or increased over the years. Thus, the Council on Hemispheric Affairs, for example, reported in December 1983 that the Guatemalan government was for the fourth consecutive year the worst violator of human rights in Latin America (a stigma shared with the government of El Salvador). New techniques may be introduced, such as "scorched earth" policies and village massacres under the Ríos Montt regime, but they are only new "efficiencies" in the war of the government against its people.

This explains the continuing relevance of the Permanent People's Tribunal, which focused much of its particular denunciations on the regime of Efraín Ríos Montt, who happened to be in power in January 1983. As of July 1984 there is a different set of generals in power, headed by Gen. Oscar Mejía Víctores (and indeed by the time this book is published, there may be a new regime). Repression and terror may rise or fall by two tenths of a percent, but there is no real change. In essence we are dealing not with any one particular regime so much as with a system that has been institutionalized.

Beyond exposing the mechanisms through which this system operates—an essential task that a number of international human rights organizations have patiently and relentlessly taken on—the Tribunal went a step further. True to its mandate to deal with the rights of an entire people, and specifically their right to self-determination, the Tribunal jury drew the logical conclusion of its deliberations in its "Sentencia" or "Judgment."

The Judgment points to a basic contradiction of the present system of international relations, the contradiction that, despite its adherence to respect for human beings and peoples in principle, "present international relations are still dominated by processes and structures in which only states and the interests they represent have both voice and weight." As a way of overcoming this contradiction, the Tribunal Judgment proposes to accord official status as belligerents to the organizations of the Guatemalan people, in order to give the Guatemalan people a vehicle to directly denounce the criminal and outlaw nature of the Guatemalan government—that is, to destroy the fiction that the Guatemalan people are represented by the Guatemalan state. In this regard, the Tribunal carries on the tradition developed at the time of the great decolonization movements, which broke through the mystification of the colonial powers attempting to treat the affairs of the colonies as their own "internal affairs," and through which the liberation movements were recognized as subjects of international law.

Thus the Tribunal in its final disposition declares that, "In the face of the perpetration of the above-mentioned crimes by the public powers of the Guatemalan government, the Guatemalan people, through their representative organizations, have the right to exercise all forms of resistance, including that of armed force, against tyrannical government powers; and that the use of armed force by the Guatemalan government to repress the resistance is illegitimate."

II. WHAT IS AT STAKE IN GUATEMALA

The magnitude of the crimes of the Guatemalan state cannot be fully understood outside the context of 30 years of U.S. intervention in Guatemala; and this interventionism, in turn, must be understood as part of the changing dynamics of U.S. imperial hegemony from the post-World War II era to the present. The most salient particularity of U.S. interventionism in Guatemala is the fact that the U.S. ruling class felt compelled in 1954 to

militarily overthrow the democratic, reformist—nonsocialist—
Arbenz government. Why? Because that government dared to
challenge the dictates of U.S.-based corporate interests, most particularly the United Fruit Company, which was affected by
Arbenz's 1952 land reform law—and whose law firm in
Washington happened to include the Dulles brothers, respectively
Secretary of State and head of the CIA at the time. Even this
slightest show of nationalism and sovereignty from the Arbenz
government was intolerable to U.S.-based corporate interests and
the U.S. government because, in its practice and as an example
to other nations of Latin America, the Arbenz government had
opened up the possibility of progressive governments acting in
the interests of their people, in an area that had been controlled
by foreign interests for decades.

In short, then, the U.S. government was prepared to oppose
any regime in Latin America which might make trouble for U.S.
investors. Further, the U.S. was not prepared to tolerate a regime
that conceded power to worker and peasant organizations, setting in motion a process of radicalization that (from Washington's
perspective) could clearly get "out of control." The Arbenz government also refused to submit blindly to Washington's dictates in
foreign policy—an unpardonable sin at the height of the Cold
War. Finally, it served as a powerful example to progressive and
democratic forces throughout the hemisphere.

The U.S. was so threatened by the least show of humanity
and independence in a Central American government that it intervened directly in 1954 to overthrow Arbenz and install a brutal
fascist dictatorship. Jeane Kirkpatrick, as an apologist for the right-
wing Reagan administration, calls such dictatorships
"authoritarian"; we call the Guatemalan regime fascist because,
while there is no movement among the people to support the
government, the brutality of its repression and the genocidal
policies it pursues most resemble the fascist government of the
German Nazis under Hitler. Furthermore, it is the establishment
and maintenance of such regimes by the U.S. that leads us to term
U.S. counterinsurgency foreign policy as *fascist:* it demands the
defense of its capital interests by insisting that agents, such as

the Guatemalan dictatorship, imposed naked, terrorist bourgeois rule to suppress working-class and peasant struggles.

The U.S. intervention in Guatemala in 1954 was successful in its immediate goal of imposing in power and maintaining a counterrevolutionary state that has lasted for 30 years. From a longer-range perspective, however, the "success" of this intervention must be questioned—for it has generated opposition and armed resistance by the Guatemalan people, which the U.S. has been able to counter only through the most massive programs of military and economic "assistance" and through repeated direct or indirect interventions. During the period 1966-1968, for example, the U.S. direct (though limited) presence was necessary to crush the growing guerrilla movement; U.S. involvement at that time included massive military assistance to Guatemalan police and army forces, as well as the creation of the system of right-wing paramilitary death squads based in the official "security" forces. Once having created the infrastructure or apparatus of the Guatemalan counterinsurgency state—which, having developed under the direct tutelage of Washington and under the conditions of modern neo-imperialism, developed into a neofascist state—the U.S. maintained a high level of direct involvement through 1977. At that time the U.S. Congress, responding to pressures from the American public, forced the Carter administration to declare a ban on military aid and sales to the Guatemalan government: the human rights violations of the Guatemalan government were too extreme and the U.S. responsibility for this situation was too clear. More recently, in January 1984, the Reagan administration resumed military aid to Guatemala. Acting unilaterally, without congressional approval, Reagan sold Guatemala the helicopter spare parts it so desperately needed—spare parts that make functional the U.S.-supplied helicopters used routinely in government bombing attacks on Indian villages and other civilian targets.

From the 1960s to the present day, a constant of U.S. policy in Guatemala has been its similarity to U.S. policies in Vietnam at the height of the U.S. war there. In order to smash the 1966-68 guerrilla insurgency, the U.S. military turned Guatemala into a kind of laboratory for counterinsurgency in Latin America, transferring all the latest technology from Vietnam — napalm, radar detection devices, etc. Green Berets and other advisers and combat forces trained in Vietnam were sent to Guatemala (and vice versa). Torture methods strikingly similar to those used by the Green Berets in Vietnam were applied by Guatemalan security forces.

More recently, in the counterinsurgency offensive of 1982, the Ríos Montt regime employed brutal techniques that also are best known to the world from the U.S. war against Vietnam: "scorched earth" policies (burning crops, forests, and entire villages to "pacify" areas out of control — one is reminded of the U.S. forces using cigarette lighters to torch entire villages in Vietnam; indiscriminate, village-wide massacres of children, women, and men; forced relocation of populations into "strategic hamlets" to clear out guerrilla areas; and so on. The appearance of Vietnam-type techniques under Lucas García and even more intensively in the pacification programs of Ríos Montt (who received his counterinsurgency training in the U.S.) corresponds to a specific U.S. plan, developed in the mid-1970s — the "Program of Pacification and Eradication of Communism" — which was publicly exposed by Elías Barahona, who served as press secretary for the Ministry of the Interior from 1976 to 1980.

Since the 1960s, the brutality of U.S. counterinsurgency in Guatemala has resembled Vietnam in yet another respect: In Vietnam, the Phoenix Program, which was by design a U.S. program of terror and torture, was justified in the name of rooting out and eliminating "the enemy," i.e., the guerrilla organization. In fact, however, this program, supposedly directed at selective targets, turned into a program of generalized and indiscriminate terror against the population who served as the base of the guerrilla organization. In exactly such a fashion, the U.S. counterinsurgency war in Guatemala, carried out locally by a U.S.-created neofascist state, has thus far been unable to destroy or defeat the resistance forces and has become a war of terror against entire sectors of the population.

From the foregoing, we must ask the obvious question: Why

has the U.S. government been compelled to maintain an interventionist stance in Guatemala, despite the fact that 30 years of intervention and institutionalized terror has generated ever-increasing instability and popular rebellion? A number of explanations are conventionally given to account for the level of U.S. intervention in Guatemala: its size and population (the largest in Central America); its resources (oil and nickel) and a relatively high level of U.S. private investment in industry; its location on the southern border of Mexico; geopolitically, as right-wing strategist Edward J. Walsh put it, "If we are to defend our interests in the region, the way to do it is to buttress the strong links [i.e., Guatemala] in order to protect the weaker ones."

No doubt, these factors are considered important by U.S. policymakers, but they do not get to the heart of the matter. The fundamental issue in Guatemala, as in Latin America over all, is popular sovereignty vs. the ability of the transnational corporations to continue their uninhibited looting of an entire continent. This issue is brought to a head in Central America today because that region is the last bastion of the American empire. A fairly rapid process of political and economic decline, which began with the U.S. defeat in Vietnam, has been yet further accelerated by the ideological extremism, military aggression, and political incompetence of the Reagan administration. Reagan's economic and nuclear arms policies have caused serious strains with the NATO Alliance. The U.S. only retains isolated pockets of influence in Asia—one of them being the largely discredited Marcos regime. In the Middle East the U.S. has been reduced to little more than an arms merchant following the rout in Lebanon and Arab refusal to enlist Reagan's support in resolving the current Persian Gulf conflict.

More generally, the decline of U.S. power is manifested in the international isolation and political delegitimation of the U.S., as well as the loss of economic domination over the capitalist world. A telling example and reflection of the decline of U.S. political/ideological hegemony worldwide is in fact the inability of the U.S. today to control the United Nations or other international political forums—and the inability of the U.S. to lay claim to representing or preserving international law or international peace, as it once did in the postwar era. Today, it is the U.S. that is defying international law (from the World Court on down); and it is the Third World nations and movements for popular sovereignty that are the foremost advocates of strengthening international institutions in defense of the principles of sovereignty and self-determination. In this context, Latin America and particularly Central America at this moment represent the only part of the globe where the U.S. retains much maneuverability, and even here U.S. influence is increasingly limited. The Reagan administration is determined to hold on in Central America, even at the risk of a major global confrontation.

The prospect of a revolutionary Guatemala is intolerable to the present U.S. administration and threatening to any U.S. regime as yet another indicator of the failure of U.S. hegemony in the world-economy. Guatemala is central to what is left of U.S. imperial policy because it is a key nation in part of an entire region that is undergoing revolutionary upheaval. Viewed as a whole, there exists in Central America today the potential for a bloc of nations independent of the U.S.—a revolutionary bloc that could challenge not only the national power of the U.S. but also, ultimately, the indirect dictatorship of transnational capital (if these countries were able to unite and act as a bloc, for example, in debtor cartels, to refuse to continue payments on the staggering foreign debt).

Furthermore, the revolutionary upheaval in Central America, and particularly in Guatemala, threatens the stability of Mexico, which, along with Canada to the north, serves the ultimate strategic purpose of providing a buffer along U.S. borders. The United States could be thought of as an island, bordered by the Pacific and Atlantic oceans to the east and west, by the vast expanse of Canada to the north, and by an unstable Mexico to the south. A bloc of revolutionary nations in Central America, which could act in concert politically, militarily, and economically, would potentially place an inimical power on the southern border of the United States. This is certainly one of the key factors that has led the U.S. government and dominant sectors of the national and transnational ruling class to raise such a furor over tiny El Salvador, and will most likely lead them to absolutely draw the line in Guatemala.

At the domestic level, since Vietnam, the U.S. government has not had support from the American people for its interventionist schemes of the type being risked in Central America. Still very much alive today is the Vietnam Syndrome—the fear of yet another senseless destruction of human life and ruthless looting of the domestic economy to support a U.S.-created, neofascist counterinsurgency state through the direct deployment of U.S. troops. Such fear of, and therefore opposition to, U.S. military intervention abroad persists despite intense propaganda efforts by the U.S. government, as has been consistently shown in public opinion polls. The fact is, the opposition of the American people is the most immediate brake on Reagan's military interventionism abroad, and in the case of Central America, it has been a crucial factor in restraining the Reagan administration from carrying out its most aggressive plans in the region.

Unlike the situation in Guatemala in 1954, and the Dominican Republic in 1965, the U.S. in Central America today faces a popular challenge so great that even direct U.S. military invasion will most likely only create another Vietnam, another no-win intervention. Therefore, if the U.S. government refuses to adjust to new realities, it will be reduced to a desperate course of military action, a policy of inflicting damage for the sake of inflicting damage and making victory as costly as possible to the revolutionary forces. This was done in Nicaragua prior to the Sandinista victory over Somoza, when the U.S. allowed the war to be prolonged well after Somoza's demise was apparent, and in the years since the 1979 revolution, when Nicaragua has had to face U.S.-orchestrated economic and military sabotage and destruction. Such is the bloody sword the U.S. can hold over the Central American peoples—but it is essential to understand that this danger is an indication and a result of U.S. weakness, not U.S. strength.

But there is yet another danger. If the U.S. intervenes directly in Central America, it will not be able to confine its intervention to one country—nor necessarily to the Central American region. Hotspots of U.S. interventionism such as Central America are the most likely detonators of a broader confrontation, including possibly a nuclear confrontation, with the Soviet Union and the socialist bloc. Indeed, such a prospect has not been so likely since the Cuban missile crisis in 1962. Therefore, it is important for American readers to understand the stakes in Guatemala and generally in Central America in the broadest possible terms. From this perspective, stopping a desperate, direct U.S. military intervention in the region becomes a question of our own survival and the survival of humanity worldwide.

We firmly believe that in their basic instincts, the great majority of the American people—like people everywhere in the world—are opposed to war and profoundly desire peace and humanity. It is our hope that in bringing to American readers the testimony of the Guatemalan people and information about the brutal role of the U.S. government, we may contribute to the realization of this overwhelming desire for peace in the region. The policies of the Reagan administration (and of all U.S. administrations since 1954) toward Guatemala do not represent the will of the American people; the U.S. government, acting on behalf of the transnational corporations, is in fact the enemy of the American people as of the peoples of Central America. A new U.S. policy that reflects the desire of Americans for peace is our hope for building a truly human society in Central America and in the U.S.

July 1984   *Marlene Dixon and Susanne Jonas*

ISLEC delegation to the Permanent
People's Tribunal on Guatemala

About the
Permanent People's Tribunal

The Permanent People's Tribunal is a public opinion tribunal that has taken its place in the tradition of similar initiatives in the Western world, beginning with the International Military Tribunal of Nuremburg. This Tribunal was followed by the Tribunal of Tokyo, which judged the Japanese war criminals; the Russell Tribunals on Vietnam (I), on Latin America (II), on the "Berufsverbot" in West Germany (III), and on the indigenous peoples of America (IV); and the Delgado Tribunal that judged the crimes committed by the PIDE in Portugal during the regimes of Salazar and Caetano.

In contrast to these tribunals, which all had certain specific contexts, the Permanent People's Tribunal is a permanent body. It was founded on June 24, 1979, in Bologna, Italy, by the Lelio Basso International Foundation for the Rights and Liberation of the Peoples. The foundation is an organization for study and research, established by Lelio Basso, who was president of Russell Tribunal II on Latin America.

At the closing of that Tribunal, he and his collaborators recognized the need to continue the analysis they had been preparing during the Russell Tribunal's three years of existence. The Tribunal on Latin America had established the violation of human rights in Brazil, Uruguay, Bolivia, Argentina, and Chile, and had begun to arrive at the conclusion that widespread torture, the disappearance of thousands of citizens, and the unpunished murders of members of the opposition to the dictatorial regimes in these countries could not possibly be the result of actions initiated by lone executioners or small groups of killers. Torture, when it is practiced in proportions reaching the point of genocide, becomes a method of government.

This Tribunal was able to demonstrate exactly how multinational economic groups and foreign governments pressure the regimes of these countries to maintain a sociopolitical system that permits exploitation—often to the point of total control—of the countries' natural resources. The conclusion of the Tribunal on Latin America was that there is systematic violation of the fundamental freedoms of entire peoples—the right of every people to self-determination, to their culture, and to the exploitation of their own natural resources. These are basic principles, which have been impressed on the international conscience during recent decades, thanks to the anti-colonialist and national liberation struggles and to activities by the countries of the Third World in the United Nations and other international bodies.

What was missing was the codification of these principles. For this reason, on July 4, 1976 in Algiers, a group of experts on international law who had collaborated in the Russell Tribunal on Latin America formulated the Universal Declaration of the Rights of the Peoples. This statement was to provide a firm basis for the battle to bring international public law up-to-date. The Declaration of Algiers became the political-cultural reference point of the Lelio Basso International Foundation, which was established a few weeks later. The Foundation, in turn, created two organizations to plan and organize the practical work with respect to problems that had been dealt with on an individual basis. These organizations are the International League for the Rights and Liberation of Peoples, now established in seven countries, and the Permanent People's Tribunal.

The Permanent People's Tribunal organizes its sessions at the request of groups that are publicly neutral in political matters or political groups united in a common program sufficiently broad to be able to guarantee the greatest possible representation. The Tribunal has its own statutes and carries out its work under the rules contained in these statutes, based on the principles of the Declaration of Algiers, as well as other international agreements and rules of international public law. When the Permanent People's Tribunal sits in session, the accused must be invited to send their representatives or written material to defend their position.

The Permanent People's Tribunal is composed of 56 members chosen from eminent personalities in the fields of culture, art, science, and politics, among them various Nobel Prize winners. For each session, a minimum of seven members are convened. The verdict or judgment of each session is delivered to the International League for the Rights and Liberation of Peoples. As a nongovernmental organization with advisory status to the Economic and Social Council of the U.N., the League guarantees that the maximum amount of information reaches the international organizations and governments represented in the U.N. The verdicts of the Tribunal, thanks to its rigor in judicial matters and its impartiality, are today published and studied at various North American and European universities.

The Permanent People's Tribunal previously held sessions on the Western Sahara, Argentina, Eritrea, the Philippines, Afghanistan, East Timor, El Salvador, and Zaire. From January 27 through January 31, 1983, it held the session on Guatemala in Madrid.

Presentation by the Permanent People's Tribunal

Petition by the Guatemalan Human Rights Commission

The session on Guatemala of the Permanent People's Tribunal was convoked in response to a petition from the Guatemalan Human Rights Commission (Comisión de Derechos Humanos de Guatemala, CDHG). The petition summarized the facts of the situation in Guatemala, particularly the systematic violation of human rights and acute repression that the Commission had observed. It called for recognition of the Guatemalan people's right of insurrection and concluded with the text below.

CONSIDERING:

1. That the people of Guatemala are undergoing severe violations of their political, economic, social, and cultural rights.

2. That the representative system has been denied, since popular elections are practically non-existent and governments are fraudulently and illegally installed by the army and the ruling sectors.

3. That the existing rule of law is violated with absolute impunity, thus creating a state of fear and insecurity resulting from the unjust and arbitrary behavior of our present rulers.

4. That social crisis and repression have worsened alarmingly since the coup d'état, and that the army of Guatemala and its representative, General Ríos Montt, are both guilty of the crime of genocide and crimes against humanity, committed against the people of Guatemala from March 23, 1982 until now.

5. That this situation legitimates the right of the people of Guatemala to defend themselves, even by means of insurrection,

and to attain their liberation and establish a democratic government that represents their interests and satisfies their just demands.

THEREFORE, considering what has been stated and considering that in Guatemala there exists a situation of violation of human rights, the Guatemalan Human Rights Commission, based on the relevant precepts of the Universal Declaration of the Rights of the Peoples approved in Algiers on July 4, 1976; on the Universal Declaration of Human Rights proclaimed by the United Nations; on the Fundamental Declaration of the Inter-American Commission for Human Rights of the Organization of American States; and on other relevant legal instruments, asks the Permanent People's Tribunal to consider the following petitions:

1. That a meeting specifically to examine the case of Guatemala in relation to the violation of human rights suffered by the Guatemalan people be held.

2. That this meeting, if possible, take place in Madrid, Spain, during the second fortnight of January 1983, since we consider that date and that location to be the most appropriate.

3. That once all the hearings have taken place, including that of representatives of the Government of Guatemala as the accused entity, and that once all the testimony, documentary proof, and other pertinent evidence have been examined, that a verdict of guilty be given against that government directly responsible for the violations of human rights in direct detriment to the people of Guatemala.

We offer to submit to the Permanent People's Tribunal all the studies, witnesses, reports, and other evidence necessary to establish the deeds that we have denounced.

For the Guatemalan Human Rights Commission
Adrían Sandoval Monroy, President

Mexico D.F., July 25, 1982

I

PROFILE
OF
GUATEMALA

Presentation
By the Prosecutor

Edelberto Torres-Rivas

The presentation of Torres-Rivas, leading Guatemalan social scientist and scholar who now lives in exile in Costa Rica, was entitled "Introduction to the Profile of Guatemala."

This is a general, introductory presentation to the problems that define and explain the nature of the Guatemalan crisis. The documentation that follows, on specific aspects of the situation, will clarify what can only be indicated here and I would refer the reader to it in case of questions.

THE POLITICAL CRISIS AS A VIOLATION OF HUMAN RIGHTS

The profound crisis in Guatemala today began in 1954 with a brutal violation of human rights and of the norms that govern relations between neighboring countries. At that time, the democratic government of Jacobo Arbenz was destabilized by the covert hand of the U.S. government, backed by the Honduran government and a group of high Guatemalan military officers. This was one of the first victories for "the Company"—the CIA.

After 1954, the crisis took on political and civic dimensions, with violations of civil rights that had been established in the national Constitution and proclaimed by the Universal Declaration of Human Rights. The military governments that followed Arbenz's fall from power applied political hatred and revenge as norms of conduct. For example, the government of Colonel Castillo

Armas (1954-1957), which led the counter-agrarian reform, forcibly dislocated 100,000 peasants from the land they legally owned and worked. In the years following 1954, there was a constant trampling on the human rights of life and safety, justified by the old excuse that order is preferable to progress.

Yet the ruling class did not in fact achieve order. Internal conflicts and power struggles made political life in Guatemala unstable for the first 12 years after Arbenz's fall, from 1954 to 1966. One plebiscite was held, in which the winner—the only candidate—was assassinated by a conspiracy of friends 28 months later. This was followed by two fraudulent elections; one successful military coup d'état, which overthrew a constitutional government; and cancellation of the electoral process. Finally, there was a military dictatorship that lasted a thousand days.

During this period of struggle within the dominant class, not only were the ballot boxes stuffed, demonstrations were machine-gunned (as in March and April of 1962), and eight military-civilian conspiracies attempted. Trade-union leaders, students, and politicians were assassinated, illegal prisons were built, and thousands fled the country. The internal crisis of the country's leadership always occurred in a political environment of extremely limited or non-existent democracy, so that the only options were the intrigues, conspiracies, and putsches. The masses of Guatemalans were completely removed from these struggles and never permitted by the government to regain the organizational levels attained during the Arbenz years.

Again and again, attempts were made to freely and democratically create political organizations and trade unions; to establish a climate in which one could think freely and express one's ideas. These efforts were futile, and were openly smashed by what we call the "counterrevolution." The fact that the defeat of 1954 had been tremendously antidemocratic was repeatedly proven and reconfirmed whenever attempts were made to legally organize the people.

After the March 1963 coup d'état, which blocked national elections, there was no longer any room for democratic or gradualist aspirations. The search for social change—for economic development and political democracy—was forgotten or put aside. In the 1960s, reformist projects and illusions collapsed.

It was at this point that popular armed struggle emerged as the only alternative: the obligatory use of force as a response to force. The first wave of guerrilla action tested not only the will of the masses, but the repressive capacity of the state. But the weaknesses of the *foquista** tendencies of that action facilitated the defeat of the armed movement.

The response of the regime was to develop counterinsurgency operations, modeled after the tactics of the U.S. forces in Vietnam. In the wake of the Cuban revolution, "Operation Guatemala" was put into effect, a sinister form of political surgery to defend U.S. security.

Looking back 20 years, the counterinsurgency operation was a brutal and disproportionate response to a series of social and political problems. Sheer force was seen as the only way of mitigating the social crisis (which for the first time took the form of armed protest), and it received hearty approval from the ruling groups. The incipient guerrilla struggles provided the state with the opportunity to develop its own particular defense of the system. The national army helped to implement that defense, based on the "logic" of counterinsurgency, which defines a political rival as an internal enemy to be eliminated.

That rationale is grounded in a Manichean vision of society and its conflicts, and backed by an ideology that was propagated throughout the world during the Cold War era: anticommunism. It is not necessary here to describe in detail this absurd rationalization—of a state policy and its consequences—by which citizens of opposing political views are transformed into internal enemies and defined as such. This is the triumph of death as a justification for order.

Since the mid-1960s, the deadly logic of counterinsurgency has inspired every step the Guatemalan state has taken. But, as with Cain, peace is not achieved by fratricide. The crisis-ridden

---

*The concept of the *foco* as a guerrilla center of operations, designed to politicize the local population and create the subjective conditions for struggle through guerrilla actions. — Eds.

institutional power of the state was not stabilized. The political
and social life of the *entire* society, however, was completely
destabilized.

This is a phenomenon worth emphasizing. The struggle for
"democracy" led to an unleashing of the most antidemocratic
methods; "order" has been imposed through the use of a fratricidal
violence that has fatally disorganized the country. In Guatemala,
the dominant groups—a fluid alliance between the medium-sized
industrial bourgeois fraction and the agrarian bourgeois fraction,
along with the upper strata of the army—bear a historic responsibility for the violence and disorder that reign today in the society.
They are the executors of a will that must be judged objectively.
It is not the subjective aspects of the actors that interest us, but
rather the results of their behavior: permanent violence, the use
of fear as a means of social control, and the constant and barbarous violation of human rights. And here, by human rights,
we refer to the right to live and work with a minimal level of
guaranteed safety and predictability.

The result of these long years of state violence and popular
struggle has been the formation of a particular kind of state power,
which is a product of the crisis but is unable to resolve that crisis.
In Guatemala we are faced with a State of Emergency *(estado de
excepción)* of a counterrevolutionary nature, which not only fights
armed rebellion with the tools of counterinsurgency but also uses
them to develop its general policies.*

These circumstances have created a central state power that
is strong in appearance only. The true nature of its power, its intrin-
sic weakness, lies not so much in its lack of social support—which
it probably does not need—as in the poverty of the resources with
which it dominates society: the permanent and indiscriminate
use of violence, the inability to respect its own legality, and absolute
intolerance for any sort of dissent.

---

*The reader will find both State of Emergency *(estado de excepción)* and State of Siege
(estado de sitio) used in the proceedings. The terms are essentially synonymous. *Estado
de excepción* is a somewhat more generic term, but both refer to the imposition of
measures that involve the suspension of rights (at the same time, they are not the
equivalent of martial law). It was specifically an *estado de sitio,* State of Siege, that
the Ríos Montt regime decreed in July 1982. —Eds.

The last pieces of this repressive structure were put in place during the government of Julio César Méndez, a lawyer who in 1966 was named the civilian president of a military government. It was thus proven once again that the important question is not who is president, but which social forces lead the state. Méndez was elected as the opposition candidate, with promises of democracy. While in office, he used the techniques of counter-insurgency and gave us the first governmental application of planned terror.

Thus, in 1966, the *second* wave of terror began, which continued during the government of Carlos Arana, a natural representative of the military and political forces that mobilized the counterinsurgency operation. General Arana can be seen in exactly the same light as Somoza II of Nicaragua, in the sense that neither did anything to stop the violence, while at the same time making off with veritable fortunes in public funds. Arana was part of an alliance, which still functions today, between an adventurist fraction of the bourgeoisie and corrupt military officers. This alliance reached pathological proportions with the government of the Lucas-García-Granados group.

We can distinguish between the first wave of terror, which took place during the 12 years following the coup of 1954, and the second because direct violation of human rights and repression were relatively less frequent during the first period. They were usually carried out by the police, took place during times when the reforms of Arbenz were particularly frightening to the ruling class, and showed signs of revenge.

The major protagonists of repression during the *second* period were the paramilitary groups created by the army and some businessmen, with the aid of the armed forces and U.S. advisers. Political crimes, the disappearance of opposition leaders, and the deaths of innocent people all increased notably. The Arana government was responsible for the death or disappearance of approximately 7,200 Guatemalans, according to journalistic statistics.[1]

For those not familiar with this obituary, it will be difficult

---

1. This statistic should not be confused with the number of Guatemalans killed between 1966 and 1970, when Arana was national head of counterinsurgency.

to understand, but a *third* wave of terror began in 1978 that was qualitatively different from the previous ones, although based on the same techniques. It began as soon as the government of General Romeo Lucas García and his team took power, and continues today, under the leadership of the born-again Christian, Efraín Ríos Montt. This third period saw the growth of armed mass resistance, and the target of the repression was the heart of the resistance: the Indian peasants, whose participation was assumed to be total by the army. Between April and November of 1982, the tactic of "scorched earth" *(tierra arrasada,* or razed land) was used. Between 28 and 32 collective massacres of indigenous villages, with no regard for age or sex, were recorded. The destruction of villages, harvests, and people in several areas of northwest Guatemala marks a new phase in state violence: open warfare against the civilian population. This is the distinguishing feature of the third period—war against civilians, not against guerrillas, as the highest stage of counterinsurgency.

The recent history of Guatemala shows us that state terror cannot be used to solve the problems of a developing society. During the 1970s, a mass movement appeared, unlike anything before. It was nationalistic, independent, and radical. Along with the guerrilla movement, it tested the militarized state's capacity to respond.

Throughout the short years of its existence, the popular movement has changed in its class structure, its demands, and its methods of struggle. Between 1973 and 1980, it went through a broad range of ideological and political/organizational experiences. We can offer a short list here, in chronological order: 1) the teachers' strike of 1973 (National Teachers Front, Frente Nacional Magisterial), supported by 19,000 teachers throughout the country, which forced the Arana government to negotiate; 2) the march of the Ixtahuacán miners, who walked to the capital and led a demonstration there of 150,000 people; 3) the February 1978 strike by public workers (Emergency Coordinating Committee of State Employees, Coordinadora de Emergencia de los Empleados del Estado), which shut down nearly the entire public administration; 4) the urban uprisings of October 1979, when urban transport fares were raised, led by the National Committee of Labor Union

Unity (Comité Nacional de Unidad Sindical, CNUS) and the Council of State Employees (Consejo de Entidades de Trabajadores del Estado, CETE), resulting in an insurrectional situation; and 5) the February 1980 agricultural workers' strike that paralyzed the 16 sugar mills on the Pacific coast and ended with a popular victory, despite the climate of sheer terror.

The role of the CNUS, the Peasant Unity Committee (Comité de Unidad Campesina, CUC), the Autonomous Guatemalan Federation of Unions (Federación Autónoma Sindical Guatemalteca, FASGUA), and other labor organizations in the leadership of these struggles cannot be explained in this paper. More than 45 trade-union leaders, who belonged to these organizations, were assassinated in 1981 alone. The political parties played a minor role, both the extreme right parties and those which try to represent a democratic and progressive centrist option. The left has not had a legal organization since 1954.

In sum, it is no exaggeration to say that the last two generations of Guatemalans have been born into and have grown up in a backward and decaying society, the result of counterinsurgency techniques being converted into a method of government. Generally speaking, in modern history, periods of crisis have provoked moments of violence that can be explained more by their peremptory nature than by their effectiveness. But our experience has been one of constant terror, 365 days a year for 20 years. It gets increasingly intense, but always has the same goal: internal order with no popular participation. The result of this state violence has been a postponement of the solutions so urgently needed for the serious social and economic problems affecting the majority of the population.

THE STRUCTURAL ROOTS OF STATE TERRORISM

The social and economic problems plaguing Guatemala are not the fruit of stagnation of the productive forces. On the contrary, they originate in the very nature of economic growth in the country. This is the effect of a "development style" concerned exclusively with the accumulation of profit. The interests of domestic and foreign private enterprise show no consideration for what can be termed the national or popular interest. Guatemala's economic growth during the past 25 years has been important, and much of the current situation cannot be understood without taking the economic factor into account.

One important development in this respect was the establishment of an industrial sector (final assembly of semi-finished goods) after the post-World War II era. This industrial development was made possible in part by earnings from coffee in the 1960s, which notably improved the gross formation of investment capital. But the most important factor was the opportunistic redefinition of foreign investment.

U.S. capital, which since the beginning of this century has owned the banana plantations and the basic services (railroads, ports, electricity, telegraphs, etc.), began in 1955 to reorient its investments toward the manufacturing sector. In 1980, U.S. direct private investment was $226.7 million, enough to control 34 of the 40 largest firms in this small country.[2] Today, however, this direct investment is less important in light of the financial credit of private U.S. banking in Guatemala. The predominance of finance capital, through various types of loans, is a new feature in the web of national dependence vis-à-vis the international market. The assets of the eight largest U.S. banks in Guatemala were $331.9 million on June 30, 1981.[3]

Industrial growth led to increased economic activity, social diversification, and a more complex stratification of the country. But there was a disproportionate social and political cost, because of the way in which industry was established and expanded. The "spillover" capacity of that growth could not cure the ailments of an agrarian society and only created serious new problems associated with the beginning of industrialization. Not

2. Of the 44 largest U.S. firms in Guatemala, 20 started off by buying Guatemalan firms. See Tom Barry, Beth Wood, and Deb Preusch, *Dollars and Dictators, A Guide to Central America* (New Mexico: The Resource Center, 1982) pp. 36, 41ff.

3. John Purcell, "The Perceptions and Interests of U.S. Business in Relation to the Political Crisis in Central America," in Richard Feinberg, (ed.), *Central America: International Dimensions of the Crisis* (New York: Holmes & Meier Publishers, Inc., 1982), p. 114.

enough new jobs were created to alleviate the chronic hidden unemployment, and the new capital-intensive industry brought open and widespread unemployment. (It is an error to say that the industrial process *creates* unemployment; it does attract and create jobs, but not to the degree necessary.)

To encourage the rapid accumulation of capital, private enterprise was granted concessions that included exemption from certain taxes, free use of foreign currencies for imports, and cheap, easy credit. State policy was placed at the service of private wealth, thus accelerating the tendency toward concentration of income into the hands of a few and monopolization of the means of production. In addition, the industrialization process in Guatemala involved the control and repression of the labor movement, with forms of exploitation taken from the era of "primitive capitalism."

Although no one could responsibly associate economic industrialization with political democracy, nonetheless it is true that in the contemporary process of capitalist growth, the creation of wealth *cannot take place* at the cost of increasing poverty, especially if, as in the case of Central America, domestic manufactured goods are aimed toward the national market. I say "cannot take place" because the state takes on the role of directing and promoting the process. This is how it happened, in our case, but the promoting was in only one direction. The state shamefully abandoned its leading role and let the "invisible hand" of the market act freely.

This method of industrialization and its effects can therefore be termed contrary to the objectives of political democracy. They strengthen the monopoly sector too much, and weaken the defense mechanisms of the labor force, increasing poverty both qualitatively and quantitatively. First- and second-class citizens are produced, and there is a tendency toward exclusive and monopolistic control by state power and the violent dictatorship of capital.

Thus the culture of repression finds a new source of energy. The experience of other societies shows us that political democracy goes along with a reasonable dose of democracy on the shop floor. Relations between workers and management should be mediated by the courts and the law, not by the police, with increasing attention given to the conditions in which the work force lives and reproduces itself.

But the so-called "social question," as a human and political problem, never appears on the agenda of a violent and repressive culture. Only in a democratic and participatory structure can there be the necessary sensitivity and opportunity to solve the many social problems that are inherent to capitalist growth. The environment created by counterinsurgency destroys this sensitivity and in a thousand ways favors the superexploitation of the Guatemalan working class, converting it into a cheap, abundant, and obedient commodity. It should be emphasized here that this process has met with extraordinary opposition from the Guatemalan proletariat, small as it is.

Today, the industrial sector is in crisis, a victim of the same factors that stimulated it in the 1960s. The Guatemalan "businessman" benefited from the broadened common market trade agreements, but the country grew to depend on its sales to the rest of Central America and did nothing to improve economic demand in its own domestic market.[4]

Since 1975, the crisis in Central America's economic integration has worsened. Interzonal trade has dropped by more than 40%, and the industrial sector is practically paralyzed. Industrialization was based on the disproportionate use of foreign raw materials and semi-finished products. The classic cases of import substitution—substituting imports for other imports—and the "wrap and pack industries" contributed to worsening the balance of trade deficit and created an enormous foreign debt. [Import substitution arose from the partial substitution of imported goods by nationally produced ones, which meant substituting some imports for others, since it was still necessary to import intermediate goods needed to make these consumer goods. —Eds.]

In the past 25 years, important changes have taken place in agriculture, the country's primary sector. The tendency to export agricultural products grew, although Guatemala moved from the

---

4. There was, in fact, a tacit agreement between industrialists and landowners *(terratenientes)* to expand industrial consumption horizontally. Hence the social limits of the market, today in a deep crisis.

sole export of coffee and bananas to a more diversified trade. Paradoxically, coffee production has doubled since 1945, and traditional agricultural production has been modernized and diversified with cotton, sugar cane, and cattle. The banana plantations disappeared slowly, leaving in their place small growers who work for Del Monte, which took over the interests of the United Fruit Company.[5] Agriculture is still the major source of jobs and foreign exchange for Guatemala.

Yet the development of agricultural capitalism has not favored the modernization of national political life. We have already mentioned a few results in relation to the political crisis and democracy. The effect of years of agriculture for export, which began during the period of the liberal republic, has been an extraordinarily heterogeneous social and economic structure.

Agricultural production for the international market did not create the necessary conditions to stimulate the rest of the agricultural sector, which produces basic grains for the people. Thus a structural differentiation was established, with distinct and, at times, complementary functions. The export capitalist economy grew, and enjoyed the technical and economic resources that the state and foreign capital offered it. But agriculture for local consumption declined, relegated to the worst land in the *minifundista* (small farm) economy. The technological level was low, and no cheap loans or state assistance were available.

Agricultural capitalism functioned for a long time in Guatemala because the relation between the large property owners and the peasant economy did not require the export economy to transfer the profits of its growth to the latter. On the contrary, the value of the rural work force and the value of the reproduction of the *national* work force were supported by the low costs (below value) of peasant supply.

This system, whose problems have always been apparent, ended with the appearance of serious deficiencies in the food supply. The small farm economy could not increase its produc-

---

5. United Fruit, as a banana firm, no longer exists. Its new incarnation, United Brands Co., has at least three outlets in Guatemala: Numar (oils and margarine), Polymer (plastics), and Unimar (marketing, etc.).

tion, and the state preferred, for example, to import corn. The combination of population growth and the exhaustion of easily grown agricultural products created difficulties that were magnified by the international economic crisis. It cannot be said that the low price of export goods in and of itself caused the crisis; rather, it was a cyclical process that demonstrated—for the last time, we hope—the inherent weaknesses of the agro-export model and the extreme vulnerability of our economy. But the real scenario of the crisis was not the price of coffee; it was the human condition of the peasants who produce it.

In the past, internal imbalances were hidden during periods of expansion of foreign trade; at the same time, the condition of the peasants slowly worsened. With each negative cycle, rural poverty grew. Today, the structural agrarian crisis cannot be forgotten, even when coffee prices bring in foreign exchange. One can no longer responsibly treat it as only a question of economics or of land. It is now a social issue, whose solution lies in power, in politics, in political struggles that are class struggles for control of the state. The time for reforms is past; land reform today makes sense only with reference to state control.

The Third Agricultural Census, carried out in 1979, was never published by the Guatemalan government. The results confirm what everyone knows to be true: the poverty/riches ratio gets worse every day, and the government has done nothing to alleviate it.

Number and Size of Agricultural Units
(in hectares* and percentages, 1964-1979)

	No. of Lots				Area			
	1964		1979		1964		1979	
	Number	%	Number	%	Hectares	%	Hectares	%
Total	417,344	100	610,346	100	3,448,735	100	4,207,864	100
Minifundio	364,879	87	547,574	90	641,631	18	678,308	16
Family Unit	43,656	11	49,137	8	650,071	19	776,083	19
Latifundio	8,809	2	13,635	2	2,157,033	62	2,753,473	65

Source: Agricultural Census D.G.E. Official terminology is used to differentiate the types of landholdings. The *minifundio* is a unit with less than 7 hectares. The *family unit* has between 1.4 and 44.8 hectares. The multi-family units, called *latifundios* here, are units of more than 44.8 hectares.

*A hectare is equal to 2.47 acres.—Eds.

The chart showing the number and size of agricultural units is self-explanatory, but even so we would like to emphasize certain points in relation to the increase in the area controlled by the *latifundista* sector as well as the increasing subdivision of the parcel economy. Despite the fact that it was clearly manipulated, the census could not hide the impact of these numerical data.

The *minifundio* category that we are using includes two types of landholdings: the *micro-fincas,* of less than 0.7 hectares, and the so-called sub-family units, of between 1.4 and 7.0 hectares. The change in 1979 is that the number of *micro-fincas* belonging to peasants who no longer live off the land grew from 85,093 parcels in 1964 to 250,918 parcels in 1979, and the average area of the parcels dropped from 0.37 hectares to 0.23 hectares.

This is the result of the free growth of capitalism in rural areas. From a social and political point of view, a very polarized social structure is produced. Throughout these years, a small but powerful modern agricultural bourgeoisie has been formed; it has never abandoned its large landholdings (which permitted the construction of the modern agricultural industry) nor its backward relations with the peasantry. Modern technology has not altered these social and labor relations, which are authoritarian, paternalistic, and poorly remunerated. In the flatlands, the result is a certain semi-proletarianization of the peasantry, who are trapped in a situation of permanent transition. The peasant is brutally impoverished, without losing his ties to the land or to agricultural work, and unable to become a permanent waged worker.

This structural situation has for years fed the social and political crisis in Guatemala. It breeds a situation in which despotism reigns in civil life and savage authoritarianism rules political life. Only by changing this form of capitalism will state terrorism come to an end, allowing a democratization of the country.

CONDITIONS FOR DEMOCRACY IN GUATEMALA

There are many reasons why democratic life has been impossible in Guatemala. We have already pointed out the long-range effects of the landholding system. The heritage of colonialism did not end with independence: we refer to the aristocracy, to the series of privileges to be enjoyed or not, according to one's skin color or last name, and to the existence of a comfortable or luxurious life at the expense of the nonpaid labor of the majority. The abundance of land and labor (and anti-vagrancy laws when needed by international demand) facilitated the creation of the *latifundio.* The liberal state, which can also be called oligarchical, was profoundly antidemocratic in its relations with the peasantry. The original accumulation, which began with the creation of the coffee economy, constituted a successful and constant offensive against traditional property rights, including the system of communal lands.

These events, which occurred at the end of the 19th century, continued on into the 20th century, and not even during the democratic period of 1944-1954 was the situation really altered. With Arévalo and Arbenz, capitalist development was stimulated, even though the methods were less despotic for the peasantry. After 1954, forced labor was not reintroduced because it was no longer historically feasible, but inequalities of social wealth were intensified during a period of relative modernization backed by the authoritarian practices previously described.

The interests of foreign capital, and particularly U.S. capital since the end of the 19th century, have not favored the construction of a democratic political system. Rather, those interests have allied themselves with sectors of the oligarchy that defended the traditional order. The rich participatory traditions of the United States, the democratic customs upon which that nation is based, had no room in Central America. The presence of the United States in the region was premature, but there is no doubt that it has acted as an absolutely antidemocratic force and supported the most conservative forces in our society. Both in the past and more so in the present, American foreign policy not only supports military dictatorships; it also seeks to eliminate democracies. It is a policy based on a conception of U.S. military security. We understand that democracy is not established in a country from abroad, as occurs with industry. But in our tragic experience, what has been imported is sophisticated technology for repression, the military ideology of security, and a Cold War atmosphere. Fascism, as someone once said, can only come from the outside.

However, internal factors play an even greater role. The external influence allowed the unimaginative copying of political models that were hard to assimilate in the absence of social forces that give them life. The concept of the constitutional separation of powers, for example, was not allowed to prosper. What did emerge was a strong, arbitrary, and personalized executive power with ritual legislative functions and dependent judiciary personnel.

The characteristics of a liberal democracy—parliament, political parties, an independent press, citizen control over government organs, and, especially, citizens' participation—are the result of a long and difficult process. In other countries, that process is often incomplete but is always the result of political struggles that end in a victory over absolute power. Constant vigilance is the price of liberty. Democratic culture always comes from the triumph of the majority and always expresses popular participation.

The struggle for democracy is thus a primary objective in the Guatemalan revolutionary program, with the understanding that it will be achieved only by means of a thorough reorganization of society and the destruction of the material and ideological forms that have favored dictatorship, violence, and segregation of peoples.

The ideology of the coffee oligarchy, which permeates the entire Guatemalan culture, must be broken. Part of this dominant ideology is *racism,* a deep contempt for the indigenous population, its values, social life, and culture. Not only are class divisions the source of social discrimination, but racial discrimination is used as well, based on colonial values that justify its practice.

The coffee republic (which ended with the fall of the dictator Ubico in 1944) founded its material progress on the revival of colonial labor practices, using indigenous peasants. The ideology of the liberal oligarchy was not liberalism at all but rather an anti-indigenism that denied basic civil rights to the country's natural inhabitants. Racism was present in every situation where domination was manifest or reproduced: the workplace, the church, the school, the family, interpersonal relationships, etc. And from then on, racism has pervaded our society as a series of conscious or unconscious practices, as a widespread prejudice against a large portion of our national population.

The Guatemalan crisis is therefore also a crisis of the dominant ideology, the ideology of racism. It is not enough to denounce its material bases without denouncing its daily manifestations as well. The liberation of the Indians will not resolve the peasant "question," but it will overcome the cultural, ideological, and spiritual subordination currently suffered by the Indians. The struggle against racism is the foundation of the struggle for democracy, and the liberation of the Indian from cultural oppression is the guarantee of majority participation in the construction of their own future. One should not forget that the indigenous population is a majority of the nation's inhabitants.

In our struggle for democracy, we are fighting a state of emergency that has taken on the form of a military dictatorship and has been unable to defeat a popular armed movement. We believe that no authoritarian structure can reform itself internally so as to achieve democracy, that is, without popular participation. The transition from the current military dictatorship to a liberal-democratic state is impossible in Guatemala if that transition is conceived of as an *internal* regeneration. Elections—a purely symbolic formality—cannot democratize a social and economic structure that produces violence *on a daily basis.*

The counterrevolution has tried to decimate the country's moderate forces, who have suffered through years of anticommunist terror. Political parties and other social forces capable of forming a democratic political *center* cannot participate in a process that has been created by state violence. The slow and gradual modification being instituted in South America, with varying degrees of success, is not likely to occur in Guatemala. In other words, a "democratic opening" led by those who have assassinated thousands of Guatemalans would be a fraud, a historical mockery, and impossible to accept.

Beyond all of these considerations, today and every day, there is a question that embodies both anguish and determination.

Societies do exist whose political structures and national economies can provide a moderately just, democratic, humane, and independent existence for their citizens. Can we assure such a society for our generation or for our children?

On the Role of
the United States and Israel

Guillermo Toriello Garrido

Guillermo Toriello has served as Foreign Minister of Guatemala under the governments of Arévalo and Arbenz (1944-1954), as Ambassador to the United States and to the Organization of American States, and as head of the Guatemalan Delegation to the United Nations. At the Tribunal, he delivered a written presentation on Guatemalan history, which is not included here for reasons of space, and also made an intervention in which he discussed U.S. domination of Guatemala. The following comments are from the transcribed tape of that intervention.

I come here, honorable members of the People's Tribunal, to accuse U.S. imperialism and the government of Israel, because they are directly responsible for the crimes being committed in Guatemala. It is not possible to find guilty only the perpetrator of the crimes inside the country. Who gives impulse to those crimes? Why does the United States do it? Why does Israel do it? What objectives do they seek in maintaining the system of domination in the region? That is fundamental, because if we examine only what happens in Guatemala, the crimes committed by the army, we would think that it is something patently national, and that is not the case.

The key is the policy of economic and political domination that the U.S. wants to maintain in the Central American area, an area it considers vital to its hegemonic interests in the region. That is the truth of what is happening in Guatemala and in El Salvador, as well as the attempts to destabilize the government of Nicaragua.

Speaking historically, how did imperialism penetrate Guatemala, what was the October Revolution, and why was it overthrown? At the beginning of the century, the U.S. imposed on Guatemala a cruel tyranny that governed the country from 1898 to 1920. During this period, the United Fruit Company made its entry and in addition established a subsidiary railroad company. Electric Bond and Share Company also came in to take over the electrical energy of the country. Thus, three companies could operate as a supranational government in Guatemala.

The government of Estrada Cabrera was overthrown by a popular movement in 1920; the United States opposed the new government because, from the moment that it achieved power, it refused to recognize the joint contracts imposed by the United Fruit Company and the U.S. Department of State. Therefore, the new government was overthrown by a military coup. Later the U.S. and the corporations imposed another general, Ubico, who governed the country for 14 years. The regime of Cabrera had lasted 22 years; add on 10 years with other generals and 14 years of Ubico. This totals 46 years of tyranny in Guatemala, supported by the U.S. Department of State.

It is important to note the situation that existed throughout Central America in 1944. In power in Nicaragua was the father of the Somozas, Anastasio Somoza García, who assassinated Sandino for driving the U.S. Marines out of Nicaragua. In power in El Salvador was General Maximiliano Hernández Martínez, who assassinated Farabundo Martí and also committed genocide against 32,000 peasants [Augusto Sandino and Farabundo Martí are the leading figures and heroes of the revolutionary struggles in their respective countries. — Eds.] In Honduras there was Tiburcio Carías, the repressor of banana workers. And in Guatemala there was Jorge Ubico. According to the U.S., during that period we were "banana republics," a tranquil term to cover the plunder of our riches and our national resources. But a populist movement, led by teachers and students, succeeded in overthrowing General Ubico. I can say with pride that I was among some young professionals who participated at that time.

A military triumvirate, again supported by the U.S. Department of State, also attempted to establish itself in power with General Federico Ponce. But people from the streets who were armed, together with a group from the army, overthrew them on October 20, 1944. Thus began a revolutionary process (the October Revolution) that was bourgeois democratic, nationalist-patriotic in the defense of national sovereignty, agrarian, and fundamentally anti-imperialist. When we took power, the transnational corporations even owned the lighthouses of Guatemala's ports, as well as all of the railroads and all international telephone and telegraph communication. This was the situation in the country; it was practically not our country. But in 1944, in a democratic spirit, we began to pass laws that favored the great majority; the dignity of workers was respected, the vote was given to women, a constitution was written that was very advanced for that epoch. We exercised a pluralist democracy that allowed all liberties.

Then a confrontation developed over the contracts with foreign business, which were supposed to run until the year 2009 without the corporations paying a single tax. We thought that the contracts needed to be re-examined. And what happened immediately? The U.S. Department of State became very upset; the new situation in Guatemala disrupted the whole scheme for political and economic domination, setting a poor example for the other peoples of America. The U.S. response was to accuse Guatemala of being a communist country, a threat to continental solidarity and to the peoples of the area, as well as a threat and a danger to the Panama Canal and to the oil wells of Texas. This came out with eight-column headlines in all the newspapers, feeding the U.S. hysteria that Guatemala was going to destroy the United States. Thus was created the climate for the U.S. to intervene in Guatemala. This was also the period of the Cold War; the U.S. had been blackmailing its allies with the atomic bomb. The alignment of forces was such that the socialist camp had very few votes in the United Nations. Guatemala was completely isolated.

I have a document that I wish to submit to the Tribunal. Written by two American journalists, Stephen Schlesinger and Stephen Kinzer, it is called *Bitter Fruit*—bitter for the United States because its prestige was undermined. But here are the fundamental facts, obtained under the Freedom of Information Act. With documents from the CIA, the Pentagon, the U.S. Marines, and the FBI, the authors show how the U.S. intervention took place, how this infamous act was planned, how special experts were brought in for the intervention. It shows how the media, which exist to transmit the truth, were prostituted in order to transmit lies day and night about the situation in Guatemala, accusing us of enormous crimes that were completely false.

Two decisions were taken by the U.S. to finish off the Guatemalan revolution. The first was diplomatic intervention, the second armed intervention. The diplomatic intervention occurred at the 10th Conference of Caracas in 1954, where I had the honor of representing the Guatemalan delegation as Foreign Minister. I opposed a U.S. resolution which aimed to destroy the inter-American system. In essence the resolution gave the right to all the governments of the hemisphere to act collectively and to attack "any country in Latin America whose institutions were infiltrated by international communism," applying the existing treaties, the Treaty of Rio. This resolution was presented to the delegations and passed with only the abstention of Mexico and Argentina and the opposition of Guatemala. This resolution is so dangerous that today, in Nicaragua and El Salvador, the U.S. wants to apply it in order to make other countries accomplices in all of its intervention maneuvers.

Naturally, after the case of the Falkland Islands, there is great distrust in Latin America toward applying this treaty, which is an instrument of U.S. imperialism to maintain hegemony on the continent. At the time of Reagan's election, a document was produced that contains the strategy for domination of all countries on the American continent [an apparent reference to "Inter-American Relations for the 1980's," prepared by the Committee of Santa Fe and commissioned by the Council for Inter-American Security in Washington, D.C. — Eds.] The strategy is based on the resolution from Caracas that we voted against, and on what they call the "Monroe Doctrine" (which is not a doctrine but only a declaration, part of a report made in 1823 to the U.S. Congress).

However, the "Monroe Doctrine" has been applied when the U.S. wants to maintain its domination under the pretext that extra-continental powers could take over in Latin America.

To maintain its domination, the U.S. created CONDECA (Central American Defense Council), formed by three armies — the Guatemalan, the Salvadoran, and the Nicaraguan — led by the U.S. Southern Command in Panama and directly subordinate to the Pentagon. With the Sandinista Revolution in Nicaragua, the system of U.S. domination has been undermined. This is why today the U.S. sends aid to the government of Honduras, arming it to the teeth as part of the deadly "iron triangle" for domination of the region: El Salvador, Guatemala, and Honduras. What is now being sought is the Lebanonization of the Central American region. Israel is acting as an accomplice and arm of the United States.

The U.S. builds bases on the Guatemalan border, on the Honduran border, and on the Salvadoran border, to maintain its scheme of domination. And the U.S. wants to lie to the rest of the world, saying the confrontation is between the East and the West. The struggle of our peoples has tremendous roots in misery, exploitation, racial discrimination, hunger, and death. Our people have the right to their own destiny without foreign interference, and this is why we are engaged in what is called a popular revolutionary war, which is a just war, a necessary war. I would like to pay homage now to an extraordinary man, Jose Martí, whose 130th birthday would be celebrated today and whose thought still inspires our revolutionary struggle. Martí came to know in Guatemala the humiliation with which our Indians were treated, and said, "So long as things do not go well with the Indians, things will not go well with America."

Guatemala is presently the only country in America where the Indian is in motion. Mestizos and Indians have entered history with the gun, to smash the insane system which the military governments imposed by the United States represent. This system was installed in Guatemala by the United States, as I said in Caracas: the first neofascist system of domination in America, which has now been extended to many other countries of the continent. This system is based on the use of violence and terror.

The frightful policies which the Guatemalan army implements with its paramilitary groups and the training in torture, given not only by U.S. advisers but also by Israelis, Chileans, and Argentinians, are part of a plan to sow terror—to play on fear. Before this Tribunal, I again denounce U.S. imperialism and the Israelis as directly responsible for the crimes in Guatemala. I do not refer to the people of the United States, because I have a great respect for them. It was precisely they who stopped the war in Vietnam, and we hope that the American people will also prevent the insane foreign policy and the fascist government of Reagan from proceeding.

We also have a great respect for the people of Israel, and the government of Guatemala strongly supported the creation of the State of Israel, with the understanding that the rights of the people of Palestine would be recognized. But the Zionists who are now in power are the new Nazis of the Middle East, where they impose a scheme of domination, occupying regions and countries that do not belong to them and practicing a true genocide against the Arab people. Israel is in complete collusion with the maintenance of domination over Central America. Moreover, the Israelis have given the Guatemalan army more than 15,000 guns. In sum, they have given the army a whole range of military assistance, including centers of computer information and radar stations to control the entire population. They have become firmly entrenched in an incredible way since 1960, carrying out the counterinsurgency struggle in all the Indian communities, while at the same time serving as an export base for Israeli arms in Guatemala; 30% of the Israeli arms that arrive in Guatemala are exported to other countries. This is how far the connivance of the government of Guatemala with Israel has gone.

To conclude, I would like to tell you that I have just been in Nicaragua for a meeting of the non-aligned nations. They reaffirmed their condemnation of the Guatemalan regime, which had been stated in June in Havana, saying that Guatemala is a dangerous focal point of imperialism in the area. In the new resolution, they say that the present regime has also supported the imperialist intervention and military presence of Israel in Guatemala. This also constitutes a threat to the sovereignty of Belize. The Guatemalan army is being armed up to the borders of Belize, with the expansionist notion of taking over Belize; this violates even U.N. resolutions.

But fortunately the people of Guatemala are in struggle, a struggle that will reach major proportions. Because in spite of the crimes, their heroic decision to change the existing structures remains unshaken.

Economic Life:
A Brief Review

Rafael Piedrasanta Arandi

The author is a noted Guatemalan economist in exile.

The governments of Arévalo and Arbenz, which followed the October Revolution, identified with the most strongly felt needs of the Guatemalan people. The Arbenz government began the implementation of significant projects, such as the agrarian reform, which benefited 150,000 *campesinos*; it constructed the modern Port of Santo Tomás, initiated the construction of the Route to the Atlantic, and planned the hydroelectric plant of Junrun. Both governments began to grow cotton, a new export item, and rejected pressure from Washington to allow foreign companies to exploit Guatemalan oil (preserved as a national industry by the Constitution of 1945).

Agrarian reform meant the loss of important stretches of fallow land belonging to United Fruit. The Port of Santo Tomás and the Atlantic Route would have served to break United Fruit's monopoly on rail transportation. Junrun meant a barrier to maintaining foreign hegemony over the supply of electricity. All this explains why the U.S. government mounted an international campaign accusing Guatemala of building an international communist beachhead, and why the CIA carried out Arbenz's overthrow with help from the high commands of the Guatemalan army.

With Castillo Armas in power, the 1945 Constitution was annulled. The Constitution issued in 1956 made it financially impossible for any agrarian reform to take place and empowered the President (no longer Congress) to grant concessions for exploiting the subsoil in accordance with recommendations by U.S. Department of State "experts." The expropriated lands were returned to United Fruit. Hanna and INCO (International Nickel Co.), foreign companies that later created EXMIBAL, were given zones rich in nickel, iron, copper, chrome, cobalt, and other mineral deposits. One government after another gave free concessions to EXMIBAL, which even drafted a Mining Code for Guatemala that exempted EXMIBAL from paying taxes on exported minerals. The government of Méndez Montenegro gave EXMIBAL free use of the waters of Lake Izabal, a beautiful body of water whose basin was then polluted by an EXMIBAL drainage system.

The pretext for all this was that EXMIBAL would create jobs for Guatemalans and improve the country's balance of payments. In fact, it has given work to barely 200 people and benefited Guatemala's balance of payments only when it operates all year round (which it often does not, because of the world nickel market), and then only in terms of the payroll. This contrasts with the $8.4 million annually that EXMIBAL promised.

Meanwhile, the extraction of oil for export brought 13.6 and 26.6 million *quetzals* in 1980 and 1981 respectively. Basic Resources, a corporation that had intervened soon after the 1954 overthrow of Arbenz to replace the old law concerning oil with a code prepared by the oil enterprises, contracted with former CIA director Vernon Walters. For $1,000 a day, he was to convince the government to allow a higher level of extraction. Since the oil fields are located in areas where the revolutionary movement has proliferated, representatives of the interested corporations offered to intercede with Reagan so that he would "renew" the sale of arms and military aid to the Guatemalan government.

The most recent military governments have encouraged hydroelectric development as never before, as a result of the rising cost of diesel fuel—the main source of energy used by EXMIBAL in processing minerals. As of 1983, the energy provided by two plants is specially earmarked for EXMIBAL. This is yet another subsidy that the Guatemalan people pay to benefit a transnational corporation.

Under Arbenz, efforts were initiated to create the Central American Common Market (MERCOMUN), with the understanding that it would involve enterprises with Central American capital (or with a lesser share of foreign capital) and that the new enterprises would be equally distributed over the five Central American nations. In the 1960s, this plan was modified under pressure from the U.S. government, resulting in the adoption of the principle of free enterprise and free commerce. In practice, this meant the establishment of foreign-owned (mainly Yankee) production branches, especially in Guatemala, El Salvador, and Costa Rica. With one sweep of the pen, they took over the Isthmus market. Gradually, old national companies came under U.S. control. In the end, a false industry was created— under foreign control—and instead of finished goods, raw materials and parts were imported for assembly or simple transfer from a large receptacle to smaller ones and then sale to the consumer. Free Zones have also been created, in which tax-free runaway shops operate, taking advantage of cheap labor.

The country's riches have also been taken over by high-ranking military officials along with the transnationals. The political and social instability have meant a fall in private investment, higher unemployment, bankruptcy for many companies, slower production rates, and a flight of capital that rose to $708.4 million in 1981. This compelled the government to impose strict control on foreign exchange, which has added new problems for the country's businesses.

A Social Analysis

Miguel Angel Reyes Illescas

Here are key points synthesized from the presentation by the distinguished lawyer and sociologist.

The regional characteristics of Guatemala have influenced the type of social conflicts generated throughout its history and particularly the last five years. The Altiplano (High Plateau), Norte Bajo (Lower North), and Norte (North) regions have the largest number of poverty-stricken inhabitants. They are composed of poor peasants in permanent and cyclic impoverishment; here the fiercest battles are waged. In the Altiplano and in the Norte Bajo, almost the entire population is composed of indigenous people, inheritors of the ancient Mayan civilization. During the last two decades in the North, there has been an intensification of government investment, the concentration and appropriation of land, and colonization of indigenous small landowners and ladinos. In the other regions, the conflicts have more resemblance to those in urban and rural societies where waged labor and emerging middle classes prevail.

Guatemalan history has been marked by a continuous struggle for the land. In an unequal conflict, the leading groups have varied in their composition and political orientation, but have always kept the majority from sharing the benefits. The result is a rigidly pyramidal society, with a very narrow apex and a very wide base, although it has not remained the same over the years and new sectors have emerged at all levels, especially since 1944.

In the rural areas, economic and political leaders base their power mainly in the consolidation of large agrarian properties and on their alliance with privileged groups in the U.S. In the urban areas, the Central American Common Market introduced a certain rhythm of industrial growth that led to a meeting of interests between the old coffee plantation owners and the economic agents of industrialization. This also generated sectors of industrial workers and slum dwellers; middle classes emerged in the cities.

THE SOCIAL CRISIS AND RISING POVERTY

The blocs of groups, which are becoming more and more polarized and confront each other on every plane, find their roots in the divergence and convergence that developed during the October Revolution and the U.S. intervention. On both sides, subgroups are becoming defined and fighting for the hegemony of their respective blocs.

The ruling groups have greater difficulty in establishing alliances. The middle sectors developed in ascending and descending cycles until they broke apart, horizontally and vertically; thus they have had little possibility of directing the political process from inside the legal political parties. The bloc defeated in 1954 has been reconstituting itself little by little, also with qualitative changes and incorporating new groups (Indians, Christians, squatters). Conditions are different now from those in 1954. Political hegemony has begun to pass from the hands of middle-class intellectuals and progressive officers, to be shared with the revolutionary leadership of the people in arms, mainly poor peasants and workers.

The ruling bloc has opted for higher levels of terror. Society entered a pre-revolutionary stage that rapidly changed to the revolutionary situation continuing today.

Poverty is on the increase. In 1980, 52% of the population lived in conditions of extreme poverty and 79% were poor. In rural areas, the situation was even worse. Over 80% of the children under five years of age suffer from malnutrition. Of every 1,000 children born alive, 81 die during their first year of life, with 60% of the deaths caused by diseases of the digestive tract and respiratory problems that, in a healthy child, would not cause death. There is a shortage of about one million homes. Of those that did exist in 1973, 57% lacked water and 72% electricity.

To the structural injustice has been added state terrorism, which has led to the forced displacement of one million poor, indigenous peasants from two thirds of the nation to other countries, mainly Mexico. State terror is also destroying the countryside, provoking conditions for the spread of disease and a decrease in food production as well as in the work force.

The government seeks to concentrate the indigenous people in "model villages" for rural development, with a clear purpose of counterinsurgency. But the government has not even been able to repair the damage of the 1976 earthquake in the rural areas. It will face the contradiction of artificially maintaining unproductive villages or taking steps toward agrarian reform that will require injections of capital. Meanwhile, its resources become increasingly scarce, because the ruling groups have moved their capital outside the country.

All in all, the social conflicts in Guatemala will become more and more acute unless their causes are attacked. The causes lie in Guatemala's history and its structures—not in those people who happen to exercise control over the government at a specific time.

Toward Understanding the Political Situation

Raúl Molina Mejía

This is a synopsis of the presentation by expert witness Raúl Molina, ex-dean and ex-rector of the University of San Carlos. He begins by discussing the conditions for the revolutionary movement—economic, social, and political—and points out that a historical-political analysis of Guatemala allows us to appreciate the righteousness of this movement, in that all democratic options attempted by the people have been completely closed off.

He then looks at the general crisis of the Guatemalan state at the end of the Lucas García period, in late 1981 and early 1982: the deepest crisis in Guatemala's history.

It was a social crisis in that Guatemala had an impoverished population whose basic needs were totally impossible to satisfy. It was an economic crisis in that there was stagnation, inflation, flight of capital, etc. It was a political crisis in that the regime lacked legitimacy, political life was disorganized, Guatemala was internationally isolated, and corruption existed throughout the state. And finally, it was a military crisis, with the army incapable of stopping the development of the people's revolutionary war, which had incorporated broad sectors of the population. As a result of the crisis, there was a coup d'état on March 23, 1982, which brought Ríos Montt to power.

The "messenger from God," Ríos Montt, has operated within a counterinsurgency model characterized by:

1. The concentration of repressive action against people who sympathize with the guerrillas or are simply indifferent to the government.

2. Military action against political-military organizations.

3. The generation of a "legal framework" to control the population, especially in the urban areas.

4. An increase in the levels of "psychological warfare."

5. Consolidation of the efforts of the state apparatus in the struggle against the popular revolutionary war.

The logic behind the repressive actions against the Indian peasant population is that the people are to the guerrilla as water is to fish; the Ríos Montt government, recognizing the validity of Mao Tse-tung's expression, decided to "eliminate the water." The massacres of the Indian peasant population have been accompanied by the most horrendous sadism: killing children in front of their parents, killing parents in front of their children, people of all ages burnt alive, heads of men placed in the wombs of women, to mention only a few examples. Along with this goes destruction of the means of subsistence for the Indian peasant communities: burning food, leveling crops, robbery or slaughter of animals, poisoning water, burning down forests, destroying homes, etc.

The forms of repressive action include: forced displacement of the population from their villages; concentration of part of the population by the army in "model villages"; militarizing the lives of the people in the rural areas by forcibly incorporating them into civilian patrols to serve as a front line in military confrontation with the guerrillas; selective repression of the controlled population by identifying those who are "less collaborative," to be disappeared, tortured, and killed; and military occupation of the urban centers.

Military action against the revolutionary forces has consisted of massive offensives in the areas of the greatest guerrilla activity, with huge contingents of infantry and special forces, supported by the air force. Parallel to military action are the civilian patrols mentioned above, which combine military agents and collaborators with soldiers (in a different role) and peasants forced into duty. They exist to control the population, confront the guerrillas, and give an image of popular support for the government.

An important aspect of the Ríos Montt government, which

results from the permanent advisership of the Reagan administration and agents from Israel, Chile, and Argentina, is increased "psychological warfare." It includes the development of counter-insurgency campaigns with such deceptive names as "Beans and Guns" (which supposedly means to feed and defend the people but has in essence meant beans for those who collaborate, guns against those who don't). Another was "Roofs, Work, and Tortillas," whose triple "T" (in Spanish, roofs, work, and tortillas all begin with a "T") will mean what it has always meant: "Torture, Terror, and Tragedy."

A massive disinformation campaign is part of this warfare; its purpose is to lay responsibility for the massacres on the revolutionary forces. To this end, all the means of communication are controlled; visiting organizations are presented with staged scenes. The disinformation campaign also claims that the guerrillas have been defeated, and tries to show there is an efficient intelligence apparat by presenting a hundred Guatemalans before a special tribunal, for example. "Operation Honesty" was another attempt at psychological warfare, using the slogan "Do not lie, do not steal, do not abuse." This little tune is violently contradicted by the same forces that have tried to popularize it, along with Ríos Montt's other Protestant homilies. He has tried in various ways to generate a confrontation of Protestantism with Catholicism, to weaken Catholic support for the people's struggle.

The program of the Guatemalan opposition is valid for all sectors not in the present power bloc. Its purpose is to build a revolutionary, popular, democratic, and patriotic government with the following platform:

1. Put an end to repression and guarantee life and peace for Guatemalans.

2. Provide a solution to the needs of the vast majority of the people, putting an end to domination by the very wealthy.

3. Achieve equality between the Indians and the ladinos, putting an end to oppression and discrimination.

4. Create a new society with a government in which the patriotic, popular, and democratic sectors will be included.

5. Develop an international policy of non-alignment with full

respect for the self-determination and sovereignty of the people.

Given the righteousness of their struggle and their political program, the people of Guatemala therefore request international recognition as a belligerent party so that international treaties and agreements with reference to war can be applied to protect the population.

II

PRESENTATIONS AND TESTIMONY

Testimony of
Miguel Angel Albizures

Labor leader

My name is Miguel Angel Albizures. I am 37 years old, and have dedicated 23 years to serving my people in different social organizations. In terms of schooling, I only went up to the sixth grade. I am the son of a peasant family who migrated to the capital looking for better opportunities to live. My father is a cabinet maker; I also have done this kind of work for several years. My mother died from lack of medical attention. In my family and in my community I have known only misery and injustice.

From a very early age I experienced exploitation and I suffered the exploitation of which my father was and continues to be a victim. When I was 15 years old, I joined the Young Catholic Workers (Juventud Obrera Católica, JOC), where I learned to serve others. It was there that I discovered a method which has shown me how to see, to judge, and to act for the rest of my life. To see reality and not to show indifference towards it. To judge reality with all of its causes and consequences, and to act in order to transform it.

I traveled through almost all of the slums in my country organizing the youth of my age, and everywhere I found injustices, some much greater than others. As part of a confessional organization, I learned about the gospel and I found strength to confront my problems and those of others. I discovered that the church in my country was not what I had previously believed, and that the gospel was being interpreted in favor of the few. I am speaking of the institutional church, which in those times restricted our rights to think and to act in service to others.

In 1962 I saw how a priest who identified with poor people, and who helped us interpret reality and confront the situation, was forcibly exiled with the approval of the bishop. From that time I told myself that something was very wrong inside the church, in the way that it distanced itself from the working class and gave it no direction. At the table of the poor, the church authorities did not find the same rewards that were guaranteed by sharing the table of the rich.

In the first five years of the 1960s, I began to relate to labor organizations and I sincerely thought that the labor movement was a real alternative for ending so much injustice. Soon after that, something happened which marked me for my whole life. A co-worker named José Angel Berreondo, who was the president of the Young Catholic Workers and had close relations with a labor union organization, fell by an assassin's bullet in front of the door to a police station, barely 250 meters from the National Palace. This was May 14, 1962.

At that time I began to realize that there was police surveillance of my house and the location where we met. Police agents openly followed us on more than a few occasions.

In 1967 I started the union in the factory where I worked. It was a cosmetics factory. Then, as now, the Labor Code existed and, in principle, it guaranteed the right to organize. However, I was working in secret for a year to prevent the bosses from finding out about our objectives. Then we held our first assembly. We formed the board of directors, on which I served as general secretary, and soon after that I experienced all kinds of pressures. I was forbidden to talk to the workers under threat of being fired. The area that I worked in was restricted and my overtime hours, which helped supplement my salary, were cut back.

We battled for three years. Many workers were fired, some were bribed, and many others were afraid to continue out of fear of reprisals. The union was finally destroyed. My *compañera* was also fired when she was a month away from giving birth to one of my daughters (this is forbidden by the laws of Guatemala concerning women who are pregnant or in a post-natal state). I had many experiences like that.

During this period, at the end of the 1960s, the public demonstrations by the labor and popular movements were very weak. Repression was rampant all over the country, especially in the eastern part and in the capital. It has been calculated that in the last three years of that decade (with the "civil" government of Julio César Méndez Montenegro), assassinations rose to a total of 10,000 people.

The weak attempts at unity by the labor movement, which were begun in 1968, failed because of an opportunistic attitude on the part of union leaders who were in collusion with the government, and also because of strong repression against labor leaders who had the interests of the working class at heart.

So we started the decade of the 1970s under General Carlos Arana Osorio with a weak and disunited labor movement. Arana Osorio had stated, "If we want to pacify Guatemala, we have to finish off half the population, and I am willing to do this." From November 1970 to November 1971, Guatemalan workers experienced a long and bloody year under the government's State of Siege. Political and union activities were forbidden, as is the case at present. Many leaders were persecuted, jailed, and killed. In January 1971, the peasant leader Tereso de Jesús Oliva and many others were assassinated.

Students and professionals also fell, like Adolfo Mijangos López, who was murdered in his wheelchair. The National Workers Central (CNT) to which I belonged was raided by uniformed police from the regime. I was interrogated along with others from the Central about our supposedly subversive propaganda, and the arms and plans to overthrow the regime that they said we had.

Let me just say that in Guatemala, the Constitution of the Republic and the labor code address the right to organize, the right to collective bargaining, and the right to strike. But to conduct and win a legal strike in Guatemala is an entire odyssey. Only one strike has been declared legal since 1954, which was that of the workers at Incatecu Shoes in August 1975. A month later, Vinicio Aguilar and his eight-year-old son were killed in a strange traffic accident. He had been one of those who, in different ways, sought to support the strikers, and he had encouraged them in their just struggle.

At the end of 1972, the workers at the Industrial Company of the Atlantic (Compañía Industrial del Atlántico, CIDASA) dared to challenge the Arana Osorio government and sought authorization for a strike. The strike at CIDASA was declared legal at first, and it lasted 67 days. Then, at the behest of the company, it was declared "unfair." The workers lost all their rights; many of them lost their jobs. In June 1973, three months after the end of the strike, the general secretary of the union, Compañero César Augusto Morataya, was assassinated.

It was my job to lead that strike, and I shared with my fellow workers all the uncertainties of the process. I knew from my own experience what a sacrifice it meant for a working family not to receive income for more than two months. But my *compañeros* and I trusted in the law, and the law as usual favored those who had the most.

I can still hear the words of the man who was then Minister of Labor. In one of many discussions, he told me, "Albizures, give it up, because we are not going to be able to declare this strike fair. If we declare it fair, we're immediately going to have a strike wave in the textile sector that we are not willing to tolerate." In other words, justice matters little; the rights of the workers matter less. What had to be guaranteed were the interests of the rich textile owners. Once again, executive power and judicial power conspired against the working class.

Just so that you can have an idea of what the right to strike is in Guatemala, I will describe some of the legal procedures.

1. Workers at a company get together and present a series of petitions through a tribunal for discussion.

2. Direct discussion begins when the owner of the company feels like it or doesn't have an alternative.

3. If an agreement cannot be reached by the direct way, they seek negotiation through the judicial avenue.

4. The tribunals call the various parties together so that workers, bosses, and a judge can discuss the issues.

5. Upon not reaching an agreement because the bosses' side does not concede (which is very common), they give up on the conciliation effort.

6. The tribunal orders a count of the vote. But this is not a vote of the people affiliated with the union; it is a vote by all the workers at the company. The bosses add onto the list of active workers their relatives, new workers, and strike breakers, who will vote in favor of the bosses. When the voting takes place, workers are pressured by the work inspectors and by threats from the bosses to vote against the strike.

7. Moreover, in order for the strike to be declared legal, it has to be based on economic demands and have the participation of at least two thirds of all the workers at the company.

8. If the union wins, the bosses try to challenge the vote. If the strike is declared legal, the union can call for it to begin within the next few days.

9. Once the strike is declared legal, it can last as long as people can hold out. But the fact that a strike is declared legal does not mean that it is "fair." In my country, when they cannot get the workers to submit by "legal" means, they get them to submit by hunger, threats, or direct repression.

I am a witness to the fact that in many labor conflicts, the labor authorities under the regimes of Julio César Méndez Montenegro (1966-1970), Arana Osorio (1970-1974), Kjell Laugerud García (1974-1978), and Lucas García (1978-March 1982) manipulated the law and ignored the rights of workers in the most crass and cynical way that this Tribunal could ever imagine. About Ríos Montt I can only tell you that on the 31st of this month it will have been six full months since he established the State of Siege and prohibited the functioning of labor organizations and political parties.

I have participated in a number of labor conflicts, among them that of the teachers, the public health workers, and the social communications workers. Together with them I suffered repression when the authorities crushed their protest and petitions with billy clubs and tear gas bombs.

On March 23, 1973, we received notification at the National
Workers Central that in Sansirisay, a village in the department
of Jalapa, more than 30 peasants from Xalapán had been
assassinated. The motive: the peasants were defending their rights
to the land.

That very day I went to the area where these events had taken
place. I talked for eight hours with another *compañero*. All I had
for protection was an identification card as a journalist. In the
various farms that we crossed, the peasants indicated that a day
before a platoon of soldiers had come through. In Sansirisay,
several witnesses talked about what had happened and accused
the army. I was stopped and told that if I did not leave the area,
I would be jailed. A peasant put me up for the night, and I spent
the night hidden because the army continued its killing. The official who directed the massacre from a helicopter was General
Efraín Ríos Montt, Chief of Staff of the army during the time
of Arana Osorio.

On May 1, 1974, we organized a peaceful demonstration for
International Workers Day. The elections in which the army
selected General Kjell Laugerud García as President had just taken
place. The demonstration was violently repressed. The toll: 7 dead,
12 wounded, and hundreds jailed.

At that moment, I was at the front of the demonstration with
other *compañeros*. I spoke with one of the chiefs of police to try
to prevent violence from the beginning. In response, they began
to throw tear gas bombs and fire guns. No one could deny that
it was the national and secret police who acted against the men,
women, and children who were commemorating May 1. Luckily,
the demonstration was authorized, because if it hadn't been, the
machine-guns that are all along the main national police station
on 6th Avenue and 14th Street in Zone One would have been acti-
vated, as well as the sharpshooters and police on 18th Street
between 6th and 7th Avenues in Zone One of the capital.

Just to illustrate to this honorable Tribunal the ravages of
repression against the Guatemalan labor movement, let me say
that in 1953, a year of democratic government in Guatemala, we
had succeeded in organizing 11.5% of the workers in the active

labor force. In 1954, after the invasion by the CIA against the democratic government of Arbenz, all of the unions were closed down by law, various leaders were assassinated, and a high number of unionists were forced into exile. In 1975, 22 years later, unionized workers constituted only 1.5% of the economically active labor force.

In March 1976, I was a witness to the brutal beating that the workers at Coca-Cola suffered. That night I was arrested by the police. I participated in the founding of the National Committee of Labor Union Unity (CNUS) on March 31, 1976. On June 25 of the same year, the National Workers Central was violently raided by the judicial police. I was able to escape over the rooftops between police bullets. Three of my *compañeros* were jailed. For a month I remained hidden; then the CNUS, of which I was part of the leadership, decided that I should turn myself in on the condition that the government would free three other *compañeros*.

I was imprisoned for several days and falsely accused of firing guns, attempted assassination, kidnapping, and robbery. These crude accusations were used to justify their repressive action. I was finally freed for lack of proof, being protected by my fellow workers.

In 1977, the labor movement and the mass movement together reached a high point. Strikes and demonstrations happened one after the other. Repression continued, but the working class was reaching a level of maturity and giving birth to new leading cadres. The cadres had been decimated years earlier by repression. In that year I received a letter from the Secret Anticommunist Army (Ejército Secreto Anticomunista, ESA), which had just begun public activity. They warned me to leave the country. A few days later, on June 8, Mario López Larrave was assassinated, a man with whom I had participated in several struggles. I mainly worked with him in the National Committee of Labor Union Unity, where he was a motivating force and main adviser. Larrave was assassinated because he did not allow himself to be bribed by the bosses and because he pointed out repeatedly the cynicism and arbitrariness with which the labor authorities acted.

In November 1977, the miners of Ixtahuacán, fed up with hunger, with the unjustified firings, with unjust salaries, with the threats of closing the mines, and with the outrageous exploitation to which they were subjected in the deep tunnels, held a protest march from San Idlefonso Ixtahuacán, Huehuetenango, to the capital, a distance of 351 kilometers. Compañero Mario Mujía Córdova was at the head of this march. I participated in the discussions, searching for an agreement favorable to the workers. Seven months later Mujía Córdova was assassinated. His crime was having accompanied the miners, having advised them, and having served the workers' cause in other factories in Huehuetenango, such as Santa Agape and Corral Chiquito. Several *compañeros* at the mines of San Ildefonso Ixtahuacán and from the factories of Huehuetenango have paid with their lives for daring to defend their rights. In mid-1982, Ixtahuacán Mines and other companies closed their doors and left hundreds of workers on the street.

At the beginning of 1978, I participated in the strikes and marches of the unions at the Oxec Mines, and the hydroelectric project at Chixoy in Alta Verapaz. In this whole region, labor unions and peasant organizations were developing very strongly. On May 29 of that same year, 119 peasants* were massacred in the Plaza of Panzós in the department of Alta Verapaz (which is very close to the Oxec Mines) when they carried out a protest over problems with the land.

I have traveled through almost all the country in my union work, and everywhere I go, injustice reigns. The ownership of the land is a chronic evil that we have attacked in various different forms. The causes of the massacre of Panzós can be found in the organizational development that existed and in the state's protection of the transnational corporations in the region, which own rich minerals such as nickel, copper, and silver and oil. Of course this is also the region where the generals own large pieces of land.

---

*The exact number of victims of the Panzós massacre, as in other massacres, varies from one source to another; this is certainly due to the repression, including the concealment of physical evidence. In the case of Panzós, the number was no less than 100 and some say over 130.—Eds.

In the first days of October 1978, there were huge mass mobilizations against the increase in transportation fares. I went as a delegate, along with others, to discuss this conflict with President Romeo Lucas García, and to demand a lowering of the fares. Authorized by Lucas García, elements from the army's G-2 entered this meeting with movie and photographic camers. They took all the pictures they wanted of the leaders, and then left. A few days later, on October 20, at the end of a demonstration, Oliverio Castañeda de León, who was general secretary of the Association of University Students (Asociación de Estudiantes Universitarios, AEU), was brutally assassinated. This assassination took place in the middle of the city, with the largest police force in our history deployed to end the life of a leader barely 22 years old. A few days later, Compañero Ciani, who had succeeded Castañeda de León in his post, was kidnapped.

The October activities lasted 10 days and the toll was 40 dead, 200 wounded, and more than 1,200 arrested. Of those of us who took part in the meeting with Lucas García, few remain alive.

From October 1978, which marks the beginning of this new and ongoing wave of repression, unionists and leaders or affiliates of other popular and democratic organizations have been assassinated one after the other. On October 16 the Secret Anticommunist Army, which is led by the Ministry of Governance, made public a list of 38 union leaders, students, professionals, intellectuals, and politicos whom they condemned to death. My name was at the top of the list.

Persecution and harassment of myself and other *compañeros* intensified. I evaded several attempts at kidnapping and assassination. The homes where I stayed were harassed. I completely abandoned my family and continued working, trying to fulfill my union responsibility. Finally, with authorization from the union organization to which I belonged, I left the country to be able to contribute to the international denunciation of the situation in Guatemala. Since then, I have returned to the country to contribute to the union movement from underground. Legal entry of the country represents death.

In mid-1980 they tried to kidnap my two daughters, who were

barely seven and nine years old at the time. My daughters quit their studies and later left the country. The psychological effects of government repression and persecution on my children are crimes for which those who have exercised power by force in Guatemala will still have to pay. They have denied the children of Guatemala the right to live in their own country and to share life with their families.

Lastly, I would like to just mention the massive kidnappings in the CNT and the present situation.

On June 21, 1980, our Workers Central was violently raided: 27 *compañeros* whom I knew disappeared, and we have not heard from them since. The majority of them were general secretaries of labor unions. On August 24, at the Emaus spiritual retreat, 17 *compañeros* were kidnapped. They also were members of the CNT, and of the School of Union Orientation. In two months, 44 leaders were disappeared with the greatest impunity and cynicism that this Tribunal could imagine in a country which boasts of being "democratic." Of these painful facts I attach a detailed report, with a list of the disappeared.

Presently the Statute written at the time of the coup d'état, which substitutes for the Constitution of the Republic, speaks for itself regarding the restriction of union rights. With the declaration of a State of Siege on July 1, 1982, all individual and collective rights of workers as citizens are suspended by decree and "the functioning of union organizations and political parties is prohibited." The Workers Centrals are closed and Guatemalan citizens have to ask permission from the army to be able to even watch over and bury their dead.

The freedom of Guatemalan workers to organize is a myth which has lasted 28 long years. Innumerable union leaders and members have had to pay with their lives to maintain the labor movement, so as to aid in the liberation of Gutemala. This is only a very small part of the bloody road that the Guatemalan working class has had to travel. Today they face that bloody road with the same conviction as always, conscious that he who names himself elected by God to govern the country is elected neither by God, nor by the people, nor by the working class of Guatemala.

Testimony of
Israel Márquez

Labor leader

My name is Israel Márquez. I am 34 years old, and I am the former general secretary of the Coca-Cola Bottle Workers Union of the Food Federation, National Workers Central (CNT), and a former member of the Leadership Committee of the National Committee of Labor Union Unity (CNUS). I began my activity in the union movement on August 11, 1975, at the beginning of the reorganization of the union at the Coca-Cola company, where I worked for 10 years.

The previous union at that company was abolished in 1954 after the overthrow of the democratic Arbenz government, when more than 600 union organizations were declared illegal. Subsequently there were various unsuccessful attempts at union reorganization, in which one of the main promoters was assassinated.

Workers for the company began to organize to try to solve our difficult economic and social problems, such as miserable wages, *compañeros* who had worked for the company for 20 years and were receiving two *quetzales* and 50 *centavos* (cents) a day, and the continuous robbery of severance pay while we were obliged to sign receipts as if we had received our full salaries. If we used the health services of the Social Security, we were fired, even though we paid dues for it. We were not allowed to study, even on nonworking time, and the treatment of us in general was inhuman.

From the beginning of this new union organization, the company was in complicity with the government. They did all kinds of things to destroy the union, such as massive firings, threats on people's lives, physical aggression, jail sentences of hundreds of days. Terror was spread by goon squads, using people who were dressed as civilians but had military licenses to carry firearms.

The personnel manager and other executives were army officers, and the workers were guarded by uniformed military police carrying machine-guns and accompanied by trained dogs. The walls were very high, with barbed wire, so that our workplace looked like a concentration camp. The company was fictitiously divided into 14 companies, in order to divide the labor force. Seven false labor conventions were held with supposed worker organizations. We labor leaders were condemned to death various times by paramilitary groups, and our identities exposed in public bulletins.

Nine labor activists were assassinated, among them five leaders, including two general secretaries, Pedro Quevedo and Manuel López Balán. Three attempts were made on my life.

The absolute partiality of the Ministry of Labor and the Labor Tribunals towards the bosses has been a constant. For example, according to the law of that time, the unions should have been granted legal status within at least two months. Instead it was granted after nine months of struggle, and when we were on strike, supported by the pressure of solidarity actions by the national union movement. This in fact was an exceptional case, since other unions spent five or six years before getting legal status, or they were destroyed before achieving it.

In spite of the conditions I just described, union organizing at this company has survived. However, that survival has been precarious and has been made possible only by the firm determination and unity of the workers, and national and international solidarity.

This situation is not an isolated case in Guatemala. Repression is both generalized and selective. Since 1978, more than 200 union leaders have been kidnapped or murdered, or have disappeared. Two mass kidnappings of leaders of the CNT and the school for labor orientation have taken place. Eight from the Guatemalan Institute of Social Security were assassinated; Damina Gomes and Rodolfo Ramírez from the Autonomous Guatemalan Federation of Unions (FASGUA); José Luis Jacome from the glass factory CAVISA; Antonio García Rac from the Workers Federation of Guatemala (FTG); Marco Antonio Cacao and José León Castañeda from the Social Communications Union (SIMCOS); Juan José Alvarado from the Federation of Bank Employees (FESEBS); the general secretary of the Federation of Sugar Industry Workers (FETULIA); and peasant leaders such as Roberto Xiguac, Alberto Gil Anona, Miguel Xil, the peasants who were killed at the Spanish embassy,* and others.

In addition, thousands of rank-and-file members from various popular and democratic organizations, particularly the unions, have been kidnapped and assassinated. This includes more than 250 teachers from the teachers' mass organization, and 49 journalists. Thousands have been fired, and organizations such as the Postal and Telegraph Workers Association and the Public Health Workers Association have been banned.

Although varying some in degree and intensity, repression has remained the same since 1954. The dictatorial governments are a product of coup d'états or imposition through electoral fraud, like the present Ríos Montt government, which doesn't in any way represent the will of the people. The brutality of the Lucas García government is well known nationally and internationally. In a little more than three years, approximately 17,000 citizens were either kidnapped or assassinated or disappeared. Massacres were sporadic, repression was selective; although all social movements or organizations, especially labor unions, were made illegal through repression, a precarious appearance of legality and constitutionality was maintained.

With the coup d'état last March, the situation substantially worsened. Massacres became systematic; in less than one year, more assassinations and kidnappings took place than in the three years of Lucas García's government. The inconsistent legality which had been maintained was abolished and the labor law created during Juan José Arévalo's time in 1947 was amended several times, each time to the detriment of the already restricted

---

*In this event, described by other witnesses more fully, a large group of indigenous peasants who occupied the embassy as a peaceful protest against government repression were killed along with other people. — Eds.

rights of workers. The illegitimate government of Ríos Montt increased the mandatory work week from 45 to 48 hours with the Fundamental Statute of Government. Under the previous labor law, although state workers had not been able to organize in labor unions, theoretically they could organize cooperative associations or employee clubs. These latter have been forbidden by the present government.

The abolition of the Guatemalan Constitution, Ríos Montt's promulgation of the Fundamental Statute of Government, and decrees such as those establishing the Tribunals of Special Jurisdiction* and the State of Siege have legalized the already existing violations of human rights and democratic freedoms: the right of workers to freely organize and associate, and the basic right to life. The present government has legalized assassination through the special jurisdiction tribunals, which legally put any form of social organization, particularly workers' organizations, out of commission. A meeting of more than three people is forbidden. The few labor unions that still function openly and legally are frozen.

Although repression has been centered in the countryside, especially in the high plains and in the northern part of the country, there are 70 known kidnappings and assassinations a month in the cities. Most of the victims are workers, with some unionists among them. The most recent case was at the Universal Textile Company, where in December two union leaders representing the workers there were kidnapped.

The situation continues to get worse, to the detriment of the workers. Unemployment has risen so drastically that presently there is an organization of the unemployed, which never existed before in the country.

Faced with this situation, a profound transformation in the organization and movement of workers is taking place. The experience of the working class has broadened during its many years of struggle. Under the country's present conditions, we can't

---

*People were taken before these tribunals, the proceedings (if any) were secret, and the accused were executed. The Tribunals were abolished in August 1983, and the executions simply continue without them. — Eds.

conceive of a traditional labor union movement; one sees new and advanced conceptions, methods, and forms of organization and struggle that correspond to the concrete conditions in the country. We think that the different forms of struggle are valid, legitimate, and necessary. The existing organizations range from clandestine to semi-clandestine to open formations, or combinations thereof. Although there are still various forms of union organizations which have been functioning in a more or less traditional fashion, generally they are frozen. In most cases, we find new types of workers' organizations: factory committees, workers' groups, and vigilance, self-defense, and militia groups.

The organization and objectives of the struggle flow from the concrete and specific needs of the workers, such as better working conditions, pay raises, the right to work, the right to life. However, we have become more and more aware of the fact that we shouldn't just struggle for our immediate needs, and that the major grievances of the workers in our country can be solved only by profoundly transforming national life and developing a new society ruled by democracy, liberty, and social justice.

By the same token, Guatemalan workers are convinced more and more each day of the need for unified and decisive action by all workers, particularly industrial workers and peasants, native peoples as well as ladinos, in unity and coordination with all the other social or patriotic sectors that struggle for democracy, social justice, and national independence.

Report on the Guatemalan Army

Gabriel Aguilera Peralta
Central American Institute
for Social Research and Documentation

The Guatemalan Armed and Security Forces were historically created to collaborate with the state as designed by the coffee growers in the middle of the 19th century. This project was based on a system of domination sustained by repression and embodied in a series of oligarchic dictatorships, which lasted until 1944. The armed forces and their personnel, the army officers, were fundamental in supporting those dictatorships.

Between 1944 and 1954, the October Revolution took place in Guatemala as an attempt to develop the country democratically. Although a sector of the army supported this effort, the majority of the armed forces refused to defend the second government of this process, that of Colonel Jacobo Arbenz Guzmán. In 1954 a subversive movement initiated by the local oligarchy and the U.S. government of that time overthrew Arbenz and suppressed the democratic experiment.

From the conservative restoration of 1954 onwards, the hallmarks of the political system of Guatemala have been the lack of democracy and the existence of a policy of state terrorism. Since the dominant social groups lack hegemony, and the state that represents them lacks legitimacy, domination rests on constant repression by the different governments against the people. This repressive policy is directed and executed by state organs, even though—as part of the psychological war—government responsibility is usually hidden, either by pretending that violent actions are implemented by extreme right, clandestine organizations or, as is happening at present, by putting the blame on the patriotic forces.

During the last decades, democratic tendencies of officers who opposed the involvement of the army in the state terrorist policy have been eliminated. Such tendencies still exist, but are extremely weak. The majority of officers at all levels consciously support the government's terror and feel part of the current political model.

In the past it was possible to differentiate between the dominant social forces and army men; the latter usually came from the middle strata and served as "instruments" of the former. However, over the last decade this situation has changed in a fundamental way. At present, higher-ranking officers tend to become an organic part of the dominant social forces as they acquire means of production.

Within the framework of the dominant social forces, hegemony is held by a monopolistic fraction, linked in particular with agribusiness and finance, and with close ties to transnational monopoly capital. The military belongs to this fraction, which controls the state apparatus and thus uses it for accumulation. This is why it is structurally impossible for this fraction to allow any democratic policies. Its permanent control over the state apparatus is implemented through a policy of terror, and through manipulation of the elections and the political parties.

These features of the Guatemalan political system explain how important the armed forces have become in the society. Since the system of domination is based on repression, the state apparatus that carries out this function—the Armed and Security Forces and their personnel, the army men—gains enormous importance, to the point of taking over functions of the civil society.

The extreme inflexibility of the political system in Guatemala and the continual use of repression as an instrument of domination have led popular sectors to resort to violent struggle in order to achieve a new democratic order. Thus, the repressive violence of the state is opposed by a counterviolence in the form of popular revolutionary warfare.

The exhaustion of today's political model and the subsequent economic crisis are the result of the development of popular revolutionary warfare. We believe that a political system based on repression can in fact sustain and reproduce itself to the extent that it succeeds in destroying or neutralizing the opposition. At that point, it tends to stabilize as it regains "spaces" of social support. As an example, we can look at the regimes based on force which emerged in South America over the last decade.

In Guatemala, the terror applied for two decades has not met its primary goal: the final defeat (during the current generation) of the revolutionary forces. On the contrary, those forces have improved their military capacity, thus preventing the consolidation and stabilization of the political system, and causing its present crisis.

The crisis emerged during the government of Romeo Lucas García because of deformations in the development of the political system that his government policies introduced. These deformations are as follows:

1. Even though the hallmark of the system is the use of state power to benefit the economic interests of the monopoly fraction, as we said, the regime of "the Lucas group" (General Lucas and his political and military backers who formed a center of power within the fraction) deformed that usage, turning it into large-scale, individual corruption. Thus the state started to implement policies that were to its own detriment and to that of the dominant groups, but extremely beneficial to individuals in the "Lucas group." (Examples we can mention are the so-called "Periférico Nacional," programs of public works, etc.)

2. As we have said, the system is based on the use of state terrorism. Under the Lucas administration, however, the use of terror in some cases also reflected personal interests (for example, the terror apparatus built up by the Minister of the Interior, Donaldo Alvarez Ruiz, who kidnapped and murdered people for

money). In general, terror — a form of counterinsurgency and at the same time a form of social control — was used in an arbitrary and unruly way, in many cases having counterproductive effects. In particular, the massacre at the Spanish embassy in January 1980 accelerated the international isolation of Guatemala.

3. It was during the same administration that revolutionary warfare developed. Lucas's government and his military commanders showed a limited capacity for conducting the war, with corruption in the high command creating several splits within the armed forces.

4. Finally, the deformations turned into divisions within the dominant social groups, and even within the hegemonic fraction which considered the Lucas group a negative factor for the system as a whole. Such divisions clearly appeared in the general elections of March 1982. The dominant sectors were divided and the election results were manipulated in favor of the candidate of the "Lucas group."

The military coup d'état of March 23 and the establishment of General Efraín Ríos Montt's government were essentially a response to these deformations — an attempt to bring about corrective measures without changing the basis of the country's political system. The power structures remain unchanged. The dominant social forces are the same; the hegemonic position of the monopoly fraction has not changed, nor has its need to maintain control over the state apparatus been altered. The aim of eliminating "the Lucas group" from government was restoration of the internal balance of the system, with the following concrete objectives:

1. To improve the international image of the country in order to obtain economic and military support, especially from the United States.

2. To improve the war strategy by eliminating corruption, revising the strategy and tactics of counterinsurgency and intelligently utilizing war propaganda.

3. To regain internal social support, particularly from urban middle strata who found themselves alienated from the system by the excessive brutality of the Lucas García regime.

A number of lower-level and middle-level officers participated in the conception and implementation of the coup, and were officially represented in the structure of the new regime. Their motivation was not progressive; rather, they wished to improve the war before they lost it.

The measures adopted by the Ríos Montt government can be easily understood within the framework of the improved counterinsurgency strategy which is being carried out.

HANDLING OF WAR PROPAGANDA

It has included such maneuvers as an "amnesty" aimed at giving the impression that the regime wanted a peaceful solution to the conflict; the formation of *civilian patrols,* * aimed at portraying a part of the peasant population as fighting voluntarily on the regime's side; *the moral and religious content* of the rhetoric of the President and his main advisers, aimed at improving the image of the government and *attributing responsibility* for the killings to the revolutionary forces themselves.

These moves are understood as part of a propaganda strategy, and therefore they do not modify reality. It is known that the amnesty was a pretext to continue the State of Siege and eliminate the possibility of prosecuting deposed government officials; the civilian patrols are involuntary organizations composed of peasants from combat zones, who are threatened with death if they do not join; the religious rhetoric of Ríos Montt does not correspond to any real Christian ethic, but is a sham in some cases and in others expresses an extremely reactionary picture of society. The real facts have not been changed, but the way they are presented has indeed been modified. This has had an impact as far as the international image and the internal situation of the country are concerned.

MILITARY STRATEGY

The main goal of the military strategy is to strike at the peasants, who are considered supporters of the revolutionary

---

*These are also called civil patrols and Civil Defense Corps units. —Eds.

forces. This includes destroying indigenous culture, with the understanding that native people are or can be the main force in the popular revolutionary war. That is why genocide on a large scale is being carried out in different zones of the country, including scorched earth tactics, confinement of peasants in strategic hamlets, etc. This strategy has a high cost in human lives and destroyed habitat. Its dimensions, and the government's demonstrated will to destroy a significant part of the population of Guatemala and radically alter the basic elements of Guatemalan nationality, remind us of fascist precedents of human destruction. In spite of these facts, the clever handling of war propaganda has helped to conceal this strategy to a certain extent.

In conclusion, it can be said that the Armed and Security Forces of Guatemala, as in the past, constantly violate the right to exist, the right to have a cultural and national identity, and the right to have a democracy in Guatemala. They have now added the massacre and persecution of the cultural identity of the native indigenous people. In doing so, the Armed and Security Forces of Guatemala commit international crimes which deserve the condemnation of the international community.

Testimony of Elías Barahona

*Journalist and former press secretary
at the Ministry of the Interior*

Gentlemen, Judges of the People's Tribunal: I am Elías Barahona y Barahona, a journalist by profession. I am one of the Guatemalan journalists who has survived the kidnappings and murders unleashed against the press by the military regime in its attempt to silence all informants who could let the world know about the reality that my people are experiencing.

I am appearing before this Tribunal to present evidence about the war taking place in Guatemala and about the direct responsibility of the Guatemalan military regime headed by General Efraín Ríos Montt. My statements are based on personal experience and information that I obtained during 15 years of professional activity and through my access to secret matters of the regime from 1976 to 1980, when I was press secretary and personal confidant of the Minister of the Interior, Donaldo Alvarez Ruiz. In the latter function, I had the opportunity to know in detail part of the security structure of the state apparatus, as regards both the police and the military.

My testimony will provide additional evidence to prove that the government of General Efraín Ríos Montt has an intimate connection with those of Generals Carlos Arana Osorio, Kjell Laugerud García, and Romeo Lucas García from 1970 to the present, and that the policies and practices of the Guatemalan military regime have had historical continuity through each successive government. Ríos Montt's military government is neither foreign to nor divorced from the aforementioned governments. Rather, it has the same objectives.

Guatemalan armed forces are directly responsible for the disappearance and/or assassination of more than 100,000 Guatemalan patriots from 1954 to the present. The systematic violation of human rights has increased in Guatemala since Ríos Montt took power, and he has continued policies of genocide that were initiated and followed by his predecessors. This has caused the majority of the Guatemalan people, faced with the institutionalization of terror as a form of government which denies all legal possibility of struggle, to exercise their right to self-defense. This policy of terror is fomented and fed by the governments of the United States, Israel, Chile, and Argentina, which have intervened in the internal affairs of Guatemala openly and covertly.

In 1970, militarization of the Guatemalan state intensified with the generals' and colonels' seizure of power and takeover of the large public and private businesses. Subsequently, their power was maintained by force against the interests of the majority through successive electoral frauds. Popular opposition grew as citizens were denied the most elemental rights and guarantees, and this opposition was countered by the regime, first with the kidnapping and murder of leaders, next with indiscriminate massive repression in the cities, and last with a scorched earth policy in the rural areas.

The military regime, presently headed by General Efraín Ríos Montt, is now trying to alter national and international public opinion. In its attempt to deal with international isolation and the general crisis in the country, it seeks to make the public believe that everything has changed in Guatemala.

To prove the historic responsibility of Ríos Montt and other military officials, it is sufficient to cite some concrete examples. Until 1970, Ríos Montt was Director of Studies at the Interamerican Defense Group in Washington, D.C., which essentially follows the principles of U.S. national security and protects U.S. ideological boundaries. Counterinsurgency plans for many Latin American countries emerge from this center. In 1971, Ríos Montt was called by General Carlos Arana Osorio to be Chief of Staff of the army. As Chief of Staff, he set up the paramilitary bands which, under various names, proceeded to combat "communism" through kidnapping and assassination.

Ríos Montt personally commanded the operation to annihilate the *campesinos* of Jalapa in the eastern part of the country. The mountain people from Jalapa had risen up because the landowners intended to evict them from their lands. Ríos Montt, from an armed helicopter, directed the massacre.

I can personally attest to this because I covered these events as a reporter for the newspaper *El Imparcial*.

Subsequently Ríos Montt served the government of General Kjell Laugerud García as military attaché to the Guatemalan embassy in Spain. Upon leaving this post, he continued on active duty in the army until he participated in the coup d'état of March 23, 1982.

Ríos Montt's present collaborators have also served in the army without interruption and occupied high positions in successive governments. There are many examples, but we will mention only a few. The present Minister of Defense, General Oscar Humberto Mejía Víctores [who replaced Ríos Montt as President through a coup in August 1983 — Eds.], served the Arana Osorio government as commander of various military bases. Later, under General Kjell Laugerud García, he joined the General Staff of the army, where he served as Under Chief and temporarily as Chief. During the Lucas García government, he became Chief of Staff of the army.

Similarly, the present Minister of the Interior, Colonel Ricardo Méndez Ruiz, has served the Guatemalan military regime uninterruptedly. He was a police functionary and later a commander of military bases. Under Lucas García he served as commander of the Cobán military base in the department of Alta Verapaz.

There is also the case of Colonel Pablo Nuila Hub, present chief of the Division of Information of the army. Under the Arana Osorio government, he had been chief of the secret police, who do essential work related to psychological warfare. Nuila Hub was the founder and the first director of Infierno-Kaibil, the elite counterinsurgency school, under the governments of Laugerud and Lucas García. Another case is Colonel Mario Ramírez Ruiz, present director of the National Police School, a post that he has had since 1980. He was previously the chief of public relations for the national police during the governments of Arana Osorio, Laugerud García, and Lucas García. He teaches counterinsurgency courses on U.S. military bases.

If we proceeded through the military and police, we would find colonels who have served these governments without interruption since 1970. Some of the chiefs who directed the attack on the Spanish embassy in Guatemala on January 31, 1980, still continue in the army and the police. Many of the agents who threw firebombs and attacked Spanish Ambassador Máximo Cajal when he was trying to escape from the fire still continue in the police. All of this leads us to conclude that the government of Ríos Montt is no different from previous governments, since it is not possible for there to have been any change without substantial modification of the military and police structures of the state apparatus, at least in regard to repression.

During my time in the Ministry of the Interior, I followed with much interest the counterinsurgency project suggested by representatives of the U.S. government to Lucas García. The project, called the Program of Pacification and Eradication of Communism, was discussed at length with a view to its application in Guatemala. It was a dossier of about 420 pages that gathered together the U.S. experiences in Vietnam, Nicaragua, El Salvador, Argentina, Chile, and Uruguay.

This project consists in essence of two phases which are: the government's public justification for selective and then massive and indiscriminate repression in the cities, under the "Theory of the Extremes," which implies a violent confrontation between the left and the right; and later a civil war. This is designed to explain what is happening in the rural areas as peasants confronting guerrillas, resulting in a civil war. In truth, it was the regime which began implementation of the scorched earth policy in 1981 under Lucas García. That action was later intensified by Ríos Montt.

I know this to be true because I was consulted on the propaganda for the first phase to the extent that I drafted the first communiqué about the resurgence of the Secret Anticommunist

Army, a sad memory, at the beginning of 1970. A list of 36 names of leaders in different sectors who had been "sentenced to death by communists" was later added to this communiqué. The chief of military intelligence, Colonel Héctor Montalván, gave this list to the Minister of the Interior. I then gave this communiqué with instructions from the Minister of the Interior to agents of the secret police, who in turn took it to the press. This shows that it was not the extremes that were confronting each other, but rather it was the government that planned and committed the murders and kidnappings.

I was also consulted in the second phase of the project, regarding its implementation in terms of propaganda through the press (psychological warfare). The regime had to reiterate repeatedly that the guerrillas were committing the massacres and that "the people" were defending themselves. In reality it was the special troops and the paramilitary groups who were committing the massacres while benefiting from the ongoing psychological warfare.

Testimony of
Pedro Luis Ruiz

Indian peasant and
former member of the Guatemalan army

I was born in 1954, and in 1960 I began school. There I became aware for the first time of how indigenous children were treated. I couldn't stand it. Because they didn't teach us much, and because my parents were very poor, I left school at the age of nine and went to work. For many years, my dream was to have a lot of money and to buy a pair of new shoes.

When I was 17 years old, I joined the military service. I was happy because I would have shoes and good clothes. But the military commissioner put me in jail for two days; then the commander arrived and stuck 60 of us into a truck and took us to Marshal Gregorio Soleres's quarters. On the road, we were beaten, and I got scared. When we got there, we encountered several hundred other men. We were beaten a lot. I looked around and saw my *compañeros* crying. A few days later, they took a lot of my friends away. I couldn't stand it any more and escaped through the kitchen window. I later returned, however, and presented myself to the Honor Guard. They arrested me, and later, by order of the service officer, they hit me in the stomach.

They began to train me. Lieutenant Pérez asked me, "What have you come for?" And I told him that I had come to serve my country. He told me that my parents were involved in political parties and that I had to be against them, "because they are against the army and against you," he said. "You are a highly valued authority, and a soldier is as good as 10 other men."

They said to us, "You can always kill your own parents and brothers if they are involved in an organization. If you don't, then

you will die." And we would respond at the top of our voices, full
of fear, saying yes to everything. And then they would punch us
in the stomach again. Every day it was the same thing. I hoped
for some change, and that they would teach me to read. But I
realized that every day they would say the same things to us: "How
does a soldier defend himself? What are his strengths, and how
does he become respected?" And the training was to beat us until
they drew blood.

In practice, you become an assassin of your own *compañeros*.
Lieutenant Germán Morales would insult the indigenous people and our customs. He wanted us to trade our parents for
machine-guns and our girlfriends for prostitutes. The lieutenant
himself would teach us how to rape women. He would tell us to
get women—we would grab those who didn't want to go and take
them to him. He would then turn them over to the soldiers; and
since we were brainwashed, we thought this was good.

When I discovered this was bad, it was too late. What I believed
to be the truth was that I was serving my country, when in fact
we were only serving the colonels, their sons, and their women.

I was a soldier first-class, then a corporal, then a second
sergeant. They made me a corporal because I had the courage
to strike my own *compañeros*, and did not feel sorry for them, and
I had the stomach to watch anything that was done.

They made me a messenger. Every day I would go to the
National Palace to leave off dispatches, one to the Ministry of
Defense and another to the Chief of Staff of the army, or to the
G-2 to deliver secret messages or requests for the kidnapping of
people. I also had to go to Marshal Zabala's, to Justo Rufino
Barrio's, to pick up gasoline; to the air force and the army com-
missaries to buy things for Colonel Gustavo Adolfo Pinto Carillo,
Colonel Aristeres Sosa, and Ruben Suárez (whiskey and cognac,
which they would later sell at a higher price).

We would have only five minutes to eat, and they fed us rice
and beans with a little bit of bread. They would feed meat and
rice to their dogs.

Since I saw myself as being in authority, it didn't bother me
to beat up my fellow peasants. The bosses would say that we had

to hit them—if we didn't, we could die for not defending our country. They also asked us to listen to gatherings of people, to monitor them. And when we heard a general or a colonel being talked about, we had to report this immediately and, if possible, take the person in.

I only understood how stupid I had been after I was discharged in 1975. Then they offered me a good salary to stay at the National Palace as an informant to persecute people. But I was in love, and I went back to my home town. However, when I got there, I felt like a nothing. I was only used to hitting and yelling.

MILITARY COMMISSIONER

In spite of this, after I had been back in my home town for five months, I was named military commissioner by the Military Reserve Command, and I accepted. I had 80 commissioned assistants under me. I was named liaison with the Military Reserve Command. Every month I had meetings with all my assistants; they would come to tell me about what was going on in their neighborhoods or villages and I would tell the Command.

My first mission was to report every eight days on the products essential to the people, on the price of corn, beans, sugar, coffee, salt. Second, I had to find out how many political parties there were, whether they were left or right, the names of the leaders, whether they were ladinos or Indians, and which party was closest to the people. Third, I had to investigate every type of religion, what they were preaching, the names of the priests and the teaching nuns, the evangelical ministers, and whether they talked about communist politics. I also had to investigate how many cooperatives there were, and who organized them. I would give all these orders to my *compañeros*, and they would keep me informed.

I was a commissioner for two years, keeping the Command informed. But I also kept a couple of priests informed, because I trusted them, and they would tell me that I was hurting my people. And, in fact, many of my assistants would tell me things that were not true, and I finally changed my mind. I was influenced,

too, by a relative who was at City Hall, sent there by the Indians.
I also resigned because I realized that I was being exploited, since
I was paid very poorly for what I did.

Captain Marín, Chief of G-2 at El Quiché, called for me and
asked if anybody was threatening me. He said that I didn't need
to be afraid, that I should just tell him—he would take care of
everything.

But my relative was a good man, and I loved him a lot. He
explained many things to me. So I left it all and went to the capital
so that they would forget about me.

The following year, I returned to my home town. There was
another commissioner. And I noticed when they started kidnapping from my town. After I had a change of heart, I began to
notice everything.

On March 29, the police from the Treasury Department killed
three peasants. I saw how they did it; half an hour later they said
it had been done by the guerrillas. I told a peasant that it hadn't
been the guerrillas but the Treasury Department police, and I
went to pick up the bodies. A few days later, the army began to
persecute me. They surrounded my house. That very day they
kidnapped my dear relative and tortured him, and they blamed
his assassination on the guerrillas.

But they couldn't deceive me. I know perfectly well that it was
the government (*la judicial,* secret police). I know the kidnapper
of my relative, I recognized his car.

The army always wants to deceive us. I know that they are
a bunch of assassins of the Guatemalan people and can only think
of how to terrorize the people.

As a former soldier in the army, I give this testimony before
the Permanent People's Tribunal, for everything that they did to
me in the army. I am a witness to the fact that the kidnappers
and torturers are the army, that now they are with Ríos Montt,
and that they are the ones who are guilty and responsible for all
the drugs given to the poor soldiers, so that they will commit such
crimes.

On Human Rights in Guatemala

Marco Antonio Sagastume
Guatemalan Human Rights Commission

The lack of economic, social, and political rights for the large majority of the Guatemalan people, and the resultant social and economic inequality, are the roots of the violations of human rights in this country.

Beginning with the Spanish conquest, the mechanisms for constructing a colonial and political system to exploit the natives and their lands took shape. An ideology of racial discrimination was established that gradually made this situation of domination acceptable. The noble and courageous history of the people was hidden from them, in an effort to eliminate their rebelliousness. Nevertheless, there were several indigenous uprisings, and these were answered with death. Villages and native people were burned in a manner similar to what occurs today.

The independence of 1821 did not alter the living conditions of the indigenous population. In fact, the mechanisms of racial discrimination were refined to deny them political participation in decision-making. The Republic of Guatemala began with a dictatorship that lasted 30 years, with liberals and conservatives alternating power; the governing oligarchy created the legal means that allowed forced labor to exist.

Cacao, indigo, cochineal, kermes, and coffee, all products for export to enrich a minority, were produced with the sweat and

blood of the large majority of peasants, who themselves were
malnourished on a diet of corn and beans.

The 20th century began with the granting of large concessions of natural resources to foreign companies. Responding to
the unfair competition of foreign capital, the local oligarchy
graciously served as intermediary.

In 1944, because of protests by urban sectors, General Jorge
Ubico handed over government authority to three generals who
were in turn overthrown on October 20, 1944, by an armed
movement. A period then began in which popular participation
was favored legally, politically, and ideologically. *As a result,
Guatemala was admitted as a member state of the United Nations on
November 21, 1945.*

Guatemala gave tangible form to its new national perspective in the preparatory meetings for the Universal Declaration
of Human Rights of December 10, 1948. It declared that the
Declaration was the greatest historical proof ever of *consensus omnia
gentium* with respect to a specific system of values; that it considered
the Declaration to be an inspiration and guide in the growth of
the international community towards becoming a community not
only of nations but also of individuals, free and equal. Guatemala
promised to proclaim, guarantee, and comply with everything
in the Declaration. It also recalled the importance of the speech
given by the President of the United States of America on
February 12, 1918, *on the necessity of the principle of the self-determination
of peoples*.

In 1948, all the nations of the world, in conformity with the
U.N. Charter, committed themselves to respect mutually contracted obligations according to *the principle of fulfillment in good
faith*. The use of *ius ad bellum* was declared unlawful. Nations would
refrain from resorting to *the threat or use of force against the territorial
integrity or political independence of any state, or in any manner inconsistent with the purposes of the United Nations* (article of the U.N. Charter
proposed by the United States).

Yet the very nation—the U.S.—that proposed the principle
mentioned above violated the sovereignty of another nation in
1954, by planning, directing, and financing an armed intervention

against the constitutional Guatemalan government of Jacobo Arbenz Guzmán.

It violated *the peaceful solution of controversies* (Resolution 2625 XXV, which states that controversies will be resolved in such a way as not to endanger peace, international security, or justice). It also violated *the policy of nonintervention*, by which all members of the United Nations promised not to intervene, either directly or indirectly, in the internal or external affairs of other nations, regardless of motive. Therefore, not only armed intervention, but also any other form of interference or unlawful threat against the nation, or the political, economic, and cultural elements that make up the nation, are violations of international law. In addition, it violated *the principles of equal rights and of self-determination of people*, consecrated in the Charter of the U.N., in which all people have the right to freely choose their own political condition and to carry on their economic, social, and cultural development without external interference.

Both Guatemala and the United States enjoy all of the rights and *are subject to all of the duties stemming from the Charter of the United Nations.*

The United States of America violated the principles that it proposed in the U.N. in 1945 and 1948, with premeditated intervention in another member state. Thus began its increasing complicity in the violation of human rights in Guatemala: in the realm of the rights specified in the International Covenant on Economic, Social and Cultural Rights; in the maintenance, support, and reinforcement of regimes that oppress and repress Guatemalan workers; and in the realm of the rights specified in the International Covenant on Civil and Political Rights, by giving all necessary military assistance to suppress the right to life of a people who are organizing and fighting for their basic freedoms. The United States is the closest ally of the oligarchy, which bases its high standard of living on the low living standard of the large majority of Guatemalans, and has taken or given away the nonrenewable resources that belong to the entire population.

All of the measures to progressively achieve the full enjoyment of those rights recognized in the International Covenant on

Economic, Social and Cultural Rights (Article 2), which were implemented during the decade 1944-1954, have been annulled by the governments of Guatemala from 1954 to this date. The laws that provided for the general well-being of the population were annulled. Along with these annulments came violations of human rights set forth in the International Covenant on Civil and Political Rights, specifically the right to life, which is the basis for world peace.

The right to self-determination is an essential condition for the existence of other fundamental rights and freedoms. Only when it has achieved self-determination can a nation adopt those measures necessary to consecrate human dignity, the full enjoyment of all rights, and the political, economic, social, and cultural progress of mankind without discrimination. The right of self-determination is a right of the people according to the Declaration [on the granting of Independence to Colonial Countries and Peoples — Eds.] approved in Resolution 1514 of the General Assembly of the United Nations.

Since 1963, the army of Guatemala has been completely in charge of the repressive machine used against the people of Guatemala, controlling all the political mechanisms that make laws affecting the people's needs. Working with the oligarchy, whose economic power is consolidated, the army maintains the exploitation of a large majority of the population, and violates the human rights of the people, who claim only their minimum rights and fundamental freedoms. In exchange, the dominant economic groups allow the army to participate in certain profits so that their interests coincide.

Guatemala, as a member state of the U.N., is legally obliged to fulfill and respect the international instruments that are in force. It has ratified the Convention for the Prevention and Punishment of the Crime of Genocide and the conventions regarding the elimination of all forms of racial discrimination. On the American continent, Guatemala became the eighth member of the Organization of American States to ratify the American Convention on Human Rights, May 26, 1978; that convention contains the human rights specified by the Universal Declaration of Human

Rights and the international agreements on human rights. . . .

In Guatemala, General Arana Osorio [who took power in 1970—Eds.] left a wake of napalm in several villages that supposedly collaborated with revolutionary insurgents who had left the national army. He also created various paramilitary squads that publicly and openly murdered people. Through a fraudulent election, Arana Osorio transferred political power to General Laugerud, who ordered the Panzós massacre of May 29, 1978, in which over 100 indigenous peasants protesting the illegal theft of their lands were massacred by the army. Political power was handed over to General Lucas García in 1978 through another electoral fraud, violating the political rights of the Guatemalan people contained in Articles 13, 15, 27, and 34 of the Constitution of the Republic and other complementary laws.

General Lucas García, owner of several large landed estates in the north of the country, began his presidential term of office with the removal of the leaders of all existing popular organizations; the mass murder of labor union leaders, peasants, students, and newspaper reporters; and the involuntary disappearance of thousands of people. . . .The government of Lucas García considered Guatemalan youth to be subversive. This was contrary to the resolution of the General Assembly of the U.N. in 1978 that pointed out the necessity to spread among the young the ideals of peace, respect for human rights, and fundamental freedoms.

The systematic and generalized violations of human rights by the Guatemalan army and the repressive squads under its orders clearly show that they have adopted measures, both on the domestic level and with the inhuman cooperation of other nations, to progressively block the enjoyment of human rights. These rights are derived from the economic, social, educational, scientific, and cultural norms contained in the Charter of the Organization of American States. Thus they violate Article 26 of the American Convention on Human Rights. The military government of Guatemala, as the representative of a member state of the U.N., cannot argue that it is unaware of the human rights that it promised to promote and fulfill. . . .

In 1980, the repression in Guatemala intensified to such

extremes that the entire world was shaken by the burning of the Spanish embassy with peasants, professionals, and diplomats inside. All the legal and peaceful roads of action taken by the people were closed to them.

In 1981, the government moved from a policy of repression by means of selective murders to widespread repression through genocide. The military operations called "scorched earth" consisted of the massacre of whole villages, the burning of dwellings, crops and domestic animals. The goal was to leave no witnesses; hundreds of corpses of Indian peasants, women, children and the elderly appeared, all marked by torture methods never before seen in Guatemala. The skulls of children were found crushed and beaten in. The squalid living conditions of the large majority are aggravated by these tortures, murders, and terror.

Under threat of death, peasants were forced to form civilian paramilitary patrols to fight against the masses who had organized in different ways. Hatred between Guatemalans was fomented. One tactic was to offer pounds of beans to starving peasants in exchange for their picking up guns against other Guatemalans. The army calls this "Beans and Guns" (Frijol y Fusil). . . .

From 1954 to 1981, international humanitarian organizations calculated that 83,500 murders were committed by the government or under its auspices. The Interamerican Commission on Human Rights condemned the Guatemalan military government as one of the major violators of human rights on the continent. At the same time, the popular organizations grew and defended themselves against government repression. The legitimacy of their struggle in self-defense was recognized, given the impossibility of defense through legal channels.

The isolation of the military regime by the world community necessitated a change in image, so that its genocidal policy could be intensified. General Efraín Ríos Montt took charge of the government by a coup d'état on March 23, 1982, pushing aside other military officials.

The speech of this general [when he seized power—Eds.] promised that his government would be based on respect for human rights. That very same day, in the villages of Parraxtuc,

Pajarito, and Pichiquil, bordering on the departments of Huehuetenango and El Quiché, 500 indigenous peasants, men, women, children, and the elderly were massacred by the army.

All the laws that contain individual and collective guarantees and fundamental freedoms, and specifically the Constitution of the Republic, were annulled by means of Decree 24-82. A return to constitutionality and punishment of the violators of human rights were promised, while at the same time political parties were suspended, as were all the political rights of the Guatemalan people.

On June 9, 1982, General Ríos Montt was named President of the Republic by the army of Guatemala and therefore is responsible before the nations of the world for the acts of the government. A political right such as popular democratic elections is not violated with impunity. Yet Ríos Montt filled by appointment all the offices that normally should be filled by popular elections, such as mayors and other local authorities. Legislative, executive and judicial functions have been fused.

Massacres based on the scorched earth strategy have intensified throughout the entire nation; the mass murders of 6,000 people were committed during the first six months of the Ríos Montt government.

Although military statutes prohibit the formation of paramilitary squads, the army has organized paramilitary squads throughout the country publicly and using threats of death.

More than one hundred thousand peasants, especially poor Indians and "ladinos" have sought refuge in Mexico, fleeing from death. Many have testified to the atrocities committed by the army. Within Guatemala's borders, one million persons have been displaced by the scorched earth strategy, concentrated in strategic villages and forced to declare that the massacres of villages, the air force bombings of the villages, etc., are carried out by organizations of the people. The "Beans and Guns" operation of General Lucas García has been further developed by Ríos Montt.

Amnesty has been offered to the members of the army and their collaborators who have acted excessively in their duties, thus absolving them from responsibility.

The destitute and impoverished conditions of the great majority of the population are exacerbated by the government's policy of genocide.

On July 1, 1982, under Ríos Montt, the State of Siege went into effect. Thus it is no longer necessary to murder so many news reporters since the army controls all general news and information. Secret tribunals have been created, based on laws that violate Articles 8, 9, 10, and 11 of the Universal Declaration of Human Rights. . . .The genocide practiced by the army and related groups shows a special cruelty to children, women, and the elderly of Indian villages, and violates Articles 2, 3, 4, 5, and 6 of the Universal Declaration of Human Rights on the protection of women and children during emergencies or armed conflict (Res. 3318 XXIX of the U.N.).

Sagastume then summarizes other international agreements signed by the Guatemalan government and violated under Ríos Montt, in particular the convention on genocide (Articles II and V) and human rights conventions. Also violated is the Convention on the International Right of Correction, through the control of information by the army, which prevents the public from being fully and accurately informed. He concludes:

The government of the United States is guilty of complicity in the above-mentioned crimes, as well as those third-party nations that have collaborated, such as Israel and Chile.

The need for a real solution to economic and social inequality, and the impossibility of obtaining a transformation of political power by peaceful and legal means, have given rise to the popular conviction that it is necessary to organize for self-defense and thus confront government repression by all possible means. At the same time, a democratic representative government must be installed that guarantees respect for human rights.

The violations of human rights of the people of Guatemala, carried out by the army and presided over by General Ríos Montt, are an offense against the world community. One does not have to "deserve" human rights; they are inherent in human dignity.

The Guatemalan Human Rights Commission declares that it does not support any one political party, but desires an alternative of peace and progress for the people of Guatemala, based on respect for those human rights recognized by the world community.

Testimony of
Guillermo Morales Pérez

Indian peasant

My name is Guillermo Morales Pérez, and I am here as a witness for my people in Guatemala. My residence is Bullaj, Tajumulco, department of San Marcos. I live between two villages: Monte Cristo and Bullaj. Today I am going to tell everything that is happening in Guatemala under President Ríos Montt.

As a witness I am going to testify before the public and the members of the jury as to how we have spent the months of 1982. When Ríos Montt became President, he announced that he was going to be democratic, but how long did the democracy of Ríos Montt last? Only 20 days, no more. After 20 days, he began to massacre, kidnap, and torture, according to the radio, and we heard that our brothers were being kidnapped and tortured.

The army entered the village of Bullaj the first time quietly, voluntarily, with affection, and what did they do? They deceived the people, they deceived us, they did what Ríos Montt ordered. He sent his army to trick us, and what happened when they entered? They killed two men. On May 15, 1982, the army entered and killed two men, dragging them out of their homes. The army men do not love their brothers, they think of us as animals. It's the same as when we go to kill a chicken. The army men no longer have mercy for Christians; they no longer have sympathy; they only think of us as animals. But it is they who have become animals, these government employees, this government, because it is the government that has declared a law to kill us for being peasants.

The army returned on July 20, and what did they do to us? The committed an injustice, because they came to the edge of these two villages, surrounded them, and started firing bullets to kill all the people who lived in the two villages. They succeeded in entering the village, and they set up camp. And out of fear, we fled. We went about 50 meters away from the houses because while we were inside, they had continued to fire at us. We left at night, without cover, dragging the children along. Women, 25 and 30 years old, pregnant, crept out of their houses. Others had just given birth only two days before. Even in their situation, they had to leave their homes, and they were very bitter, what with the bullets and all. Filled with fright, we had to leave, with the army on top of us, and we, what could we respond with? We are nobody, and they called us guerrillas.

And what type of guerrillas are we if we have nothing, if we only work in the fields? Our struggle is to work enough to be able to feed and maintain our families and to live through the year. Because if we do not work, we cannot live. The condition of the land where we live is bad. We don't have 300 or 1,000 *cuerdas*; we have scarcely one, five, or 10 *cuerdas* [one *cuerda* is the equivalent to 350 square meters—Eds.]. There is nowhere to put any livestock, or any other type of animal. We don't have that possibility. Thus, we can only work the land; it's the only way we can earn a living. . . .

The shooting lasted from July 20 to July 22, almost three days. Then we returned to our houses. We proclaimed that we had not committed any crime because all we do is work in the fields. This is what we did. But what did they do? The set up camp in the village of Bullaj; we remained in our homes and continued working. On July 24 they began to bombard, bombard, bombard. They shot bullets all over, it was a noise like one hears when it rains on the coffee trees, like one hears in the *charunales* [trees that are used to provide shade for the coffee trees—Eds.]. We heard the shots very well, and they fell like a light rain. We ran away in fright, in terror, because we had never heard so many shots before.

Two more men were killed: Marcos Cash, 65 years old, and Luciano Chávez, 35 years old—they killed them, they hung them up. This evil army hung them, they knifed them in the neck, and at the same time they stuck them in their sides. They did all this

the way they wanted, just like killing an animal to eat. This is
what they did to our brothers.

We ran from the fear that we felt, with this constant bombardment that lasted two more days, July 24 and July 25. The
following day, July 26, they camped in the village again. On
July 27, they began burning all the houses. They burned the
houses, they burned everything that was inside them—clothes,
beds, our personal documents, money—all these things were
burned. And at the same time, they ate all the animals, and what
they could not eat, they shot full of holes. It lasted almost seven
days, ending on August 2. From July 20 to August 2, 1982, 45
houses in all were burned. During this period, 300 or more army
soldiers were in the village.

They returned November 24. And they returned in another
way, trying to deceive us again. What did they do? They entered
the village without making any noise, they came without firing
a shot, very quietly, and we trusted them. Perhaps they were not
going to do anything. Perhaps everything was over. Because according to what Ríos Montt said on the news, everyone was supposed to return to their homes and to rebuild them. The army
was not going to continue burning; he said, "I repent for having
burned your homes." In a note sent to the mayor of the Tajumulco
he said, "Rebuild your homes, don't be afraid of the army, when
they come, they will come in peace, they will not repeat their acts."

We felt safe and trusting, because we really felt that we had
not committed any crime. We thought that we had not wronged
Ríos Montt; we only claimed our rights to live well with what
we earn from our own work. What did the army do on November
24 in the village of Monte Cristo? That afternoon, around
4:00 p.m., they divided up to go to the houses of the village, and
captured four families, little boys and girls, teenagers, old men
and women. They took them to where the army was camped and
brought them before their commander. What did the commander
of the army say? "Kill these lazy good-for-nothings, because they
are with the guerrillas." They were then killed with machetes and
knives, without using firearms. They cut off the head and arms
of one of the women; they left her without head and arms, and

they cut open her chest with a knife. Her name was Luisa Martín. And in this manner, they finished off all members of the four families, 18 people in all. The names of the dead people are: Joaquín Martín, Emiliano Martín, Juventino Hernández, Felipe Chávez, Jesús Ramos, Lucía Martín, Chavela Martín with three children, María Ramos, Esperanza Ramos, Oracio Martín and four other children from two to five years of age.

The following day, they continued burning houses and robbing whatever they found, things that the people had worked for. There were around 150 soldiers who entered the village on November 24 and 25.

We have heard the news that Ríos Montt wants to end the war with "Beans and Guns." There in our village, we see very clearly what the army does — bombard, shoot, burn houses, kill people, and destroy all the food supplies in the village. We have never seen this offer of beans that the news speaks of. . . .

So many of our friends and family have died, and in addition to this, Ríos Montt has given orders for the creation of groups to patrol under his orders. On December 23, these patrols killed Santiago López, 55 years old; Rafael Chávez, 35 years old; and Rosalía Chávez, a 14-year-old girl. What did they do to this girl? They raped her and then killed her. They killed her 10 meters inside the Mexican border, but they took her out again and buried her 10 meters inside the Guatemalan border. This is what the patrol did under orders from the army. . . .

The landowners have also acted in an evil way toward us. They give us a task which takes two days to do, and we only earn one *quetzal*, 50 *centavos*. Meat with bone is one *quetzal* for half a kilo, and pure meat costs one *quetzal*, 65 *centavos* for half a kilo. To be able to buy this half kilo of meat, we must work for two days. In reality, we do not eat any meat, and our families eat only a little tamale with salt. We cannot eat anything else the way the rich people can: milk, meat, eggs, vegetables, avocados — all the things that are at the market, that the land produces.

The rich people have all of this. And they have us like slaves, like animals, like beasts of burden, and they ride us. We carry them on our backs and give the rich man what he wants — we do everything.

Our personal dignity is dominated; and because of the lack of schooling and food, our children are the way they are, like me, with little schooling, even to explain this message I am giving. The majority of the country is also like this. We have no teachers, and at the same time, we do not have enough time to learn. There is much injustice in Guatemala. This is what I came to testify here in this country of Spain, so you will help us, because we can no longer stand the situation in Guatemala. Just as we are together here today, all together, we are brothers. We believe in this brotherhood and for this reason we plead for help and aid, to help our Guatemala be healed, that we may live in freedom and tranquility, and that we may all live together as brothers. Thank you.

Testimony of
Regina Hernández

Guatemalan Committee for
Justice and Peace, refugee program

My name is Regina Hernández, and I am a member of the Guatemalan Committee for Justice and Peace (Comité Pro-Justicia y Paz de Guatemala). I have come before the Permanent People's Tribunal to give testimony about the displaced persons, or refugees, inside Guatemala. Before leaving Guatemala, I spent several months with these refugees, sharing their life of terror and anguish.

They are the survivors of massacres perpetrated by the army in the villages in the highlands of Guatemala. They are those who managed to escape when their houses and crops were burned. Many of them witnessed the murders of their parents, brothers and sisters, spouses, and children.

Some are entire villages or communities who scattered to hide in the mountains when they heard that the army was near, to avoid being massacred like neighboring villages.

Others discovered earlier that the army was approaching, and because of the terror sown by the soldiers wherever they go, these people preferred to seek refuge in the capital or in other regions of the country, with the idea of returning to their villages when things settled down.

Others are families who have some relative or relatives connected with the opposition or "people's organizations" in Guatemala, and are thus "guilty by association."

The majority have no place to go and continually flee from one place to another. In their letter celebrating Holy Thursday, the bishops of Guatemala calculated the number of these refugees

or displaced persons inside the country as more than one million.
They also said that more houses have been destroyed by the current repression than were destroyed in the earthquake of 1976.
The number of refugees has grown, because the repression—
instead of decreasing—has become more acute.

* * *

HOW THE DISPLACED PERSONS LIVE

The conditions of our lives are very bad. If once we lived in
misery, under inhuman conditions, today our situation is worse—
it is indescribable. We try to survive by imitating little wild animals,
fleeing constantly in self-defense like hunted rabbits or deer. But
the difference is that we are people, and it is difficult for us to
move around—the colors of our clothes, especially the *huipiles*
[traditional blouses, known for their beauty—Eds.] of the native
women, make us targets, and we travel from place to place in
groups of hundreds and sometimes thousands.

There are families with five or six children, small children
who must be carried. To see a woman with one child on her back
and one at her waist is very sad. Children who can walk carry
a few clothes or a little food.

You fall and scramble up again. You hurt yourself on the thorns
along the path, and then salty perspiration runs down into these
cuts. This burns, as you can imagine! Then, when you decide
to rest a little, the mosquitoes and flies crowd around to suck up
your blood.

It is incredible how the children tolerate this without crying.
What they can't stand is knowing that the army is near. I remember
when we were in a small village and it was rumored that the soldiers
were coming. All the children began to shout with fear and
anguish.

When we found a place away from the soldiers, we would sit
down to eat and share whatever we were able to bring along. We
were so hungry that a cold corn tortilla and a little salt (if we had
any) tasted wonderful. When we ran out of tortillas, we would

go a day with only half a glass of corn meal mixed with water; this was all we had for the whole day.

We would also search for herbs we recognized and eat the leaves. This was during the winter, the season when the herbs grow. Sometimes all we had was a raw ear of corn that we found in those places where the crops had not been destroyed by the army. In the mountains, the refugees eat anything to survive.

Imagine what disease you find in these places where everything is lacking, where we must sleep exposed to the rain and wear our clothes wet until they dry out again. So many children have died of diarrhea, measles, pneumonia! If they don't die at the hands of the army, they die from disease.

So we move on, in growing numbers. In the mountains there are places that resemble the settlements constructed after the earthquake, where you find 1,500 to 2,000 families, places where you might eat only tortillas once or twice a day. Sometimes you wait a long time before getting to taste a little salt. There are places where people have gone to the extreme of drinking their own urine, because the rivers might be poisoned. We have also quenched our thirst with the dew that forms on the leaves of the plants.

Nevertheless, in the middle of all the anguish and terror that the army causes us, we try to encourage and inspire each other, to cheer each other up. One time we organized a little party, with guitars and violins, sharing with each other some of what we had left. We do this to have a few joyful moments and not to go crazy from anguish.

It's during these times that we live the Gospel—with deeds, not only with words. When we get to a place, we look around and check to see that everyone has arrived, that someone has not gotten lost along the way, that none of the children are missing. We all worry about each other. If we plan to stay in a spot for some time, we share what we have brought along to eat, and the few blankets or plastic covers that we managed to carry along to cover us at night. This is how we celebrate our faith, by sharing everything: sorrow, grief, suffering, and joy.

THE FEAR OF MODEL VILLAGES

All the things our people need are, for the government, a means of pressure to force us to turn ourselves in. They trick the international press into believing that the government is a savior, regrouping people and offering them "shelter, food, and work." But you don't know how much sorrow there is in the hearts of the people that the government has relegated to "model villages." How can people agree with a government that has murdered their families and burned everything they had? If they are living in these "model villages," it is because they are there under threat. Men must be part of the civilian patrols; if they don't do it, they are killed.

DAYS OF ANGUISH IN CHIMALTENANGO

I would like to tell you what happened on July 16, 17, and 18, 1982, when the army entered the village of San Martín Jilotepeque in the department of Chimaltenango. They entered the village on July 16, at 11:30 a.m., accompanied by civilian patrols. That day I was with a friend who had asked me to come to her house. We couldn't get there, because in the road we met all these people running away from the soldiers. It began to pour down rain that afternoon. We ran from the village and regrouped in a village nearby, with about 400 others, while the soldiers went from house to house, killing chickens to eat and trying on the men's clothes. The soldiers had also gotten wet in the rain and they were nonchalantly changing their clothes.

Meanwhile, in the next village, we got an enormous pot and prepared food for the children. We couldn't sleep because of the shots we heard throughout the night. The next day the soldiers approached the village where we were staying and all of us had to flee again. I remember the dawn of July 17, when we heard the cry, "Run, the soldiers are coming!" The children began to cry, terrorized, but after we started walking, they calmed down some. Each person carried his belongings, his poncho, some tortillas, corn meal, or whatever he could find. Each child who could walk also carried something.

The people of three villages came together in one place. We were resting when we again heard shots nearby. Once again we fled. Finally we came to another place farther away, where we found more people from other villages. There we rested again and shared what we had. We ran out of water and ate dry corn meal. We became nauseated from the lack of water. There were too many of us, so we decided to divide up into smaller groups. Each group went to a different village where we knew there were no soldiers. But in all this activity, families got divided up. In my group, there was a child carrying his mother's clothes and a poncho, while his mother went off in a second group carrying their tortillas. Her oldest child was in a third group, and the father—with the rest of the ponchos—went with yet a fourth group. I also saw a little girl about five years old who had lost her parents. But there we were!

We found a little orange tree loaded with oranges. We picked them all. They were very acidic, but they helped a lot. After a long walk—all day long—we came to another place about 9:00 p.m., and slept there. At this place they gave us hot tortillas, water, and a little salt.

On July 18 at 5:00 a.m., we were all up and ready to go. We washed with the dew from the plants. We found yucca and some other food and we each ate a little. We gave the leftover tortillas to the children. We were busy doing all this when we heard shots. We had to run again. Minutes later we saw the soldiers come running down a road. We had separated into groups of 20. What hurt me the most was seeing the old people with their canes, but thank God we managed to get away. From a distance, we saw the village burn.

When we heard that the soldiers had left our village, we returned home. We got there at 4:00 p.m. It was so sad, watching families find their houses and possessions reduced to ashes!

HELP FOR THE REFUGEES

All this suffering has forced me to leave my country to seek help. We need your help to cry out and denounce what is happening in Guatemala, where they try to smother our cries with massacres. We need your help to survive and to resist this war.

Inside Guatemala, the service that I performed for my people was to bring them a little medicine, some food and clothes that I got from my friends. By sharing I have learned much from them. This little assistance meant risking my life; I knew that if I was found delivering these things, I would disappear forever. Many times I have been on the edge of death, sometimes from bullets and sometimes from flames, when they set fire to the forests. I have had to cross burning forests, practically suffocating from smoke inhalation.

What sadness! In Guatemala, the assassins of the Ríos Montt regime can go everywhere. And we, who have not stained our hands with blood, who have only tried to help, to defend ourselves, and to survive, must travel oh so carefully, hiding as if we were thieves. We are certain that someday there will be justice and that peace will come to Guatemala, with the help of all the people of the world.

The Committee for Justice and Peace has made a promise to bring help to 11 departments of Guatemala. It is one of the urgent tasks that we as Christians must undertake now, in this moment of struggle for our liberation.

Testimony of
Carolina van den Heuvel

Deputy, the European Parliament

The following resolution was adopted by the European Parliament and presented to the Tribunal as testimony by Mrs. van den Heuvel.

The European Parliament

A) Recalling its resolution of September 17, 1982 on the violation of human rights in Guatemala;

B) Alarmed at the scale of the campaign of repression which, in the guise of an anti-guerrilla operation, is mainly aimed at the defenseless rural populations, particularly the Indians;

C) Considering the repeated condemnations by Amnesty International and the recent conclusions of a fact-finding mission by the U.S. National Council of Churches reaffirming the genocide against the Indian population;

D) Whereas 40 political prisoners are liable to be executed at any time;

E) Whereas some one million people are forced to be continually on the move to avoid the massive slaughter;

F) Whereas thousands of Guatemalans have fled from this violence and have sought refuge in adjacent countries, mainly in Mexico, where there are now 250,000 refugees living in wretched circumstances;

G) Having regard to the fact that in the last 18 months, these actions, carried out by government troops, have cost 15,000 innocent citizens their lives;

H) Disturbed by the trajectory of the new regime, which is failing to provide the necessary guarantees for the launching of a genuine process of democratization:

1. Condemns the criminal actions of the Guatemalan authorities, who are controlling and covering up these operations;

2. Asks its President to take measures so that a Parliament delegation can make a visit in order to study firsthand what support can be given by the Community and to call on the United Nations to set up an international committee of inquiry;

3. Regrets the fact that Mexico has returned to Guatemala a thousand refugees, who were shot by the Guatemalan army as soon as they crossed back over the border, and calls on the Mexican government to give all possible aid and reception facilities to refugees trying to escape from these massacres;

4. Calls for urgent humanitarian aid to be granted by the EEC [European Economic Community—Eds.] to the displaced populations who are threatened with famine and to those who seek refuge in the Mexican border area;

5. Calls on the Commission to ensure that European aid reaches the affected populations, through organizations that are independent from the authorities, and with full guarantees as to the management and delivery of this aid;

6. Asks the Council of Foreign Ministers, in political cooperation, to strongly protest these massacres to the Guatemalan government and make joint diplomatic representations to the Guatemalan authorities;

7. Calls on the Council to ask the U.S. government to take this resolution into consideration with regard to its policy of aid to Guatemala;

8. Instructs its President to forward this resolution to the Commission and Council, the Council of Foreign Ministers in political cooperation, the Secretary General of the United Nations, the U.N. High Commission on Refugees, and the governments of Guatemala, Mexico, and the United States.

Testimony of
Philippe Texier
Magistrate

During June 22-29, 1981, a mission composed of the International Movement of Catholic Jurists, Pax Christi International, and the International Federation for Human Rights came to Guatemala to conduct an inquiry about the general situation regarding human rights.

Bearing in mind the terror that reigns in this country, the mission decided not to conduct any interviews with the government authorities, in order to have a wider margin to maneuver in terms of contacts with the people. In spite of the fact that these contacts were difficult and necessarily clandestine, they were made in a broad range of sectors: the church (and, in particular, with Monsignor Ríos Montt, whose brother would take power one year later), peasants, Indians, popular and labor union movements, intellectuals, and jurists.

Guatemala, which is called the land of terror, had not had any demonstrations for a year. The demonstration of May 1, 1980, was the last public expression of the labor unions and popular organizations. In the capital, the military, police, or paramilitary presence produced feelings of great terror. General Lucas García's junta had not taken exceptional measures (declaring a State of Emergency, State of Siege, or curfew). But when night fell, the streets of the capital were deserted and the hotels were empty, in a country of great tourist riches.

MASSACRES OF THE POPULATION

According to the local newspapers, in the first half of 1982, there were an estimated 30 assassinations and a dozen forced disappearances or kidnappings per day. In other words, there were more than 5,000 dead and 1,500 disappeared in six months. All of the population has been affected, but perhaps the most severely hurt are the peasant and indigenous populations of El Quiché, San Marcos, Quezaltenango, Huehuetenango, Sololá, and Chimaltenango. The press echoes these massacres daily, but gives the junta's official version. (For example, the Coya massacre, which took place on July 14, 1981 with a death toll of about 300 peasants, children, and villagers, was reduced by the government to 25 "subversives" killed by the army.) These huge massacres (in particular Coya and Panzós) very concretely raise the question of the juridical concept of genocide, as it is defined in the December 1948 convention on genocide.

Regarding the composition of military forces and the magnitude of the massacres, we have submitted a written report from the mission, but we would emphasize the systematic character of political assassinations carried out by the government. Unlike other countries in Central and South America, in Guatemala there are no political prisoners. Those who oppose the government are physically eliminated.

TORTURES, DISAPPEARANCES

Very few witnesses survive torture, and therein lies the difficulty in obtaining testimonies. The evidence of torture can be seen in the state of the bodies that are discovered daily in ditches, in hidden cemeteries, in the fields, or in the cities. The majority of the bodies are mutilated or burned; pregnant women are cut open. The only direct testimony that we could obtain is included in our report.

Involuntary or forced disappearances, which in Guatemala are numerically very significant, began in 1960. From 1980 to 1981 they increased, but it is impossible to give the exact number because a systematic study could not be made. Sometimes the bodies of the dead are found, as in Comalapa in 1980 (30 in a hidden cemetery), or 23 in 1981 in a common grave. In general it is difficult to identify them because they are tortured, mutilated, or completely shot up by bullets.

In theory, the 1965 Constitution provides recourse to habeas corpus or the "Recourse of Personal Exhibition" [the right to demand to see the physical evidence of a person—Eds.], Article 79, but this text is never applied. The police never submits itself to serious inquiries, and the magistrates confess their impotence faced with the scope of the phenomenon.

A lawyer (who still works clandestinely in defense of union rights) told us about the impossibility of presenting a case to the judges. Out of fear, the judges do not dare either defend or accuse the plaintiffs. In 1980, three judges and six lawyers were assassinated.

In June 1981, recourse to habeas corpus had not existed for a year because all those who could present it, lawyers and others, were in danger of being killed. No lawyer appeared in public anymore. In order to identify dead bodies, or to denounce disappearances, lawyers must assume false names or pass as relatives of the dead.

THE PROBLEM OF THE INDIAN AND THE FORCED DISPLACEMENTS OF THE POPULATION

The forced displacements are very important. They were important in 1981 and their importance increases constantly, whether we are talking about migration toward border countries (particularly Mexico) or internal displacement toward the capital or zones that are far away from people's place of origin. These displacements occur primarily among the indigenous peasant communities of the regions of El Quiché, Quezaltenango, and El Petén.

In the space of several days, we met numerous peasants, unionists, and Indians who lived underground in the poor neighborhoods of the city, under very precarious conditions. Having been forced to leave their birthplaces, most of them lived separated from their families. They have had to give up their traditions and their forms of dress to avoid the army or the security forces.

There are many who seek refuge in Mexico or try to, even risking their lives. On June 17, 1981, in the region of the

Usumacinta River (department of El Petén) many Indians were massacred by 120 armed men, identified as members of the Secret Anticommunist Army (ESA). The majority of the inhabitants of the region, 4,000 people, chose to cross the Usumacinta River and seek refuge on the Mexican side. Mexico has offered political asylum to 1,150 of the 4,000 peasants who have asked for it.

THE STATE OF CIVIL AND POLITICAL LIBERTIES

While all civil and political liberties are theoretically guaranteed by the 1965 Constitution, we can say that as of May 1, 1980, not one of these rights can be exercised. Public expression by labor, peasant, Indian, Christian, or popular organizations does not exist.

Labor union freedoms and the right to strike do not exist any more. In 1980, more than 80 labor union leaders were assassinated or kidnapped, and no competent labor union cadres remain in the companies.

The right of association is no longer respected. To issue any communication, all organizations must take out paid advertisements in the press. This involves great risk for the responsible people, who must personally present themselves with identity cards. Since they cannot distribute their literature, organizations resort to "propaganda bombs" in the neighborhoods of the city. The audio-visual press belongs to the government and is censored; the written press is also censored, and opposition newspapers are circulated clandestinely.

Freedom of religion is not respected either, and Catholic organizations such as the Guatemalan Committee for Justice and Peace or the Confederation of the Religious of Guatemala (Confederación de Religiosos de Guatemala, CONFREGUA) are obliged to exist underground. Simply possessing a Bible has become a subversive act in a country that is primarily Catholic.

In just a few days we perceived very strongly that we were in a country under terror. This impression has been confirmed by the elections of March 1982, which, far from producing a solution, brought about a coup d'état followed by General Ríos Montt's accession to power. The massacres have not ceased, and violations of human rights were as grave and flagrant in 1982 as they were in 1981.

Testimony of Harald Edelstam

Former Swedish Ambassador to Guatemala

During the years 1969 to 1971 I was the Swedish Ambassador in Guatemala. During the latter part of this time, General Arana Osorio was President. He carried the nickname "the Butcher of Zacapa," since in 1967 he had several thousand people killed in the province of Zacapa, where he was military commander. The reason for the killing was that people had given shelter and food to resistance fighters. During the time of President Arana, as well as during earlier periods, injustice, persecution, terror, kidnapping, disappearances, and killings by the military, the police, and right-wing extremists were frequent. A small upper class owned most of the good land and the industry. The Indians were exploited as workers on the coffee, sugar, banana, and cotton plantations. They had little or no schooling and no social or medical services.

No wonder that armed resistance movements emerged to protest the bad living conditions of the poor and to fight against the injustice and persecution. The outside world begins to understand more and more why there are resistance movements, and there is a growing tendency for sectors of international opinion to support their demands and condemn the rulers.

Amnesty International has revealed that the new military junta under the leadership of General Ríos Montt does not respect the minimal human rights. A mission of inquiry sent to Guatemala in July 1982 by the American Public Health Association, the National Association of Social Workers, the Institute of Medicine and the National Academy of Sciences concluded that human rights in Guatemala again were being eroded by a return to repressive measures characteristic of former regimes. A new report from Oxfam America, the international development agency, speaks about the enormous impact of increasing political violence in Guatemala.

It is often argued that the violation of human rights is justified for internal security reasons and by a need to overcome the subversion of political dissidence that threatens the unity of a nation or its economic development. Acceptance of the argument that violations of human rights are justified by a superior interest is a sign of a moral double standard. National security cannot be attained at the expense of human rights and fundamental freedoms.

We must oppose violence as a method for solving political or social problems. We cannot accept the argument that a whole people striving for social and economic reforms should be classified as terrorists.

This session of the Permanent People's Tribunal has an important task to fulfill. That is, to reveal the flagrant violation of human rights occurring in Guatemala and to inform the world about these violations with the hope that the military regime in Guatemala will find it advisable to end the State of Emergency and move towards democratization and greater freedom for all its citizens.

Testimony of
Juan Velázquez Jiménez

Indian peasant and mineworker

My name is Juan Velázquez Jiménez, from the municipality of San Ildefonso Ixtahuacán, department of Huehuetenango. I come as a representative of the people of Guatemala to tell what is happening with the Ríos Montt government. But before that, I would like to speak of what has made my people famous: the problems of the mines at San Ildefonso Ixtahuacán, and the four-day march to the capital of Guatemala that my people made to hold a demonstration.

Work in the mine began when the government signed a 40-year contract with a gringo man [i.e., foreign—Eds.] named René Abularach. The people protested with a demonstration, saying that they did not want the mine. A lawyer came, but the government showed no respect to him. Then the army troops began to arrive at the mine. The army had no respect for the people, but instead began to beat and slaughter them. The municipal mayor was immediately informed of what the army was doing but the mayor did not come, out of fear of the army. Later, the army arrested 15 men from the village, whom they took away. They also took prisoner a priest and a catechist and brought them by truck to the Huehuetanango department seat.

The army charged that the priest was guilty because he was giving guidance to the people. The priest responded that the people were only seeking their rights. The soldiers told the priest that he should not get involved in politics and let him go. The other men were struck, beaten, and kicked, and then were allowed to return to their village.

Later the gringos came to work in the mine and extracted tons of minerals in trucks. The people did not want the mine to continue because it was dangerous for the community. People thought that the community was going to cave in because the miners dug tunnels under people's homes. Tunnels were dug 4 kilometers under people's houses and some of the land in the community did cave in. Then, many people left to go to other, more faraway towns: to Cuilco, Ixcán, and La Costa. We were afraid, thinking that the whole town was going to cave in at once. We also did not want the mine because the lifeblood of the land, a very valuable mineral called tungsten, was being taken to another country.

People formed a union and went to demonstrate at the capital, walking on foot. For four days, they walked to the capital to demonstrate against the mine. Later, the same problems with Mr. Abularach continued. He claimed that the mine was not worth anything, while he was really trying to keep the miners from unionizing.

Now I would like to continue telling about what is going on with the Ríos Montt government. On May 6, 1982, the soldiers left Huehuetenango, and arrived in my town of San Ildefonso Ixtahuacán at noon. Along the road, they grabbed one of my brothers, took off his shirt and his pants, and left him naked. The soldiers tied him up and stuck him in a car. A red truck was in front and two olive green trucks were in back. They arrived at a crossroads where the trucks remained. They also left my brother there tied up in the car, with five soldiers to watch him.

Later, the soldiers arrived at a church where we were having a celebration. They started kicking us around and made us leave. At the celebration there were 45 adults and our children. The soldiers then gathered us together in the basketball court. Later, more soldiers arrived and surrounded the whole village. They began to drag people out of their homes until 10:00 p.m. Then they put us in a school, locked us up and told us to stay there while they ate, saying they were exhausted because of us. They locked the door real well and went to eat.

When they got back, the soldiers began to talk to us: "Now we sure did catch you today, you subversive thieves, you disgraceful

Indians, you savages." We answered, "We are not stealing. We are celebrating the word of God." The second lieutenant said, "There is no God here who will bless you." They grabbed a 22-year-old peasant, and the second lieutenant told him: "All of you are bums and gossips. You are the teachers of all the subversive people here." Then one of the soldiers threw a lasso around the peasant's neck, and they hung him right there from a beam in the school. But the rope broke and the peasant fell to the ground. The second lieutenant kicked him, told him to get up, and then they tied him up again. They hung him again, and beat him all over until he died. Then the soldiers laid his body down.

The second lieutenant asked, "Where are the catechists?" The soldiers grabbed two of them and then three more people. Outside the school, the soldiers began to fire their guns, and those soldiers who were inside the school began to steal watches and money from the people. Then the soldiers took the dead man's body from the school and they brought some bombs inside, saying to us, "Be careful that you don't leave, because you will die." They grabbed 11 people from among those at the school, and took them to prison. My brother, whom they had left in the truck, also was killed. Five soldiers remained at the school, but then they left, with us locked inside. We stayed there crying. At 7 a.m. we broke down the doors of the school, and went home.

The soldiers went to Cuilco but later they returned to Huehuetenango, to the settlement called Laguneta, Aldea Alta in the municipality of San Ildefonso Ixtahuacán. I was working in the cornfields when they came. There were two peasants from the village of La Cumbre Papal, going to work in Chiapas. The soldiers grabbed them and searched their bags; they took away some hats that the peasants had, and then the soldiers tied them up by the neck. Five soldiers pulled at them from one side, and five soldiers from the other. The peasants were left there dead, tied to a tree. The soldiers cut off a piece of flesh from their legs, pants and all, and they left it hanging on a stick. They did that to both of these men.

Then they climbed up on a building and began to shoot. I was trembling with fear. When they arrived at the village of La

Cumbre, they began to burn houses. I went to Laguneta and there I found a municipal employee. I told him that the soldiers had already killed two peasants. "We are not aware of it," said the employee. This happened on June 12, 1982. On June 13, 20 of us got together and went to see the bodies of the dead men. We took off the rope, dug a hole, and we buried them. And this I saw with my own eyes, because it is not good to tell lies.

On June 15, 1982, I was buying medicine in San Ildefonso Ixtahuacán when the airplanes went over. There were two in front and one behind, another two and then one, two and then one. There were a lot of planes and I was not able to count them all. I counted only eight. That day they went to bomb Nentón and San Pedro Necta, in the department of Huehuetenango. On the 16th, they were still bombing. The next day, one of my cousins arrived who had escaped death in the bombings; he was crying. Many people were killed in the bombings. There were many children killed, my cousin said.

On August 18, 1982, the soldiers came to organize civilian patrols in the village of Akjel, in the municipality of San Ildefonso Ixtahuacán. They ordered the assistant mayor to convene the people. When people arrived, the second lieutenant began talking, saying that by order of the Efraín Ríos Montt government, they were going to organize the civilian patrols. People asked him, "What are these civilian patrols for?" The second lieutenant answered, "To take care of the people so that the guerrillas don't come in." Then people asked: "Well, what are these patrols going to defend themselves with?" He answered, "You are going to carry machetes, rope, and a piece of wood. And if there are a lot of guerrillas, you are going to ring bells, sound horns, and yell, so that people come to grab the subversives."

People then said to the second lieutenant, "Second lieutenant, but we have to work on the farm. How are we going to eat?" He answered, "If you do not want to patrol, then you are subversives. You are going to respect the law, because it comes from the government. And if you don't respect the law that I have announced to you, I will kill your entire village." Then he showed us some bombs, and told us: "Here are your avocados, we are going to use them on your family." The people became very frightened and they agreed to patrol under the barrels of the soldiers' guns.

The second lieutenant said that the patrols had to receive identification cards that he himself, and the commander of the San Ildefonso patrols, would issue. On November 3, people from the village presented themselves in town and 100 identification cards were given out. The second lieutenant announced that all youth of 18 years old or over would have to go away to serve in the army. He also said that every patrol group had to bring its flag and identification cards when it was patrolling. "If you don't carry your flag and your identification cards, then you are guerrillas, and the army will kill you." That is how the civilian patrols in my town were organized.

On October 5th, I went to sell some oranges and bananas to the village of La Cumbre Papal. The civilian patrols were there, together with the soldiers. The soldiers asked for my papers, and told me that I had to go with them to the village of Papal. While I was in the village, the soldiers removed a man named Juan Ordoñez from his house, and another neighbor, and they set both of their houses on fire. The houses were made of straw. As the houses were burning, they threw both men, who were tied up very tightly, into the fire. And then they took me down farther, and we ran into two children who were eating corn on the cob in their homes. One ran off and hid in the *tamascal* [a steam bath used by the Indians—Eds.], and the other, a five-year-old, stayed inside the house. The soldiers set the house on fire, and burned it down with the child inside. The dead child was left in the house. The other child who had hidden in the *tamascal* was also killed. The soldiers then began to burn the other houses in the village. I could not count them all. I counted at least 20 houses that were burned by the soldiers. Then they let me return to my home.

In the month of November, a white pickup truck arrived. When it came to the Sevillaj bridge near the Cuilco mound, it stopped in front of Sr. José López's house. Soldiers from the truck set his house on fire and then they machine-gunned Sr. López, who was 60 years old, and all of his family. They killed a total

of 10 people in that house. There was not one single person from
José López's family left. Then they forced the civilian patrols,
who were accompanying the soldiers, to bury the dead in 6-foot
ditches.

Throughout Guatemala, in various places and towns, our people cannot stand so much repression any more. People find dead
bodies thrown at the side of the road. We find dead bodies without
heads, without hands, without legs. We do not want any more
killing. We cannot stand Ríos Montt's repression, his misery, any
more. We cannot work, we cannot do business, we cannot eat,
because of everything that Ríos Montt is doing. And now we
peasants want Ríos Montt to resign. We cannot stand him any
more. I hope that you ladies and gentlemen can help us so that
this Ríos Montt government will resign, along with his army, which
is finishing us all off in Guatemala.

Culture, Genocide, and Ethnocide in Guatemala

Arturo Arias

Alaide Foppa Association
of Guatemalan Cultural Workers

For some years, the regimes that have governed Guatemala since 1954 have been denounced systematically for their violations of human rights. But today, under the regime of General Ríos Montt, these violations have reached such gigantic proportions that genocide and ethnocide have become the basic cultural policy of the government.

A national policy for culture establishes, among other things, guidelines for the state to follow with a view to shaping a national identity by which the majority of its citizens may be recognized. In this light, the cultural policy carried out by the present government of General Ríos Montt appears to be one of consciously and deliberately negating, and destroying by fire and sword, that cultural identity with which more than 60% of the Guatemalan population is identified—the indigenous culture. Indeed, centuries of native culture are being annihilated: language, history, myths, legends, and artistic expression.

The indigenous people of Guatemala have never forgotten that the preservation of their culture is fundamental to keeping themselves alive as a people. Neither the barbarity of the Spanish conquest, which imposed new and dominant cultural patterns, nor the subsequent contempt shown for native expression and creativity by the "ladinos" (all the non-indigenous Guatemalans), with their European and North American cultural models, could conquer the indigenous people—descendants of the Mayan civilization, one of the brightest stars in the history of mankind. On the contrary, the native population continued to gather together and transmit their ancestral cultural traditions in spite of the oppression they have suffered since the colonial period.

But today this group is the prime target of the army. Because the army had difficulties in finding the armed guerrillas under the regime of the brothers Romeo and Benedicto Lucas García, the present government has instituted a systematic and coldly calculated policy that directly affects the cultural base of the majority of the Guatemalans. This policy has become true ethnocide.

Ethnocide means that an ethnic group is not allowed to enjoy, develop, or transmit its own culture. This implies an extreme violation of human rights, particularly the rights of ethnic groups to their cultural identities, as established by many declarations, pacts, and covenants of the United Nations and many regional inter-governmental and nongovernmental organizations. But the case of Guatemala goes far beyond an attempt to deny to ethnic groups the right to enjoy and transmit their own culture. There is massive extermination of the population, carried out through the destruction of villages and the razing of cultivated lands. This is genocide combined with ethnocide.

For the above reasons, the Alaide Foppa Association of Guatemalan Cultural Workers (Asociación de Trabajadores de la Cultura de Guatemala, "Alaide Foppa," ATCG) has placed special emphasis on the study of indigenous culture, which has always given the country its distinct, rich heritage. It is only through historical study that we may understand the exceptional importance of culture, the efforts to prevent its development, and its systematic destruction.

If culture is an essential element in the history of a people, it becomes absolutely strategic when diverse ethnic groups live together in one territorial space, as is the case of Guatemala. There is a necessary differentiation and inequality between the dominant culture and the so-called dominated cultures. In regard to culture, the dominant Guatemalan sectors do not have an identity of their own; rather, their identity is a mixture of features from the diverse centers of hegemony that have controlled the country politically and economically, and from the ethnic elements of the dominated sectors. Thus in Guatemala one cannot talk of one culture; one must speak in a dialectical dimension of various cultures. To do the latter signifies the existence of a dominant culture and various dominated cultures, with a basic contrast existing between the first and the second. None of these cultures is found in a pure state; rather, there is a continuous movement of elements that mix together and separate in the process of dialectical opposition.

The indigenous culture of Guatemala results from a system of colonial oppression and exploitation, and the response of the oppressed to this situation. The language, customs, forms of family, communal and social organization, values, traditions, psychology, etc., that have survived from the original Mayan-Toltec civilization with the inevitable modifications caused by four and one-half centuries of colonial domination, distinguish Guatemalan indigenous culture. The ethnic-cultural particularity of the indigenous people today is expressed in variations of idiom and dialect, differentiation in clothing, and distinct regional and local celebrations. It originated not only in the situation of domination by the conquistadors and the Spanish colonial regime; in addition, from that time to the present, the principal burden of producing wealth in Guatemala has rested on the shoulders of the native. For this reason, the ethnic condition of the native is equivalent to the economic condition of the exploited.

Popular culture is a means of resistance and struggle for sovereignty. The ideological domination of the popular cultures was carried out in the colony through the Catholic religion. But this same religion is a prime factor (although not the sole one, nor separate from an overall political process) in the transformation of the consciousness of the people. Thus it reactivated the oppressed ethnic culture, first as an instrument of resistance and second as an instrument of struggle. This determined, quantitatively and qualitatively, the recent recognition by the immense majority of the Guatemalan people that the popular revolutionary war is the ultimate and inevitable means to achieve their definitive liberation. Religion was a key element in the transformations that occurred, especially beginning with the decade of the 1960s; this is not surprising if we recall that religious belief was always at the center of the indigenous communities from prehispanic times, and played a preponderant role in shaping the worldview of the different ethnic groups.

The origins of this process go back to the emergence of Catholic Action (Acción Católica) in the 1930s. It began with the indigenous traders, who developed as a sector through the emergence and growth of regional markets. With the triumph of the bourgeois democratic revolution in 1944, representatives of the various political parties went from the capital to the Guatemalan highlands, creating power centers in the indigenous communities for the first time. The church, having close ties with the right-wing political parties of that time, also began a reorganization on a national level. But the movement of Acción Católica did not acquire strength until 1954, when the right overthrew the government of Jacobo Arbenz.

At this same time, the Guatemalan Christian Democratic Party (DCG) appeared; it became the link, directly and organically, to the groups of Acción Católica, which in turn became the base of the DCG. In spite of its anticommunist ideology, the DCG was from the very beginning opposed to the government, as became more evident during the years when the government made the DCG illegal (1961-1966). In the meantime, the Spanish missionaries who reached the highlands after 1954 gradually discovered, under a religious cloak, a cultural defense of an ethnic character, in the face of a fear that allowing any kind of "modern" penetration would signify the disintegration of the community. The missionaries began, with the support of Acción Católica, a reform process that, little by little, moved into open conflict with the existing system.

During these same years, the first guerrilla experience occurred. The incorporation of the first natives into that movement provided the practical basis for the thinking of the left with respect to the ethnic-national question to be revolutionized. The development and gradual radicalization of Acción Católica, united with the revolution in the philosophy of the new left, enabled the indigenous masses to see that the root of the problem was their exploitation as poor people and the discrimination they suffer as Indians. The entire movement of Acción Católica, encircled by the increasingly reactionary and violent positions of the government, was compelled to join the war. At that moment, to save the system of exploitation, the policy of systematic genocide and ethnocide against the entire indigenous population of Guatemala was initiated. . . . It is the most disgraceful genocide carried out on the American continent since the extermination of the North American Indian population.

Along with their effects on all indigenous groups, the counterinsurgency policies have particularly affected professionals involved in the diffusion of culture. Reporters, artists, and university professors from various fields have traditionally been considered "heads of subversion." Their professional training, with its affinity for 18th-century European humanist traditions, necessarily conflicts with the violence of the colonial and neocolonial systems. In addition, many have publicly and repeatedly denounced the repressive spiral on a national and international level, even at the risk of their lives.

If the indigenous groups chose the road of popular revolutionary war as a last resort—as the only way to save themselves as people, as a social group, and as a human species, collectively making the decision to be free by means of prolonged and martyrizing war—then the dominant sectors from 1524 to the present have chosen the road of violence as their first resort, their road to self-enrichment. They are totally indifferent to the human condition of their victims, indifferent to their culture, indifferent to the effects of a political and social system maintained by means of constant oppression and racism. In the history of the modern world, this represents, without a doubt, one of the most atrocious crimes ever committed against humanity.

We Charge Genocide
Ricardo Falla

A priest and anthropologist, Ricardo Falla offered a remarkable presen-
tation (196 pages in its long form) that begins with the definition of genocide
as stated in the convention adopted by the General Assembly of the U.N.
on December 9, 1948: any act perpetrated with the intention of destroying,
totally or in part, a national, ethnic, racial, or religious group as such.
(Emphasis ours — Eds.) Organizations such as Amnesty International have
condemned the Ríos Montt government for illegal massacres of noncombatants,
but none of them have condemned it for genocide in the strict sense of the
word. The difficulty in doing so lies in the term "as such." The aim of
destroying a group must be because it is a national, ethnic, racial, or religious
group and not, for example, because it is a political opposition or economically
competitive group.

To prove his charge of genocide, Fr. Falla begins by telling what occurred
at the village-farm of San Francisco in 1982.

The best-documented massacre under the Ríos Montt regime
was perpetrated by the army at the totally indigenous village-farm
of San Francisco in Nentón, Huehuetenango on July 17, 1982.
An estimated 352 people were killed, of whom we have 302 names,
220 of them with the person's age and/or parentage. This village
appears on Map Number 1:250,000, to the north of the village
of Yalambojoch, not far from the northern border of
Huehuetenango with Chiapas, Mexico.

The survivors have been interviewed by the Christian Committee of the Diocese of San Cristóbal de las Casas in August 1982,
by myself at the beginning of September 1982, by members of

the Guatemalan Committee for Justice and Peace, and by Alan Riding, a reporter from the *New York Times* for an article published on October 12, 1982. On different dates, to different interviewers, the two main survivors have given absolutely consistent versions of the events.

In addition, at the beginning of September 1982, I myself interviewed people from various neighboring villages. Their populations had fled to Mexico between the end of July and the beginning of August 1982 because of that massacre, which produced a terror that catalyzed the flight of almost 10,000 refugees. A movement of such scope does not occur unless there are proven facts behind it.

In addition, a few days after the massacre, Father Ronald Hennessey, a Maryknoll missionary and the priest of San Mateo Ixtatán who is responsible for the zone of Nentón, went to the site. He saw the horrifying spectacle of burnt, decapitated, shot-up, and macheted corpses that were scattered all over that village-farm area of 60 homes.

Your Honors, the reality of this massacre is absolutely incontestable, although the Guatemalan ambassador to the U.S. said that it was contrived because, according to him, the site does not appear on the maps of Guatemala.

The pattern of the massacre, as in other massacres, was as follows. The soldiers separated the men off to one side, telling them that there was going to be a meeting, and locked them up in the courthouse of the village-farm. The soldiers then rounded up the women from their various homes and locked them up at another location along with their children, both those having the use of reason and those not yet having it (the survivors make this distinction very clearly).

At about 1:00 p.m., the soldiers began to fire at the women inside the small church. The majority did not die there, but were separated from their children, taken to their homes in groups, and killed, the majority apparently with machetes. It seems that the purpose of this last parting of women from their children was to prevent even the children from witnessing any confession that might reveal the location of the guerrillas.

Then they returned to kill the children, whom they had left

crying and screaming by themselves, without their mothers. Our informants, who were locked up in the courthouse, could see this through a hole in the window and through the doors carelessly left open by a guard. The soldiers cut open the children's stomachs with knives or they grabbed the children's little legs and smashed their heads against heavy sticks.

Some of the soldiers took a break to rest, eating a bull—the property of the peasants—that had been put on to roast. Then they continued with the men. They took them out, tied their hands, threw them on the ground, and shot them. The authorities of the area were killed inside the courthouse.

It was then that the survivors were able to escape, protected by the smoke of the fire which had been set to the building. Seven men, three of whom survived, managed to escape. It was 5:30 p.m.

The massacre continued, and when about six people were left, the soldiers threw grenades at them, killing all but two. Since it was already night, these two escaped through the window, covered with blood but uninjured. One of them was shot, the other lived. He is the surprise witness of this horrible deed. It is said that he arrived in Chiapas, Mexico, at 11 a.m. the following day, but because he had such a darkness in his soul, he did not even notice that it was daytime:

> *Eleven in the morning it must be,*
> *And I came here to Santa Marta,*
> *But I'm like an idiot.*
> *I don't see anything clearly,*
> *I'm not even sad.*
> *I don't think anything.*
> *I haven't eaten, I haven't eaten.*
> *I have no coat, I have no clothes.*
> *This is what I see.*
> *Nothing, Nobody!*
> *I have no hat,*
> *nobody.*
> *Entirely.*

What would Otto René Castillo say if he heard this nocturnal poem of the spirit of the people? What would Alaide Foppa—the poet, but before that a woman—say? What would Sor Juana Inez de la Cruz say.. ."on a dark night/with desires for inflamed love.. ."?

The informants—survivors, inhabitants of neighboring and sister villages—are unanimous in attributing the massacre to the army. There were 600 soldiers with 6 officers, wearing camouflage uniforms and boots. They were accompanied by a helicopter that landed in the soccer field with boxes of food. The helicopter's previous trips were known. The army men started out in Barillas, where there is usually a detachment of approximately 250 soldiers. They traveled from Barillas to San Mateo Ixtatán in a truck, then to Bulej; from there, they set out on foot. They were in Bulej on July 15, when a captain killed the "animator of the faith" of the village, because his guerrilla brother had supposedly fled. The captain also forced the civilian patrol to kill four others with sticks. Five days later, 30 of them went to the priest to confess, as they were terribly remorseful. In other words, it is completely proven, Your Honors, that the crime was perpetrated by Ríos Montt's army.

The people who were interviewed by others and by me have their explanations of the army's motives for its actions. We do not believe the reasons given by the army, which has changed its version of what happened.

The main explanation given is political: the army was searching for a nearby guerrilla camp, wiping out the population that supplied cattle from the farm of Colonel Víctor Manuel Bolaños to the guerrillas, punishing the guerrillas, and generating terror in the area to make the people stop giving logistical support to the guerrillas and/or flee to Mexico. This left a whole area empty of any population except in a few controlled strategic hamlets, such as the village-farm of Ixquisís.

Some give economic motives: the rich pay the army to remove the people, either through giving credits that can then be used as pretexts to seize the land, or through massacres that drive the population away. Then that land, some of which isn't even titled yet, reverts to the state, and is bought by the rich to extend their grazing lands.

But there are also motives of racial discrimination. Although the generation of terror is a political reason for total massacre, an ideological bridge is lacking to legitimate the massacre of clearly innocent people such as the elderly and, above all, the children. The latter cannot even be construed as "collaborators" of the guerrillas. However, in Ríos Montt's opinion (*New York Times,* May 20, 1982, and API Agency) they can be executed by the army even if they are not legally combatants. The ideological bridge is the concept that guilt and crime are transmitted biologically. It is racist.

This concept is utilized by the army men in their statements, especially when they announce that as punishment, they will finish off a village, *"not leaving a single seed."* For example, this was said by the lieutenant in a village of Cuilco on September 10, 1982, as corroborated by one of the witnesses of the Tribunal. At a higher level, it was said by the reserve commander of the departmental seat of Huehuetenango around June 21, 1982, when he was threatening the responsibles of the village who had brought lists for creating civilian patrols. He told them that if they let arms go to the guerrillas, "We're not going to leave a single seed, we are going to make a clean sweep there."

The behavior of the soldiers presupposes a racist ideology, in the way they treat their victims as animals. This is shown in the threats, gestures, and actual incidents of cannibalism. I don't know if even the Nazis went this far. On September 30, 1982, Salpress published an interview with a deserting soldier, who said that the "Kaibiles," the special troops, are forced to drink the blood of their victims. On December 26, a refugee told me that a friend of his from Ixtahuacán fled the base in Huehuetenango because of his refusal to drink the blood of the kidnapped as part of his training. The refugee heard this because the army was persecuting his friend.

On January 16, 1982, a ladina woman heard the lieutenant in the plaza of Santa Ana Huista say: "Now I want blood. Blood tastes sweet to me." One of the survivors of San Francisco saw with his own eyes a soldier or officer (he did not specify) take out the heart of a warm corpse, and bring it up to his mouth. The witness says he lowered his eyes in anger and did not see if the person bit into it or not. In Todos Santos, a peasant from Santa Ana Huista told me in the beginning of December 1982 that the lieutenant or the captain, in front of the civilian population and his soldiers, cut open a victim, took out his liver and ate it raw. The peasant heard this from the victim's brother. He did not give the date of the occurrence.

This racist ideology is found at the top level of the government itself. In December 1982, a journalist in San Pedro Sula asked Ríos Montt, following his meeting with Reagan, who we should believe is telling the truth about the army's massacres: the peasants or Ríos Montt, who flatly denies them (in May he did not deny them, but evaded the issue). Ríos Montt responded that the truth is relative. That in Nicaragua there is one concept, in El Salvador there is another, in Guatemala yet another, etc. "Where does the real truth lie, on which side? *This is exactly why there is a state.*" Although he might say that he forbids his troops to commit massacres of innocents (as opposed to collaborators from the disarmed civilian population), his ideology is fascist because he sees the state as being the source of truth and the source of right—not man, and of course not the peasant. Man is depersonalized, that is to say, he is converted into an animal. The people are considered to be biological tissue, and if one part is infected, it is cut off in order to save the whole. However, the whole is not the people, but rather the state.

Finally, there is a motive of ethnic discrimination in the repression and the massacres of the innocent in their totality, which makes this policy genocidal, as was stated by the American Anthropological Association in its General Assembly of December 7, 1982, in Washington, D.C. (although without much discussion and precision). The target of the genocide is the Indian people, not just a village as an ethnic microgroup. The intention is not one of total destruction, because the Indian people are necessary to the economic system of the government as labor power, among other things. Rather it is one of partial destruction. It is a different level of genocide from that which is committed against the massacred villages, although they complement each other.

Ethnic discrimination is part of the economic and political

motives for these massacres. This is proven by the fact that these massacres take place almost exclusively in the indigenous zones of the country. If ladinos are also hurt, it is because they are located within the zones of Indian influence. The army does not choose these zones because they are Indian, but rather because that is where the subversion is found. However, in that struggle against subversion, there is a discriminatory motive, since discrimination is linked to the subversion.

Why, then, is subversion found primarily in the indigenous zones? There are historical reasons. The destruction of the guerrillas in the eastern part of the country (in the ladino zone) during the 1960s caused the revolutionary leaders, in particular an enlightened army leader, Luis Turcíos Lima, to include in their strategy the incorporation of Indians and the struggle against cultural oppression, ethnic discrimination, and racist marginalization. This dispersed guerrilla group chose the department of El Quiché as the area of its resurgence.

At the same time, in the indigenous areas along the coast that are linked to the highlands, similar programs (although implemented differently) draw Indians into the struggle against "racism," as it is called in these zones that have suffered since the Spanish conquest.

Discrimination also operates negatively in the growth of the revolutionary movement. The movement does not spread everywhere with the same force. This is because defamation of the Indian (that is, discrimination) on a national level slows the growth of confidence and organization in the eastern ladino zones. The cadres who come to organize there are Indians and not, as many would like, students or lawyers from the capital. In the indigenous zones, although different languages are spoken, the movement spreads with a faster rhythm than in the ladino zones.

In the light of these considerations, which are better explained and better documented in our written paper, we have drawn our conclusions, gentlemen of the panel, after a careful examination and consultation with jurists (not being one myself, but rather a humble priest and modest anthropologist).

We conclude that the Ríos Montt regime should be condemned for genocide in the strict sense of the word because: a) it has perpetrated killings of ethnic groups (population microgroups) with the intention of destroying them completely as such, that is to say, not only for supposedly being guerrillas, but for belonging to particular ethnic groups (a case in point being the children who do not yet have the use of reason); and *b) it has perpetrated killings of members of the indigenous ethnic group (the majority rural population of the country) with the intention of destroying it partially as such.* That is to say, not only because within that group the majority have become involved in subversion, but because the nature of that subversion has been liberation from cultural oppression and ethnic discrimination.

A final note: The Nazis were accused of and condemned for genocide, but it would be an error to believe that economic and political motivations excluded the motivations of ethnic and racial discrimination that were present.

Testimony of
Rigoberta Menchú

Indian peasant and catechist

My name is Rigoberta Menchú. I am 24 years old. I am a
Quiché Indian, a peasant, and a Christian. I have experienced
repression personally, and this is why I am going to tell you about
my life, and what is experienced by the great majority of
Guatemalans. Mine is not the only case.

My parents were Vicente Menchú and Juan Tun. There were
nine children, and I am the fourth. I had no childhood from eight
years old on because I had to work on the farms, picking coffee
and cotton. I was paid 20 *centavos* (cents) per job. There were times
when I couldn't finish the job and I would not receive the 20 *centavos*. This is what my life was like for three years. All this effort
was to help out my parents, for whom the support of our family
was very difficult because there were so many of us. My parents
could not send me to school. I spoke only my first language,
Quiché.

From the time I was very little, I was aware of my father's
struggle for land, since frequently we were threatened by the landowners with being dispossessed of our small plot in the high plains.
For us, the Indians, the land is our lives. We depend on it, and
we owe our lives to it.

When I was 10 years old, I began to assume my Christian
commitment and responsibility to be a real catechist in my community. The catechist in Guatemala is a leader who is responsible to look out for the welfare and seek solutions to the problems
of the community, and at the same time to preach the gospel. Concretely I did this with children younger than 10 years old. Little
by little I grew in this function, and when I was 13 years old, I

continued working with young people of my own age. In this way I got involved in my father's struggle, that is, the struggle for land. I traveled to the farms of the large landowners to help support the family, and to carry forward my father's struggle, which is the struggle of the community and which was, and is, the struggle of our people.

Two of my brothers died in our travels to the farms on the southern coast. Nicolás was only two years old when he died, after the cotton plants where we worked were sprayed with pesticide. Felipe had not had his first birthday, and he got all swollen up; since we didn't have any medicine or money to buy any, there was nothing we could do.

We buried my brother Nicolás on the farm, and that is why [taking the time off—Eds.] they kicked us off the farm, and we lost our jobs.

In 1973, my father was put in jail because he gathered together and organized the community to defend our plots of land. They sentenced him to 19 years in jail, the main purpose being to pressure us and scare us. He was actually only in for one year and two months. My mother paid bail and they took away our land.

In 1975, six armed men, whose faces were covered with handkerchiefs, kidnapped my father. With support from all the communities, we searched and found him several kilometers from the house, tortured and thrown in the road. The community carried him the 4 kilometers to town and, with the help of the priests, we sent him to the Santa Cruz, El Quiché hospital. While there he was about to be kidnapped by people from the army, so we got him out of there, and he stayed with some of our friends until he was well.

We continued organizing ourselves to defend our land and our things, to defend ourselves from the Brols and the Garcías, who surrounded our village more every day with their bodyguards.

My father continued our struggle, and he sought help from the labor unions. In 1977, the authorities arrested him and jailed him. He was accused of being a communist. They sentenced him to 30 years in prison or to accept being executed.

Religious people, students, and the labor unions denounced this action, and they helped us save his life. We managed to get him out of jail, and in private the judge told him they had intended to kill him anyway for being a communist.

In jail he met a peasant from the Peasant Unity Committee (CUC) and he got more ideas about the struggle. He continued the struggle, with more strength than any of us, in many villages and towns. He traveled to many places in El Quiché, Chimaltenango, and Sololá.

When they did not find my father at my house, five armed men kidnapped my brother, Patrocinio Menchú Tun. They tied him up and they beat him. Blood came out of his eyes, his ears, and his nose, and he showed up in the Xejul-Uspantán camp, tortured. They put him in a well full of water, and they gave him electric shock; they pulled out his fingernails and they hit him on the head. When he was in the well, they gave him a little bit of food to subsist. Later the army accused him of being a guerrilla, of being armed and uniformed. The army called other people to come and see the punishment that they were going to give the guerrillas.

When we went to Chajul-Quiché, the soldiers stopped us and sent us to the park where a lot of people were forcibly gathered. The army held a meeting and threatened people so that they would not fight. Out of a truck, they took 20 tortured people in soldiers' uniforms, among them a woman who had had her head shaved and her breasts cut off.

They had all been tortured in one way or another, and many of them were swollen up. The army explained the tortures and threatened the crowd. Some of the captives were dying. Men, women, and children, all were crying. Another group of soldiers gathered together all the tortured people and poured gasoline on them, and burned them. The army was yelling, "Long live the army! A guerrilla seen is a guerrilla dead!"

The people picked up their machetes and wanted to drive the army out. We abandoned our house. Several weeks later, the army burned my house and all of our things. Then the army ran the people out of San Pablo Baldío and La Esperanza. They kidnapped many. Several clandestine cemeteries appeared. Repression increased in almost all of the villages.

We decided to keep struggling. We sought out students, labor unions, ordinary people. In September of 1979, we went to the Congress, but they didn't listen to us. My mother went along. They told us that it was not a place for Indians. They beat us, they pushed us, and they removed us. We had already gone to other places and in January 1980, we looked for ways to make them listen to us. They persecuted us and they wanted to kidnap us.

This whole long history of denunciation was suppressed. It had to be brought to light, and that is why our *compañeros*, including my father, occupied the Spanish embassy on January 31, 1980. When the government set fire to the embassy and 39 people were burned alive, the savagery with which our country has been governed became clear to the world.

After that massacre, all of the children of the people who died there were pursued and persecuted, in different parts of the country. As a result, we had to seek refuge in other people's homes in different departments. Three months later, on April 19, 1980, my mother was kidnapped by four armed men. The next day, her clothing appeared on the streets of Uspantán; later, in the municipal headquarters, her clothes were put on display so that the rest of the family would come to pick them up. We knew the danger that our lives would be in if we did this, so we did not claim our mother's clothes.

According to the testimony of a cousin who tortured my mother, and who also guarded her corpse for four months in the hills, she was tortured for almost 12 days. They dressed her in a military uniform, they cut off her hair, and for 12 days, she was cruelly tortured. They slowly pulled out her fingernails, they cut off different parts of her body, and they put her in a black well where they also put other tortured people. And they gave her a little bit of food so that she could survive and they could continue torturing her. When she was dying after several days of torture, an officer ordered the army doctors to give her an injection, and intravenous feeding. After recovering her health for three days, they began to torture her again in the same way, to rape her again. They asked her where were the rest of her children, where was the part of the community which had fled, and they asked about certain people who had left the community. They told her that if she pointed out the location of the guerrilla camps, they would let her live. She did not say anything. She denied that she had any children left alive.

Little by little, my mother lost her will to live. When she was dying again, they took her to an embankment 15 minutes from the town of Uspantán, and they left her there in the bushes still alive. The soldiers guarded her corpse constantly for four months. My mother died slowly. She was eaten by animals, by vultures, by dogs. Only the longest bones of her body remained. The soldiers would not let anybody get close to the area.

Little by little, the army withdrew from the area, until my mother's remains could no longer be found. We could not gather even one little part of my mother's remains. At that point, we could not believe the savagery to which the soldiers had resorted. We did not know where my mother's grave was.

We had to find ways to survive and protect our own lives. When my mother was kidnapped, we were separated from my two little sisters. My only hope was to find them still alive. Not long after, I did discover that my sisters were alive. Today I have the hope that they are still living.

Ever since I was left an orphan, I have experienced many things. Last year, in February, there were barely 50 people left in my village of Chimel, and they were massacred. My sisters-in-law were there with their little children. I know that my other brothers have been assassinated in other places, but no one has given me complete information.

I have also gone from house to house, fleeing from the massacres, together with other Guatemalans who have experienced the same fate. We have found several corpses of mutilated women, including Petronila Xoná. She too was from my village.

I couldn't live anywhere afterwards, because they looked for me everywhere in Guatemala. They burned several houses where I had been, and I put people in danger.

In Guatemala, repression is generalized everywhere in the

country. I have had occasion to talk to men, women, and children—survivors of their communities—and they have told me of the terrible things that many of them experienced. We could talk hours and hours about the genocide against my people.

I am clear that the army is not going to change with a different general in the government. They are the same, those who killed and tortured my parents and relatives. In the same way that my parents died, they have finished off my cousins, my uncles, along with so many others from my town.

Testimony of
Gabriel Ixmatá

Indian peasant and migrant farmworker

We, the peasant descendants of the Maya-Quiché, are here to address the entire world, so that all will know the kind of life and treatment given to the poor peasants of Guatemala.

International public opinion knows that in our Latin American countries, governments exist that do not represent or respond to the interests of our people. We, the peasants, already know and have known these governments. We cannot be deceived. They are the governments of a few wealthy people who are taking advantage of the majority of the people of the nation. This is the case in Guatemala, where General Efraín Ríos Montt proclaimed himself President in June 1982.

It is truly shameful and painful to have to state that in this year of 1983 which has just begun, the situation in Guatemala for the peasants who work the land becomes more difficult and bitter, day by day. Our suffering has gone on for more than 450 years, and now it has increased, especially for the indigenous people and all the subsistence workers.

The small plots of land that we still have in the cold lands or high plateau do not want to bear crops any longer. The soil is worn out, and corn and beans do not grow because fertilizer costs more than 20 *quetzals* for 100 pounds [one *quetzal* has traditionally been $1.00—Eds.] and is sold only in "Bandesa" (Banco Nacional de Desarrollo Agrícola—National Bank of Agricultural Development) and in the cooperatives that were militarized under the regime of Lucas García. Of the animals that we have left, the majority are dying because we cannot take care of them and because of having to go from place to place looking for food.

The work for us peasants on the coffee and cotton plantations is limited and complicated. We are given work for 15 days only — then the bosses send us home. This is when the army takes advantage and makes the men participate in its civilian patrols.

As coffee pickers, we want to testify to the lives led by our families, our neighbors, and our people on the coffee plantations in the harvest of 1982-1983. The plantation owners have become more and more repressive against us workers. Some give us work and others do not. Those who give work to the peasants say that we must accept the rules of the plantation and that the jobs must be done perfectly. They say that he who does not clean the coffee well enough will not be paid and will be fired from the plantation, because there are more than enough workers. This happens daily. The consequences of this treatment are more and more peasants out of work and more suffering for the families.

The bosses want only men to work on the plantations, not women or children. For our wives and sisters, the pay is half what the man earns. Our children are not given full food rations. The bosses say that the children do not give them any benefits.

The ration consists of three or four ounces of beans, approximately equivalent to an eighth of a kilo, and one kilo of corn a day, which must be paid for at the end of one month's work. There are times when the money earned is not enough, and one has to go deeper into debt to the boss. Here we must say that there are bosses who allow us to continue working, and there are bosses who make us pay the money no matter where we have to get it from.

With respect to the tools needed to do the work, the boss, as always, never supplies them. The worker must buy and bring his own work tools with him to be accepted as a worker. Life on the coffee plantations is really difficult at this time because not only are the bosses depriving the workers of work, but they also are depriving us of our existence. The government's security agents and the bosses are constantly questioning the workers, forcing us to say things that we do not know or making us admit that the government is bad so that they can finish us off or make us disappear.

THE COTTON PLANTATIONS

The cotton picking begins in December. The owners of the cotton plantations offer a wage of one and one half to two *quetzals* for 100 pounds of cut cotton. As on the coffee plantations, the foremen, stewards, and administrators have their controls, mistreating us and saying that we must accept what the owner says—and we do—because it is thanks to the owner that there is work for so many people. They continuously rob us at the weighing stations where they take in the cotton. For defects, they deduct 15 to 20 pounds for each 100 pounds of picked cotton. None of this is new. This has been going on every year, but in the last few years the robbing of the workers has become more acute.

We are also exploited in other ways. There are a variety of work rules. For example, in work for a day wage, the men are paid one *quetzal* 50 *centavos* for a 10-hour day, and women are paid one *quetzal* 25 *centavos*. In piece work, the tasks take various forms. If it is by meters, 30 square meters form one "piece," whether we are picking coffee, cotton, etc. The pay is one *quetzal* 60 *centavos* or two *quetzals* for the piece. But the work usually takes two or three days, and if it is not done well, payment is not received. A ton of cut sugar cane pays one *quetzal* 60 *centavos* or one *quetzal* 80 *centavos*. It is not easy to cut a ton of sugar cane in one day.

As a result of the strike by more than 80,000 peasant workers in May 1980, the regime of Lucas García authorized a minimum wage of three *quetzals* 20 *centavos*, which to this date has not been put into practice by the bosses and owners.

I was a witness to an event that occurred December 18, 1979, on a cotton plantation called the "Acacias" in the municipality of Gomera, department of Escuintla, where we were picking cotton. From the first day on the plantation, the owner—Mr. Milton Molina—had treated us like lowly animals and our children like pigs because they could not work. On December 18, Mr. Milton Molina ordered the spraying of his plantation with *tamaron* and other pesticides to kill the insects in the areas where we were working. As a result of this, five of our children died of poisoning in two hours. We were all taken to the Guatemalan

Institute of Social Security at Gomera, where two more fellow workers died.

The report by the plantation supervisors said that this had happened because the workers were very careless, not washing their hands before eating or feeding their children, and that for these reasons, they became sick and died. Of course, this was never known outside the Institute of Social Security. The dead were buried as victims of common diseases and malnutrition. These are very few examples, but they are sufficient to show the kind of life that we peasants live and the kind of treatment to which we are subjected.

In those areas where the guerrilla organizations are strong and can exert pressure, the rich are forced to pay higher wages and provide better treatment to the workers. But in those areas where pressure is not exerted by the guerrilla organizations, the owners pay miserable wages, treat us cruelly, and constantly call the army to control and persecute the workers, because all the indigenous people of the high plateau are suspected of being in opposition to the government. . . .

We, the peasants, also wish to proclaim that all the mistreatment, work rules, and actions by the owners against the peasant workers—in particular, those indigenous descendants of the Mayans—have been and are being used to divide the poor people of Guatemala. They want to divide the indigenous population and the mestizos so they can continue sacking, robbing, and squeezing the workers and the people. We must expose and denounce these despicable acts of racial discrimination, which the rich and oligarchic Guatemalans use as a weapon to divide us and to crush the indigenous as well as the non-indigenous peasants.

We peasants are aware that they have attempted to keep our people divided in two. But they have not succeeded and they never will, because now the indigenous, the mestizos, and all social classes of our country are united hand in hand and shoulder to shoulder. We are fighting a war of liberation for our people, with our grandparents, our brothers and sisters, and our minds. We are capable of leading ourselves, to seek the well-being and the dreams of our people who are one and will remain one. . . .

Testimony of
Juan José Mendoza

Indian community leader

A high point of this testimony was the story, which follows, of a community organization in the well-known tourist town of Santiago Atitlán, whose population of about 25,000 spoke Maya-Tzutuhil—Eds.

. . . In Santiago Atitlán, a group of Atitecos who had suffered and knew the pain and suffering of their people organized in 1966. They were catechists of the Catholic Church. With the help of the parish priest, Father Ramón Carlin (a missionary from Oklahoma, USA), they began a campaign to teach reading and writing to the population. In 1970, with 300 members, we organized the Radio Association of the Voice of Atitlán. All the villages on the banks of Lake Atitlán participated; together we would seek a just and humane life.

We organized groups to teach reading and writing. We organized cooperatives: handicrafts, agriculture, and savings and loans offices. We began programs of health information and adult education, cultural programs and religious programs preaching the Christian gospel. We had a radio station to transmit the programs to all neighboring villages. Peasant children, young people, women, men, and the elderly participated. We all respected the sacred right to life of our relatives and neighbors; we shared our grief and our suffering as well as our happiness. All of the members of the Radio Association of the Voice of Atitlán voluntarily worked together to bring happiness and well-being to the lives of our oppressed people. Then, for trying to come out of our life of misery, the hatred of the government and the wealthy landowners destroyed us.

In June 1980, the army set up camp in the village of Cerro de Oro, eight kilometers from the town of Santiago Atitlán, with seven truckloads of soldiers, 50 soldiers in each truck. They interrogated the villagers of Cerro de Oro, to find out who were the collaborators in the Radio Association of the Voice of Atitlán and who were the influential people of the village. But the villagers did not give any information. So the army moved their camp to Cantón Panabaj, two kilometers from the village of Santiago Atitlán, on September 5.

On September 30, at 7:30 p.m., a paramilitary squad in a red car, coming from the department of Sololá, kidnapped the catechist Juan Ixbalán on a public street of the town of Santiago Atitlán. On October 10 they kidnapped another catechist, Manuel Coché. They tied his hands, beat him up, and dragged him from his house. Then the army forced the population to attend a meeting on October 15, at 11:00 a.m. They announced that the army had been sent by the government of Lucas García to protect and take care of the town of Santiago Atitlán. The people were prohibited from walking on the streets after 7:30 p.m., were forced to return from their work in the fields early in the day, and were forbidden to go very far from the town.

On October 24, at 4:30 p.m., the army and the national police surrounded the building of the Radio Association of the Voice of Atitlán, leaving after half an hour. But at 1:30 a.m., on the 25th, a group of soldiers, dressed in civilian clothes and well armed, kidnapped Gaspar Culan Yataz, director of the Radio Association; he was beaten savagely and shot in the head. His wife and daughter were also beaten. The soldiers carried the unconscious Mr. Gaspar to the camp; nothing more was heard of him.

The building of the Association was searched and plundered by the army on November 12. They stole radios and office machines, destroyed doors and windows. They hid a bag of firearms inside the building. The following day, Father Francisco, who had been the parish priest of Santiago Atitlán since 1969, told the mayor what had happened. The mayor called the army and, together with the army, he entered the building. The colonel ordered the soldiers to search the building, and they found the sack containing firearms. The colonel told those present that the Association had used arms and that they were accomplices of the subversives.

Four members of the Association were kidnapped on November 15, and savagely tortured. Three were buried in Chimaltenango in graves marked "XXX." The body of the youngest was found by his relatives, whose names are Nicolás Ratzan Tziná, Juan Pacay Rujuch, Diego Sosof Coché, and Esteban Ajtzip R. We had to hide in the ravines and hills and could not work. Many of our houses were sacked, we were victims of persecution. Ever since the kidnapping of the director, we have had to abandon our work as the Radio Association of the Voice of Atitlán. . . .

The murderous army was always looking for ways to terrorize the population of Santiago Atitlán. In September 1981 there was new persecution of ex-members of the Radio Association of the Voice of Atitlán. The army sent letters to every one of the ex-members telling them to give themselves up at the camp. If they did not turn themselves in, their houses would be burned, their families would be killed, and they would be prosecuted according to the law of the army. To save their families, 15 ex-members of the Association turned themselves in.

They were held in the camp for 15 days. They were threatened and forced by the Minister of National Defense to declare to the international and national press and to Guatemalan television that they were collaborators or members of the subversives and that all of them had gone to the camp to seek refuge and ask for protection by the army. On November 18, the army gave the interview to the press and television in the camp of Panabaj, Santiago Atitlán; they also forced many people to go to the camp and pretend to be subversives seeking shelter and refuge in the camp. All of these lies hide the crimes of the Lucas García regime from the eyes of the world.

In the face of this difficult situation, many of us had to flee to Mexico at the end of November 1981.

Following the coup d'état of March 23, 1982, Mendoza returned to Guatemala hoping to find more peace but instead found even greater insecurity.

He came to live in the community of Nahualá, where the following incident took place: an example of the Guatemalan people's indestructible defiance. — Eds.

The military commander had received an order from the army saying that the civilian patrol should not go out at 7:00 p.m., as was the custom, but should wait until 10:00 p.m. for that night only. However, the civilian patrol disobeyed the military commander and went out at 7:00 p.m. At that moment, the army was about to kidnap someone.

A group of well armed soldiers dressed in civilian clothes passed by, accompanied by a person with his head covered who was going to point out the house where the kidnapping would take place. The civilian patrolmen recognized the voice of the hooded person, and when the two groups met, a member of the civilian patrol unhooded the person. At that point, the soldiers machine-gunned the civilian patrolmen and also killed the hooded person. But members of the civilian patrol had prevented the kidnapping and unmasked the army as the author of the kidnappings and massacres of the indigenous population.

Testimony of
Miguel Morales Ordóñez

Indian peasant

This witness, from the village of Corinto in the department of Huehuetenango, began by describing how the army came to his town and forced people to "volunteer" for the civilian patrols, leaving them without a way to make money to support their families. Shortly after that, about 150 soldiers returned, and the witness was taken from his home under armed guard to a "meeting" of some 60 villagers. Several peasants were then brought before the people, with their hands tied behind their backs. A second lieutenant spoke.

He said, "We have come to clean up this place, because we know that there are people here involved in subversive activities." We became very sad because we really did not know what subversive activities were. He said a few more words, referring to the men who were brought in with their hands tied behind them: "Look. You know why we brought these 'people' here—these turds. Because they were involved in subversive activities. We'll see what happens to them, to these shits who have committed sabotage along the roads and who have sabotaged the electric power lines."

Right then, he aimed at the three men that he had brought in all tied up, and fired three shots into each one. In all he fired nine shots, three at each person. Then he said, "Now you saw what happened to these shits and if you don't clean up this subversion, this is what will happen to you. I know that among you there are some who are responsible for subversive activities."

Then he forced a man among us to count all the people and asked, "Hasn't Francisco Salas come today?" "No," said the man.

"Then he must be involved in subversive activities," said the second lieutenant, "Let's wait until he comes." So he waited long enough for Salas to come and he really did appear, with another man— there were two of them. "He's the shit who is in charge of the subversion here, he's the responsible one," said the second lieutenant. Salas said, "Good morning, Sir," and the second lieutenant responded, "No 'good morning's' for me, you son of a bitch." He pushed Salas aside and made him stand alone, to one side, and he shot and killed him . . . .

This is what the government's army is doing in Guatemala; there is no respect for human rights. Instead of respecting human rights, they kill us or they accuse us of being guerrilla fighters. So we have come here as witnesses to what has happened in my village. We ask the governments of the world to condemn this government because of the massacres that they have committed with their army.

Please excuse my Spanish—we speak another language, Mam. I would like to greet you in my language:

Ma chinule k'ol jun colb'eb'el kee tej'e tnám ja tsájna k'in wee aj'e tnám te Guatemal que kkiak'il k'e kiee aj' atee—tsalú irx nchi b'ine wiije-irx jun k'olb'eb'el que j'a kawél aj'téc tsalú krxel nc'ano ke kiak'il wiirxón kie kiak'il—tnám twits txotx tun kionom te tnám te Guatemala aj'a—tnám toxrx tjak' moyb'il irx tj'ak tk'ak'al kiub'el k'inam irx ke wiirxonnáje tnám nnípán waíj irx k'aj aj'e tnám aj ma jaw tion tib tun tkanet j'un k'olb'el tetchomclal chj'ontek'e key.

On behalf of my people in Guatemala I greet everyone here today and the gentlemen of the Tribunal, and I ask that you implore all the governments of the world to help the people of Guatemala, who are suffering so at the army's gunpoint, and who are also suffering from hunger and need because they have risen and want their freedom. Thank you.

Testimony of
Pablo Ceto

Indian peasant

My name is Pablo Ceto. I come from the municipality of
Nebaj, in the department of El Quiché in the northwestern part
of Guatemala.

Nebaj, Chajul, and Cotzal are communities that have stood
out in the last 10 years of revolutionary struggle. One could almost
say this region was the cradle of one of the great currents of the
people's struggle, which strengthens and guarantees the people's
advance.

I am the fifth of 11 children from an Ixil family. We are one
of the branches of the Mames who mainly live in Huehuetenango,
and also in Quezaltenango and Retalhul.

My testimony will not be the story of 1, 2, 15, 20 more
massacres. My *compañeros* have already said enough, enough so
that the suffering will always remain in the consciousness of our
people. Furthermore, this is confirmed by the opinion of
international institutions and organizations such as Amnesty
International, Americas Watch, the National Council of Churches,
the American Association of Anthropologists, and others. I don't
think it is necessary to describe all of the facts in order to com-
prehend this regime.

I want to describe not only how our people have suffered, but
also the paths their lives have taken. I want to give a picture of
the future of the children who are descendants of the great Mayan
civilization.

I am from a poor Indian family. I began school when I was
nine years old, after helping my grandfather in the cornfields and
in the mountains growing beans. During the first years of primary

school, Indians were the majority, and in the last years we were in the minority. I learned to read and write the alphabet, and I also learned humiliation and contempt, that is to say, discrimination against the Indian.

After my primary education, I received a scholarship and attended secondary school outside of my town and its mountains. In Santa Cruz, El Quiché, during those six years, I learned about Central America, America, the Old World, etc. But above all, I learned to ask about the causes of suffering—for example, hospitals with a capacity of 200 beds and three doctors to care for 40,000 inhabitants. Miserable wages. Kidnapping of peasant Indian youth so that they would serve as soldiers.

Our first step against discrimination was in Santa Cruz, El Quiché. Instead of only "Miss Quiché," a ladina, receiving 100 *quetzals* in the patron saint festival, we succeeded in also getting 100 *quetzals* for the Indian queen (then called "Princesita Utatlán"), who had previously received 25 *quetzals* from the authorities.

In addition to our Association for Maya/Quiché Culture, I also got to know other groups—youth, Christian, Indian, and pastoral organizations. We began to work with indigenous organizations on a national level. We also began to encounter the aspirations of religious people and students who were joining together with the peasantry and the Indians in search of a different future. It was a time of beginning to learn the reality of our people in all our peasant communities of El Quiché. It was a period of consciousness raising; of groups for Christian reflection, for the study of human rights, for the study of the paths that we had just traveled—the peasant leagues, the cooperatives, the struggle within the juridical and legal framework. In subsequent years, we would not be able to travel those paths.

In 1974 I went to study at the university on a scholarship. I studied agronomy for five years, but the force of my people, of the Indians, of the peasants, was calling me. Every weekend I would go back to my town until I finally returned to my place of origin, my personal, cultural, and political reference point.

In 1976, with other *compañeros*, I was helping out in the emergency caused by the February 4 earthquake when the army kidnapped more than 50 leaders from the Ixil Chajul, Cotzal, and Nebaj communities. But the awakening of our communities grew greater every day. The earthquake revealed reality all the more and increased the solidarity between Indians and ladinos, between peasants from the southern coast and the high plains. It helped us to know other people, other groups, other places. It allowed our horizons to be broadened; it gave us greater clarity about the reality of our country. And we would hear from the countryside and we would help the Coca-Cola workers who were on strike. We helped with the formation of the National Committee of Labor Union Unity (CNUS); we helped in whatever way we could.

Later came the demonstrations of May 1 and October 20. In 1977, there was the march of the miners of Ixtahuacán. In 1978, we founded the Peasant Unity Committee (CUC). The men would show up in their straw hats, with their machetes, their hoes and their placards made of straw and nylon. It also revealed to the Guatemalans and foreigners that the rich color of our Indian *huipiles* (women's blouses) was not just for folklore, that we Indians are not only good for carrying loads on our backs, but that we have developed equal or greater strength for pushing forward the struggle to win better wages, better working conditions. Indians and poor ladinos appeared together, and we have begun to weave this alliance forever.

That same year, we brought our strength to the CNUS by affiliating. In 1979, along with other popular and democratic organizations, we decided to join our forces to struggle against repression, and the Democratic Front Against Repression (Frente Democrático Contra la Represión) was formed. Later it became more and more clear that there were no more avenues. Only force opens up avenues, the force of the people—of the masses—of the fighting masses.

In 1980, we decided to occupy the Spanish embassy. Above all, this decision showed the greater clarity and conviction that we had attained: that if it is necessary to give our lives for others, we will give them. What good does life do us, if the rest of our people don't have it? We cannot and we will never be able to live just to live, and for nothing else.

We also headed up the strike on the southern coast, the one

made up of 70,000 volunteers, farmers, and farmworkers. Pablo Bautista, a ladino peasant, lit the spark. Subsequently, Ixil, Quiché, Mam, and Cakchikel [Indian groups—Eds.] people gave the strikers strength, and we won. In that way, we honored our fallen comrades at the Spanish embassy.

In 1981, we founded our January 31 Popular Front, an extension of the unity of thought and action of our fighting organization.

Every day I see that the road is becoming more difficult and longer. But the heart and the fist have also become stronger. I see that my *compañeros*, my people, walk with feet of lead and fists of steel. Each time that we evaluate ourselves, we see that there are more of us, that we are more convinced, that we are stronger in convincing others and stronger in our decisions.

I went on to contribute my small part, along with writers, professionals, artists, Christians, and other leaders of popular, democratic, and patriotic movements. For the peasants, for the Indians, together with other *compañeros*, we became members of the Guatemalan Committee of Patriotic Unity (Comité Guatemalteco de Unidad Patriótica, CGUP).

For me, it was setting foot outside Guatemala to push forward the denunciation of this regime, and international solidarity with the people of Guatemala, that have given me strength and support.

This is why I always feel that we are moving forward. We are many, and the confidence of my people is large. No one can be isolated. Whatever can be achieved, no one is capable of achieving it alone. It always requires the support of others, and that is what I have learned in these last 10 years. In the struggle, we have forged many ways of moving forward, which are based on the community life of our people, the spirit of sharing not only sorrow but also a vision of the future. There you find the essence and values of the cultures of my ancestors. . . .

There is an uprising in Guatemala. It is the people who cry out, and the path of their steps is already taking shape.

On the Persecution of Christians and the Church in Guatemala

Julia Esquivel
Guatemalan Committee for Justice and Peace

1. COLONIAL PERIOD, PERIOD OF INDEPENDENCE AND PERIOD OF LIBERAL REFORM

Historically, the Catholic Church emerged in Guatemala committed to the military conquest and the extermination of the indigenous masses. The entire first stage of the Spanish Conquest was expressed in the words of Father Francisco Vázquez: "Don Pedro Alvarado with his soldiers and a Catholic priest came to wage war against those of Atitlán. . . ."

But not all people of the Church served the interests of the conquistadors. There were men like Fray Bartolomé de las Casas and other members of the Dominican Order who opposed the voracity of the colonists. The Dominicans achieved the abolition of slavery by the proclamation of the "New Laws" of 1542.

However, the work of the preachers was soon institutionalized and placed in the service of colonization in the "Indian reduction project." For the last quarter of the 17th century, the majority of the Orders were caught up like the rest of the colonizers in the dynamic of accumulating land, Indians, and privileges. Thus a gap between the hierarchy and the people was slowly created, a characteristic that has remained constant with greater or lesser intensity throughout our history.

Faced with independence (1821), the ecclesiastic structure split apart, taking diverse political positions, but none embraced the need for social change demanded by the oppression in which the people lived. The Church participated directly in the achievement of independence.

During the post-independence period, the situation of the Church varied according to the evolution of the inter-oligarchical struggle between Liberals and Conservatives for control of political power. The ecclesiastical hierarchy generally allied with the Conservatives; for this reason, when Liberal power was consolidated, the Church suffered relentless persecution. An important event was the promulgation of Decree 93/1873, issued by the regime of General Justo R. Barrios, which established the "Freedom of Sects," thus permitting the entrance of Protestantism. The purpose was clear: to neutralize the popular influence of the Catholic Church and permit North American economic expansionism with its Protestant ideology. It was not until the government of General Ubico (1930-1944) that the Catholic Church slowly began to recover its prestige and initiated a pastoral program, principally in rural areas, along the line of Catholic Action (Acción Católica).

2. ROLE OF THE CHURCH AND CHRISTIAN ACTIONS IN THE POPULAR MOVEMENT AND ITS PROGRAM (1944-1983)

With the bourgeois democratic revolution of 1944, the Church found itself restricted in its functions, losing the prerogatives that Ubico had restored to it. Unhappy with this situation, the anticommunist Church hierarchy represented by the person of Monsignor Mariano Rossell supported the wealthy—both national and transnational—in their efforts to overthrow the government of Arbenz. In June 1954, that government was overthrown and in July of the same year, Colonel Carlos Castillo Armas was placed in power. Thereby began a period of good relations between the Church and the government.

During these years, many "pastoral agents"* arrived, all with instructions to fight communism; but what they actually found was a people submerged in exploitation and misery. In the face of these circumstances, they began projects of social assistance. In the decade of the 1960s, the Church was transformed from a typically anticommunist Christian church to one based on a social Christian model.

In 1962, with the explosion of social contradictions and the increase of guerrilla activity, the Bishops wrote a collective letter stating that communism is "a false solution" and legitimating private ownership as a natural right. In 1963, the army intervened and by means of a coup d'état imposed Colonel Enrique Peralta A., under whom the first wave of repression was carried out. Monsignor Rossell published a letter praising Bishop Francisco Marroquín (who had favored the Indians and opposed the colonizers) and indicating the injustice of the economic, political, and social structure toward the indigenous majority. This act provoked serious reprisals against him.

During these years, Protestantism began to grow, and its adherents increased from 25,000 in 1953 to around 100,000 by 1962. Evangelist campaigns, like Billy Graham's in 1958, were of great importance to this growth.

Monsignor Rossell died in December 1964, and his position was taken by Monsignor Mario Casariego, an ultra-conservative with a great lust for power. During the government of Julio César Méndez Montenegro (1966-1970), the hierarchy assumed a dual posture. On the one hand, Monsignor Casariego pointed out that "the Church has the duty to respect the authorities and to collaborate with the initiatives that promote the well-being, progress and peace of the people." On the other hand, the Bishops Conference pointed out that there was a climate of violence in the country and unjust distribution of wealth.

In 1968, the Vatican II and Medellín documents [key to the evolution of liberation theology—Eds.], together with the

---

*This term has acquired a particular meaning in Latin America where it refers to clergy (and also lay people) who are concerned about and minister to the material and spiritual concerns of the community—Eds.

institutionalized violence, fostered an increasing awareness—a compelling conscience—in the pastoral agents. They proposed to develop a program of teachings responding to the needs of the exploited majority. Beginning in that year, they trained hundreds of catechists and social workers. Thus the Church began a new process at its base, a process of discovering the role of Christians linked together with the needs and struggles of the people.

During the government of General Arana Osorio (1970-1974), the Church showed a lack of cohesion in pointing out the roots of sin in the social structure. In February 1971, the Bishops issued a statement on the State of Siege, condemning violence in all its forms. In December, various Catholic and evangelical pastoral agents called for ending the State of Siege, which at that time had been in effect for months. The regime persecuted and threatened these clerics, and several were forced to leave the country. The Arana regime was characterized by the beginning of the enthronement of military cliques in power, the same cliques who urged the development of counterinsurgency policies.

The government of General Kjell Laugerud García (1974-1978) continued Arana's work but strongly encouraged a reformist program and tried to obtain social support. He achieved neither. The constant of this period, in the face of repression, was mass organization. Thus emerged the Peasant Unity Committee (CUC) and the Coordinating Committee of Settlers [i.e., squatters— Eds.] (Coordinadora de Pobladores, CDP), whose origins included a significant background in the Christian faith. The National Committee of Labor Union Unity (Comité Nacional de Unidad Sindical, CNUS) and the Robin García Student Front (Frente Estudiantil Robin García—Universidad y Secundaria, FER S-U also came into existence.

In 1976, an earthquake uncovered the real social volcano upon which our country has lived for hundreds of years. At this time, the Bishops Conference issued a historical document: the Pastoral Letter, "United in Hope." This Pastoral Letter began with an analysis of reality, denounced the accumulation of land as a sin, recognized the intra-ecclesiastic problem, reaffirmed its choice for the poor, and emphasized that the Church should participate in the post-earthquake reconstruction on the basis of the values that inspired the Church's own work. This letter won the antagonism of the government and the wealthy, who began a direct attack against it.

It is important to note the emergence of the Guatemalan Committee for Justice and Peace, formed in November 1977 and composed of priests, pastors, and other religious and lay people of ecumenical spirit. The committee initiated a struggle in defense of human rights, acting as the voice of those without a voice, thus trying to work with the people in constructing a Church that is born from the poor.

On June 30, Father Hermógenes López was murdered in order to silence his courageous denunciation of the army's abuses and for defending the natural resources of his community, San José Pinula. Another important event for the Christian community was the massacre at Panzós on May 29, 1978. More than 130 indigenous peasants were murdered in connection with the seizure of lands being carried out by members of the military and large landowners. In the face of these acts, priests and other religious and lay people strongly protested, denouncing those responsible and declaring the murders to be the consequence of sin in the entire social structure. As a result, the Minister of Defense accused the priests and other religious people of inciting the peasants; Sister Raimunda Alonso, among others, was expelled from the country, accused of participating in political activities and of being the cause of the Panzós massacre.

The coming to power of General Romeo Lucas García (1978-1982) brought general instructions to end all struggles for justice and rights and to implement a "Government Program of Political Assassination," moving from selective repression to massive repression.

On December 20, 1979, Father Carlos Stetter was expelled from the country. He had replaced Father Guillermo Woods, who had been murdered in 1976. Both had worked on a project of equipping lands and organizing cooperatives with more than 2,000 families in Ixcán, Huehuetenango.

The struggles of the people's movement went beyond economic

demands and became demonstrations of repudiation of the regime, thus acquiring a political character. On February 24, 1979, the Democratic Front Against Repression (Frente Democrático Contra la Represión) was formed. Great hopes for the Latin American people were born on July 19, 1979, with the triumph of the Sandinista National Liberation Front in Nicaragua. The Christian communities strongly supported the Nicaraguan people, while the Archbishop publicly criticized the participation of priests in the fight against Somoza.

On the occasion of the Third General Latin American Conference of Bishops in Puebla (Mexico), the base communities initiated a deepening of the documents and "rescue" of Medellín. At this point, the government accused the Church of being "communist" and of fomenting subversion. The Jesuits were directly threatened and responded to these threats: "We place ourselves under the sign of choosing for the poor."

On January 31, 1980, a delegation of indigenous peasants from Quiché, accompanied by workers, students, and city residents, peacefully occupied the Spanish embassy to denounce the repression they were suffering in their communities. In response, they were machine-gunned and burned alive in the embassy. The Bishops Conference, the Conference of the Religious, the Christian world in general, and the international community repudiated this act. The massacre was understood by the people as a blood marriage uniting various sectors of the populace.

On May 1, the last workers' demonstration was held. That day, more than 100 people were kidnapped and forcibly disappeared, among them Father Conrado de la Cruz and the catechist Herlindo Cifuentes.

The most relevant incident of 1980 for the Church happened following the murders of Father José María Gran and Father Faustino Villanueva and the assassination attempt against Monsignor Gerardi, Bishop of the Diocese of El Quiché. The priests responded by closing the diocese, thereby manifesting their protest against the repression suffered by the people. In August the Guatemalan Church in Exile (Iglesia Guatemalteca en el Exilio, IGE) was founded, bringing together the pastoral agents who had been in El Quiché with the other pastors to continue working with the people and to denounce the repression. On December 20, the government denied Monsignor Gerardi, who was returning from Rome, entry into the country.

In Escuintla, Father Walter Voordeckers was murdered and Bishop Mario E. Ríos Montt was threatened and persecuted. On the southern coast, on November 19, the Evangelical Pastor Don Santos Jiménez was murdered while he celebrated a religious service. For years he had supported the people's fight to obtain a piece of land.

Faced with this repression, the hierarchy finally spoke out, but was conciliatory and did not directly point to those responsible for the repression. The Guatemalan Committee for Justice and Peace initiated activities reflecting the true situation, and the experiences of the first Christian communities were explored. The "Church in the Catacombs" is no longer merely part of history; it has been resurrected in our country.

Lucas García continued with his policy of destroying everything and everyone in opposition to his government's program. Yet the people took another step forward. On January 31, 1981, the Popular Movement (Movimiento Popular) announced the creation of a new Revolutionary Mass Organizations Front (Frente de Organizaciones Revolucionarias de Masas) that embodied the goals and experiences of the people who died in the Spanish embassy. The January 31 Popular Front (Frente Popular 31 de Enero, FP-31) was formed, based on the concepts of "Deeds, Secrecy, and Self-Defense." The Revolutionary Christians, part of FP-31, aspire to be "the voice of all the Christians who are in different trenches of the battle and who therefore are unable to express themselves."

The Church suffered another wave of repression. Father Juan Alonso was murdred in El Quiché in February. On June 9, the Jesuit Father Luis E. Pellecer Faena was kidnapped in broad daylight. On July 1, Father Tulio Maruzzo was murdered in Izabal. On July 28, Father Francisco Stanley Rother was murdered in Sololá. The bodies of the missionaries Angel Martínez and Raúl Josef Leger were exhibited by the government, which claimed that they had been killed in a skirmish with the guerrillas; in fact, the autopsies proved they had died days before.

On September 30, 1981, the government held a press conference with a great deal of publicity. Suddenly Father Pellecer appeared to testify to his "repentance and conversion," confessing that he had belonged to a political-military organization. He accused the Church of being infiltrated by communism at all levels. The objectives of the government in presenting Father Pellecer were to legitimize repression of the Church and to launch a direct attack on liberation theology, following the postulates of the document of the Santa Fe Committee [right-wing policy recommendations prepared in the U.S. shortly after Reagan became President—Eds.]. These objectives were not achieved despite the sophistication of the event, since the testimony contained basic contradictions that could not be cleared up. . . .

Since General Ríos Montt took power in 1982, the repression against Christians has acquired other characteristics. In addition to striking the pastors, the repression strikes entire Christian communities, often when they are in the midst of celebrating their faith.

On January 5, 1982, the priests Roberto Paredes and Pablo Schildermans were kidnapped and their sexton, Don Eladio Aguilar, was murdered. On January 6, Sister Victoria de la Roca was kidnapped in the Esquipulas Convent; General Benedicto Lucas said: "She is tied in with the guerrillas and we have abundant information." On January 13, Brother Santiago Miller was murdered in Huehuetenango. The missionary Sergio Berten was kidnapped and disappeared in the same month. On February 19, the body of the Evangelical Pastor José Humberto Alvarado was found.

In those cases where it was possible to break through government secrecy, the following massacres committed inside churches and chapels have come to light: March 20 in Lacamá Tercero, Chichicastenango, El Quiché; March 28, Pachay and Las Lomas, Chimaltenango; March 30, Chupol, El Quiché; July 17, San Francisco, Nentón, Huehuetenango; and July 18, in Rabinal, Baja Verapaz.

On March 31, the Bishops issued two documents. One was a letter addressed to the military junta expressing their hope that the promises made to the people would be carried out, asking a guarantee of freedom for the development of evangelism and manifesting their desire for dialogue. The other letter was on the occasion of Holy Thursday, in which they denounced the situation of the refugees and displaced persons both inside and outside of the country, calculating those inside the country to number more than one million. In addition, they denounced the repression of the populace. On May 27 they again denounced the repression and indicated that it had reached the extreme of "genocide."

The Conference of the Religious pointed out as guilty of genocide "those who do not wish to change the situation of oppression prevailing in the country." On May 13 and June 13, the national press published two news releases from the Committee for Justice and Peace denouncing the fact that the massacres "have continued with the consent of the authorities."

To bloody repression has been added manipulation of the people's faith and religious belief. With Ríos Montt the government has become a theocracy. In his person is not only the President but also a pastor who says that he governs "not by votes nor weapons but by the will of God." Some fundamentalist sects of North American origin have viewed the coup d'état and the government as a "miracle of God" and a defeat of Satan. During the campaign it was called: Guatemala—Miracle on the Move!!! But the manipulation of the Evangelical Church by small allied groups in power has not been shared by the rest of the evangelical churches. Prophetic voices such as that of the Evangelical Fraternity of Guatemala (Confraternidad Evangélica de Guatemala) have been raised, saying, "It is our duty to unmask, before the people of God, those who traffick in the name of God." They cite as an example General Ríos Montt's manipulation in trying to legitimate the death and pain that he is causing the country.

3. THE HORIZON OF THE NEW SOCIETY
AND THE PERSPECTIVES OF THE CHRISTIANS

In spite of the policies of genocide and "scorched earth," the people continue to make giant steps in their struggle to free themselves. On February 9, the Guatemalan National Revolutionary Unity (Unidad Revolucionaria Nacional Guatemalteca, URNG), which forms the vanguard of the revolution, was introduced to the public. That same month, the Guatemalan Committee of Patriotic Unity was formed, composed of popular and democratic civic notables who have responded to the call made by the URNG for the need to form a national patriotic front.

The URNG and its program are the alternative to genocide, to the dependence and antidemocracy in which our people live. In its proclamation, a five-point Program of Government was announced. Several sections contain special mention of the contributions and perspectives of Christian participation in the struggle to forge a new society. Point Four is particularly important: "The revolution recognizes the Christian community as one of the pillars of the new society, insofar as their beliefs and their faith have been put in the service of liberty for all Guatemalans."

With this perspective, we wish to manifest our unshakable decision, rooted in our faith, to continue accompanying the people. Our martyrs are the mark of this participation and they show us the way, they appeal to us and give us strength. Our contribution will be present in the new society. Our communities, living the sacraments and celebrating the faith, analyze and reflect on reality by the light of the gospel so that our contribution may be illuminated by the Word of God. As individuals we shall give our testimony by joining popular organizations to work for better and more fraternal social, economic, and political structures.

We are also conscious of the right that our people have to fight for a more just and fraternal society and the need for the support of the international community. We ask for this solidarity from our fellow Christians of the universal church and from all men of good will.

Testimony of
José Efraín Rosales

Indian peasant and
Delegate of the Word

Compañeros, receive a fraternal greeting from the Christian, poor, peasant, and Indian people of Guatemala, and please receive my own greeting as José Efraín Rosales from the village of La Estancia, Santa Cruz, El Quiché, Guatemala, as a peasant, an Indian, a Delegate of the Word, and a member of the Guatemalan Church in Exile.

I would like to give testimony about what happened in my community, in my family, and in my town. Everything that I tell here, I have seen with my own eyes and I myself personally have experienced it.

In my community there are 2,000 inhabitants: 75% of them are Catholic Christians, 100% are Indians, 65% are peasants, and the rest are weavers and businessmen. The peasants have an income of barely $75 per year. There is a lot of economic and educational poverty. The children begin to work when they are seven and eight years old. They are forced to work by the very situation of poverty. The village is situated six kilometers from the departmental seat.

The religion that existed was very traditional—that is to say, we learned only to pray, to go to mass, to have processions, to visit the statues, etc. The rich, the government, and the army were happy with this. But every day, exploitation, oppression, discrimination, and enormous injustices against the people got worse and worse. Then the Church changed, through the needs of the people. It now opens doors for us, takes the blindfolds off our eyes, and plays a very important role—that is, it begins to help the people denounce injustices, poverty, exploitation, discrimination, and oppression.

The community had good leaders and organizations, for example: cooperatives, committees for the betterment of the community, Catholic Action, and the Peasant Unity Committee (CUC).

In 1972, spies began to infiltrate the existing organizations, and to accuse and slander our leaders to the authorities. There was a case in 1973. I was a leader in my community. I was called before the governor of my town, Colonel Oswaldo Echeverría, who threatened to send me to jail if I continued talking about injustice, freedom, exploitation, poverty. He quoted from the Bible: "Blessed are the poor, because theirs is the kingdom of Heaven," and he also told me: "If the poor did not exist, the rich would not eat."

In May 1979, spies from the government and from the rich people locked 250 people who were Delegates of the Word in a Catholic church, terrorizing them and threatening them that if they continued talking about injustices, they would be assassinated by the army. This occurred in my community.

On April 9, 1980, a very strong repression began in my community. And on that same date, Fabián was assassinated by 15 men armed with machine-guns and dressed as civilians. They were the death squad, with their faces painted or masked; this took place in the Utatlán ruins, on the road halfway between La Estancia and El Quiché.

That same month, a young man, Mauricio Ramos, was jailed and then kidnapped. He was accused by the guards of the Department of the Treasury of making and selling illegal liquor. But this was a lie, because he was a weaver of traditional cloth. The authorities colluded with the kidnappers, and after they kept him in jail for a week, they took him out at 8:00 p.m., so that he could be kidnapped and made to disappear.

Every 15 days, on the road to the community of Santa Cruz, the selective repression and assassination of our comrade leaders continued.

On September 26, 1980, the kidnapping of my brother X took

place. At 5:00, 30 well-armed men with machine-guns arrived. They took my brother out of the house. He was half-naked. It was wintertime; they put him into a well of water and took him out again. They tortured him, and they took him to the house of his uncles, his relatives, his friends, and to the home of his in-laws; each time the kidnappers would ask if anyone knew this man. He had cancer in his right foot. He was a leader of Catholic Action, and treasurer of a reconstruction committee after the earthquake. Two kilometers from the house, at the edge of an embankment, there were some trees. They tied his hands with some ropes, and they strung him up in the form of a crucified person, and they hanged him and they stuck a knife in his ribs. These were people from the death squad, from the Secret Anti-communist Army (ESA). On that same day, in different ways, the following people were assassinated: my brother, Ambrosio, Marcelo, María, Marcelino, Justo, and Julián.

On October 24, 1980, 34 people were massacred in Chuimatratz, Sacualpa, Santa Cruz, El Quiché. Among them were my relatives Petronila, Luisa, and four children: Virginia, Cruz, Miguel, and another who still did not have a name because he was only 17 hours old. They were burned with gasoline.

On a Monday in April 1982, repression by the government of Ríos Montt continued against the community. Forests were burned, houses were burned, food and crops and animals were burned and damaged.

In my community, more than 200 leaders of cooperatives, Delegates of the Word, peasant leaders, have been killed. I want to make a clarification: not all of them have died right in La Estancia. People who are traveling have been taken off of the buses; others have left the community because of repression and have been killed in other towns or villages, because it is a constant persecution.

I also want to clarify that other organizations often give different facts about how many people have been killed. For example, in my community, they killed the grandfather. His name is Pedro, his son is named Pedro, the grandson is named Pedro, and they all have the same last name. This happens a lot in rural communities.

Regarding the church, our religious people, together with the people of the town, had built schools for the education of our children, in the department seat of Santa Cruz, El Quiché. But in August 1980, the army closed the schools, they removed the nuns and our priests from the church, and they also removed Bishop Juan Yerardí. The cooperatives that the church led were also closed down, and their leaders were kidnapped, tortured, and decapitated.

As proof of this, there is the assassination of three priests from El Quiché. On June 4, 1980, the army killed Father José María Gran in Chajol, Santa Cruz, El Quiché. Father Faustino Villanueva was killed on July 10, 1980. Father Juan Alonso was killed on February 13, 1981. They are all from this country.

For these same reasons, our priests and the Delegates of the Word cannot carry forward the pastoral work, the liberating evangelization of our communities. This is why the Guatemalan Church in Exile exists.

Lastly, we will not become tired. We will follow the example of our martyrs, of our first Christians, and the example of Christ. He chose to be on the side of the poor, to denounce injustice, and he died for telling the truth. . . .

Testimony of
Carmelita Santos

Indian Catechist

INTRODUCTION

My name is Carmelita Santos. I am an indigenous catechist and a member of the Guatemalan Committee for Justice and Peace.

I present my testimony to this People's Tribunal in the name of my Guatemalan brothers and sisters who are unable to lift up their voices today, and who suffer under the military dictatorship of General Efraín Ríos Montt. I wish to speak in the name of all the men, women, children, and elderly people of my country, so that the world will know about the terrible injustices that we suffer there, and so that our right to live on this earth as people and as children of God will be recognized.

MY WORK AS A CATECHIST

I work in communities, talking to the people about God, and the people like that. I also teach people how to sing. People like to sing or to shout, because they fill their lungs with air and it makes them happy.

In 1970 and 1972, some good priests came here, who were honestly committed to helping their brothers in need. They weren't like the ones before them, who only talked to the "ladinos" in the village. They took care of us all. They came to our village to evangelize us but on seeing our communal lands where we all ate the same corn, they were the ones who were evangelized. When there was happiness, we all shared in it. And we all shared the same sorrows.

The priests wanted to improve our plight, but because we were many, two priests alone could not carry out improvements for all. The best thing they did was to set up schools, to train community leaders. These schools were established in various regions of Guatemala, since the priests could not cover every town. They and the nuns would visit each school, and then return two weeks or a month later. Those of us who were trained were called catechists, or community leaders.

The catechist works with the community, spreading the Word of God, allowing everyone to participate. The Word of God leads us to organize and make our demands together, because we will not be listened to on an individual basis. We organized a demonstration, protesting our oppression by the rich. But they said: "What's going on? The downtrodden Indians are acting up. Those who open their mouths will be killed."

HEALTH EDUCATION

The nuns taught us the importance of hygiene. When children have rashes or intestinal parasites or diarrhea, it's because of bad health conditions. But there are even worse problems in villages like Canchún Chitucán, where there is no water because it sank after the earthquake. There is hardly enough to drink. Where could the people go? A priest said: "Let's dig a well."

But the religious people's love for the poor and their total devotion were not well-received by the rich. Neither they, nor the police, nor the judges, nor the soldiers like it when someone is concerned about the poor. They accused the priest of being a "guerrilla chief" and tried to capture him and kill him, but he managed to escape. He had to leave the country.

THE CHURCH, THREATENED AND PERSECUTED

First they threaten the community leader. If he doesn't leave immediately, he is kidnapped during the night and killed in the ravine. This has been done to catechists and to people who have listened to their sermons. Now we cannot hold our masses, or recite the rosary or the Novena of the Sacred Heart of Jesus, because we are being watched. In our village there are two strange men; they are not from the village, but they appear and disappear in the evenings.

Who persecutes the Christians? The big judges, paid by the governor or the ex-governor of Salamá; the soldiers stationed in the town of Rabinal; the national police; an employee of the city who is a friend of the soldiers or the national police; or a military commander.

This happened during the time of Lucas García, who said that there was freedom for the Church but who really persecuted it. They watched the villages and took away our leaders, killing them one by one. Oh! But Lucas went too far, and it was known that he was an assassin. The rich say that there was a change in government. They put in Ríos Montt, saying that he was "better," but he has the same heart as Lucas, and sharper nails. He's "democratic" but he's smarter than Lucas. Oh! "The envoy of God," Ríos Montt calls himself. Is he like God, powerful and merciful with the poor?

TESTIMONY OF THE COMMUNITIES' SUFFERING IN THE GENOCIDE CARRIED OUT BY THE RIOS MONTT GOVERNMENT

Ríos Montt shows his power to the poor. When he took over, he ordered his soldiers to eliminate from the map of Rabinal, Baja Verapaz, several villages that no longer had inhabitants. The people there had been slaughtered by soldiers and 10 commando squads from Xococ: Río Negro, Camalmapa, Canchún, Buena Vista, and the village of Chichupac, where there were only about 20 survivors. . . . In each of these villages there had been 300, 400, 500 or more inhabitants, not counting children. I say this because I have been in these communities many times, singing, praying, and celebrating the Word of God, or we would dance to the *son* of San Pablo or Rabinal. It hurts me that my people have left me alone. And I say this because I burn inside from the injustice of Ríos Montt against my poor people of Rabinal and against all the other poor people of the indigenous regions of Guatemala. Let them kill me for speaking the truth. I am not afraid.

Ríos Montt says that he is governing in the name of God. For those who believe in him, he is a Christian and belongs to an evangelical sect. But the repression got much worse for the poor with the arrival of Ríos Montt.

1. Plan de Sánchez, July 18, 1982

It was Sunday. Before, no one would go to the town to do their shopping. But that day, July 18th, in various villages—Concul, Irchel, Xeciguan, Chiac, and the whole village of Plan de Sánchez—the people decided to come with their baskets on their heads, filled with *macuy* and *chiquiboy* [foods—Eds.] to sell and exchange for corn. Women came with chickens, or baby pigs, to trade for food to feed their families. Other women from the mountains brought cheeses to exchange for corn from Rabinal. Some merely wanted to go to Sunday mass. It was around 10 a.m. The soldiers stationed there had mortars and began to fire bombs on the villages around the town of Rabinal. Then a helicopter flew over us and dropped more bombs. There were two little planes, very high up, some distance from the helicopter, and we had the impression that they were watching over the helicopter.

When everyone saw this, and heard "boom! boom! boom!," they all got up. Some were crying because they had left their children in their village, children of 3 or 4 years who were too little to run away. Others said, "Mine are 8 and 10 years old; maybe they've run to the ravine." "But what about the elderly, who can't run?" So they decided to go to the villages.

But down the path, a village called Plan de Sánchez was surrounded by soldiers who would not let the people go by, telling them to wait for the captain, who was going to tell them something. Some, seeing the crowd from a distance, returned to the town. Others hid in the ravines and the hillside. Meanwhile, the soldiers were searching the houses in Plan de Sánchez, taking away the good clothing and the valuable old jewelry, stealing it all. Then they set the houses on fire and rounded up the children and the old people, all in one group.

In the afternoon, they began raping the women and torturing the men. What terrible screams could be heard two mountains away! Then they piled everyone up, poured fuel on them, and set fire to the people. Women, old people, and children were turned to ashes. One of the burning people managed to escape, and ran around like a cat until she finally fell into the ravine. The soldiers howled when they saw this naked person doing that; it was just a joke for Ríos Montt's soldiers.

Then they piled up the dead bodies and went to get Lorenza, the woman who had survived the fire. They sat her in the middle of all the bodies, they cut her lips, and made her watch the soldiers as they placed the burnt children at their dead mothers' breasts and the men's heads between the women's legs.

Lorenza was a preacher in the village, along with Narcisa. They belonged to the church choir and gave sermons. Narcisa had been burnt alive. But Lorenza had survived, and the soldiers asked her if she believed in God. "Let's see if He saves you!" they shouted. Lorenza, lying in agony, heard but remained quiet.

On Monday, July 19th, the soldiers went down to their barracks, taking with them some pigs, chickens, clothes, and jewelry from the dead people's homes. Some of the villagers managed to sneak down and bury some of the dead, and they found Lorenza dying. Jacinto, Lorenza's father, came and took his daughter to the health center. But the soldiers caught on immediately and they captured Jacinto and Lorenza. They said, "Hand over that shit, let's burn it some more." And Jacinto yelled that he would not hand over his daughter to the soldiers. At last he managed to get into the health center. A nurse wanted to help, but a soldier stopped her from doing anything. He took a needle out of his bag and gave Lorenza an injection. She died, leaving behind a baby girl 11 months old. In just one afternoon, 225 men, women, babies, and elderly people were killed, all burnt to death.

2. The Siege of the Church

One day we were working in my village. I can't remember the exact date, but it was a bit before what happened in Plan de Sánchez. In the afternoon a group of soldiers entered, shouting, "Well, well, what's going on with the Indians? Yours is a happy life. Why are you quiet? Where are the *marimbas,* your drums and *chirimía?* Eh? Go on with your customs, go to the chapel, celebrate the Word of God. Sing, and pray for peace." They told us a date, and said they would return, to see if we had done what they told us. We all asked each other, "Should we do it? My God, would they kill us during the mass? Maybe we shouldn't." "But they'll kill us anyway if we don't," said someone else. "Just yesterday they bombed a village." So we decided to do what they had said.

We took the *marimbas,* but played only one song, because almost all of us cried when we heard our song. We began the celebration of the Word of God, and we sang. When we had finished, our chapel was completely surrounded by soldiers.

The captain entered and came to us. "Well, folks, we want peace," he said. "But if you make trouble, we have this for you," and he showed us a big rifle in his hand. "This is for you if there's trouble." Our Bibles were on the altar. And he went up to the altar, took the Bibles and set them on fire. (For the soldiers, the Bible is subversive literature. Many people have buried theirs.) He took a hymnal, opened it and read a song which says:

> It is not enough to pray.
> Many things are needed
> for there to be peace.

The captain was furious, and he shouted, "Subversives! It's true, we have to kill all the Indians. And it doesn't matter if they are all gone. Don't worry, the village won't be empty—we can bring foreigners to live in your villages. There are plenty of people in the world!" I wanted to answer him, but I knew I would have been killed on the spot. I said to myself, "No foreigner could live in our village. We have no beds in which to sleep, all we eat is corn, we have no nearby water, no baths, no latrine, no electricity. No foreigner could live in our villages." And I wanted to answer, "They could not stand to live like we do, and work so hard. But riches do not fall from the sky, as my mother says, so we must work hard." I was so angry, but I didn't say a word, thank God.

The captain had a notebook, with a list of names in it, and he began to call out the names of all the members or Delegates of the Word of God. They were all poor peasants. When they heard their names being called, they humbly stood up, took off their hats and said "Here, I am here." They didn't understand why their names were being called. Quickly, the soldiers stood behind each person who answered. There were many men, each one with a soldier behind him. Some people thought maybe they were being called to form a commission. Some of the women had packed lunches, and went up to their husbands to tell them to take the food with them. The soldiers got very angry and almost kicked the women out. Then the men were taken outside. Their hands were tied and they were lined up below a pole near the chapel. The children cried out to their fathers, wanting to go with them, but the soldiers dragged the children away without pity. "Do you want us to kick you?" they asked. But the children did not understand what the soldiers were saying, and they continued crying. The mothers consoled their children.

The soldiers took the men down to a creek. They tied them with a rope around their necks and hung them from the trees, beating them with sticks and branches. At first, we heard screams, but little by little the voices grew fainter because the ropes cut off the men's breathing. Night fell, and the men had not died. The soldiers stayed, sitting there shouting and laughing. Who knows what they were laughing about. Maybe Judas knows. This is the story of Christians from the base communities and how they were killed. That day, 32 men died.

Jesus preached and helped the needy. He was persecuted to death, nailed to a wooden cross. Jesus still suffers today on the heavy cross of Guatemala, from the terrible repression by Ríos Montt. The Christian base communities represent Jesus, and they are killed, dragged out of their churches for celebrating the Word of God.

3. Chichupac, April 19, 1982

On the 18th of April, soldiers entered the village of Chichupac, telling the people not to be afraid. "We are defending the country," they said. "You must trust us. We want to talk to you in a group. The government we have now is good. We will return tomorrow, but we want everyone to gather together in the church.

If you have old people who are sick, take them to church tomorrow, because we will bring two doctors with us. If they have problems with their lungs, or a toothache, they will be cured tomorrow. Take the children as well: we will bring them toys to make them happy."

Some people believed the soldiers, and they went to church. Many soldiers arrived and they passed out used plastic toys. There was no doctor.

After the toys were handed out, the soldiers did not respect the statue of Christ that the catechists had put on the altar. They began to destroy the statue with their machetes. The people were surrounded and could not leave the church. Then the soldiers called out people's names, including children, and took them to the clinic nearby. All the names were of people who had learned how to read and write. (During the time of Lucas García, all peasants had been ordered to learn how to read. People signed up to learn, and the catechists signed up to teach, but the soldiers killed them. One catechist was killed while carrying a notebook with the names of the people who were studying, including the names of children who could not go to school but who had signed up to learn.)

The women were raped before the eyes of the men and the children in the clinic. The men and the boys had their testicles cut off. Everybody's tongues were cut out. Their eyes were gouged out with nails. Their arms were twisted off. Their legs were cut off. The little girls were raped and tortured. The women had their breasts cut off. And the soldiers left them all there in the clinic, piled up and dying. Those who were not on the list were prohibited from burying the victims. I only remember that 15 children were killed. I cannot remember how many adults were killed. A woman who was there told me all this. . . .

Testimony of
Irma Consuelo de Azmitia

Religious worker

Irma Consuelo Dorantes de Azmitia began her testimony by telling of how her family had always been very united and active in the Christian family movement. They included her husband Mario, her married 23-year-old daughter Dora Clemencia, who was three months pregnant, her student son Mario Federico, and two teenagers: Irma Graciela and Juan José. Dora Clemencia, in particular, had been active as a catechist and teacher of illiterate people as well as youth groups: "She was such a good person for the young people because she always had this radiant sparkle of happiness and gave service at the same time."

On September 19, 1981, my son, Mario Federico, 22 years old, was dragged out of a friend's house by a group of heavily armed men driving large, dark-windowed vehicles with short-wave radios. All day, we had no news of him. It was the morning of September 20 when we heard the details about how these men, dressed in plain clothes, had taken him, after beating him. But we still had no news of him.

The morning of September 21 we tried our utmost to find out where he was, and around 10:30 a.m. a telephone call came to my husband's office. My son's voice asked for the telephone number of his fiancée. As my husband did not know it, he said, "Here is your sister, if you want to talk to her." He immediately said yes, and asked her the same thing. I do not know if she gave him the telephone number, but in any case it was decided that they would meet at 1:00 p.m. at the church of the Hospicio on Fourth Avenue and Fifteenth, Zone 1 of the capital. Immediately, they called me at my office, very happy that at last they had talked with him and that soon we would meet.

At 12:15, my daughter and my husband came and we got the family together. Since we did not know from which direction he was going to arrive, we divided up on the adjoining streets so that we would not miss him. After half an hour had passed, we began to wonder why he had not arrived. Where could he have called from? Why did he call? Suddenly we became anxious and called to my daughter, looking for her at the corner where she had stayed to wait for her brother. We could not find her. We had grave premonitions.

When my husband reached the corner where she had been waiting, he described my daughter to a person who sold sweets there, and asked if he had seen her. He was told that some men in a car had taken her. Now two had been taken from me. Desperate and not knowing what to do, we asked and asked for help to find them, but it was no use.

Then, on the morning of September 22, 1981, I went to my office to tell them that I could not work under these circumstances. Afterwards, we went to visit the Cardinal with whom my husband worked, to ask him to help us find our two children. First we went with my two remaining younger children and their father to the Cathedral. We all held each other's hands and together asked God for strength, to help us through these difficult moments. Then we went to the Cardinal's quarters and explained to him what was happening. He said that he did not believe it, that it was not possible, that undoubtedly it had happened because my daughter had gone with "Operation Uspantán" (a project to educate and help the poor of El Quiché).

Our desire to find our two lost children increased by the minute. The Cardinal said that he would call on the Minister of Defense that very day and that he would talk with the lawyer Donaldo Alvarez to find out about them. By midday, he said, he would have a report. We left there with the hope that we really were going to find them, but something even more terrible happened. When we were scarcely a block and a half away from the Cathedral, a car suddenly cut in front of us going the wrong way on the street, at Seventh Avenue and Ninth Street. Our two

younger children were scarcely four meters behind us. I was with
my husband, who was holding my arm, when suddenly six armed
men drew their pistols and surrounded us, saying to him, "Come
with us." I screamed at them like a crazy woman, but they did
not listen to me.

Then they tried to put him in the car where two armed men
were waiting. With their threats and their pistols, I thought they
would kill us on the spot. That did not happen, but it was
impossible to stop them. The closer they pushed us to the door
of the car, the closer they held their pistols, until one of these men,
dressed in plain clothes, said to me, "Do not feel sad, lady." This
was when they took his arm, pushed him into the car, and headed
east. I lost my head, screaming like a mad woman, "They have
taken my husband, they have taken my husband," and I did not
know what to do.

I went back to the Cardinal's quarters and ran in to tell him.
At that moment, he came out, saying, "This is not possible, what
is happening?" I told him what he already realized, that not even
10 minutes had gone by since we had been there talking with him,
when the gunmen had threatened us and taken my husband. He
immediately called the secretary of Donaldo Alvarez. Attorney
Alvarez was a minister in the government. The Cardinal said,
"Miss, I am sorry to bother you again, but the mother of those
two young people that I just spoke to you about is here, and now
some gunmen have taken her husband at Seventh Avenue and
Ninth Street. I would like to know what is going on. Tell attorney
Alvarez to please help me find out what is going on. It is a family
for whom I have a great deal of respect, and it is very important
for me to know what has become of them." After this conversa-
tion, he told me to go with someone and to take care of myself.

I felt a terrible pang of fear at the thought of going out there,
that some men would take me also. As I left, I again went into
the Cathedral to ask God for strength because they had destroyed
me. It was at this moment that I remembered my two young
children. I did not know what to do, but I asked God to give me
the strength to carry on and find them. I was afraid that they
had been taken, but no. I went to hide in a friend's house and

I asked her to look for my two young children. They looked all over, asked relatives and friends, and they could find out nothing.

Eight days later, I found out that they were all right and were hidden, and that nothing had been done to them, thank God. Immediately, we were reunited and stayed in another house where several people helped us to leave the country, because it was now just impossible. My two children and I felt the constant persecution against us. Therefore we left our country in October, one month after my family had been kidnapped.

I want to emphasize that there were six men who attacked us. One was driving, one was beside him, two aimed at us from in front and two from behind. The car they used was a type of small truck, and when they stopped, they blocked the street so that no other car could pass. The circulation of these vehicles has always been notorious throughout the city. It was all so sudden. It happened in an instant, a matter of seconds, when they got out of the car to do their work. We must also recognize that, up to now, the present government has done nothing about these missing people. A year and four months have passed and we still have heard nothing about them.

Testimony of Manuel José Arce

Writer

If it were not for the fact that repression in Guatemala has surpassed all known limits and become an authentic war against the people, with the dimensions of genocide, one could say that the repression of thought—whether in journalism or artistic and literary creation—is one of the most important functions of the government. My testimony here comes from personal experience in journalism, literature, and the theater and from the experiences of my colleagues.

CENSORSHIP OF THE PRESS

Censorship of the press has become a norm, and is exercised on levels ranging from the most disguised to the most openly brutal; let me mention some notable examples.

Internal Censorship

Publication is repressed of anything contrary to the ideology of management, which in turn governs itself by the norms of a far-right organization of employers, the Association of Publicity Media (Asociación de Medios Publicitarios).

Economic Censorship

It is exercised by two organizations, the Chamber of Advertising and the Chamber of Publicists, and consists of blocking the submission of paid advertising to press, radio, or television companies that do not adhere to the political line of the CACIF (Chamber of Farmers, Businessmen, Industrialists and Financiers—Cámara de Agricultores, Comerciantes, Industriales y Financistas). Thus financial ruin can be imposed.

Clandestine Censorship

It is exercised by paramilitary gangs (of the government and the extreme right) through anonymous or signed threats, and includes shootings, fires, and explosions against the physical plants of news enterprises. The most frequent victims have been *Diario El Gráfico, Nuevo Diario, Diario Impacto,* Radio *Nuevo Mundo.* There is also kidnapping, torture, disappearance, attacks on the street, and assassination of journalists; the list is very long—Mario Monterroso Armas, Irma Flaquer, Oscar Arturo Palencia, Marco Antonio Cacao Muñoz, Didier Martell. . . .

Official Censorship

Openly imposed by the government, it consists of centralizing "approved" information in the public information department of the army or the President. Publishing information not coming from these departments is prohibited; the penalty is fines, closing of the company, and/or imposition of in-house censors.

Self-Censorship

For reasons of personal security, all journalists are obliged to ignore certain topics or not to treat them freely.

IDEOLOGICAL BOMBARDMENT

In a parallel way, the public is submitted to a systematic, ideological bombardment in a variety of forms:

—Official propaganda: obligatory advertising campaigns on the radio, TV, press.

—Propaganda of the extreme right: financed by political groups. Includes censorship of films, especially of their political content.

—TV programming from the U.S.

—Comic strips of obvious ideology.

—Reactionary, consumption-oriented radio programming.
—Commercial advertising controlled by the owners
mentioned above.

LITERATURE

In 1954, immediately after the CIA-organized intervention,
there was an exhibit of "proofs of Soviet penetration of
Guatemala." It contained books, films, and records published in
the U.S.S.R. and other countries on politics, science, art, and
literature. Among them were books by Pavlov, Gogol, Dostoyev-
sky, Turgenev, Chekhov, and other Russian writers, as well as
Ortega y Gasset *(La rebelíon de las masas)* and Jean Jacques Rousseau
(The Social Contract). Films of Eisenstein and of the Bolshoi ballets
"Swan Lake" and "Coppelia"; records of Kachaturian, Stravin-
sky, Tchaikovsky, Mussorgsky, Prokofiev, Rachmaninoff, Rimsky-
Korsakov. . . . All this material was publicly burned, in an act that
marked the beginning of the cultural era in which we now live.

Possession of any of those books, records, or films was sufficient
reason to imprison the owner and subject him to interrogation
and torture by the Committee for Defense Against Communism
(Comité de Defensa contra el Comunismo). I personally went
to prison in 1955. From that time on, possession of works that
could be considered "subversive material" was grounds for
assassination.

The massive and uninterrupted exodus of Guatemalan intellectuals after 1954 speaks for itself; I will give only a few major
examples. Miguel Angel Asturias, a few days before he officially
received the Nobel Prize and while still Guatemalan Ambassador
to France, received in the mail and before my eyes a threat from
the ultra-right organization, MANO, that he would be killed if
he returned to Guatemala. Otto Rene Castillo, Roberto Obregón
Morales, Julio César de la Roca, Alaide Foppa, Juan Luis Molina
Loza, Mario Botzoc, José Maria López Valdizón, Huberto
Alvarado, Oscar Arturo Palencia, along with many other writers
and poets, have been assassinated. . . .

The Theater of University Art was shot up during the opening of a new exhibit of paintings and many of those present were

gravely wounded. The Theater of the People's University was set on fire and one of its most brilliant actors, Miguel Angel González, was shot to death in the street. Threats have prevented the staging of many theater works when not directly prohibited by the government. The National Theater Festival of 1979, which carried my name and was dedicated to me as a tribute from the theater workers' union, was expressly prohibited from presenting any of my works.

Juanita Loza de Molina, the actress, was imprisoned in an insane asylum for having publicly demanded to see the body of her son, the intellectual Juan Luis Molina Loza. Many theater people, whose names I have omitted because they still live in Guatemala, have been the victims of pressure, prison, and beatings because of their work. Following the courageous flowering of a theater that dealt with reality, today in Guatemala there are only costume comedies and "boulevard theater."

ILLITERACY

Another means of intellectual isolation, another aggression against culture, is the policy of illiteracy. The illiteracy rate, which had been reduced in 1944-1954, has been intentionally increased since then as part of the overall policy of domination through poverty and isolating the people and the intellectuals from each other.

MY EXILE

I left my country because of threats against me and the impossibility of self-expression as a writer and as a citizen. The campaign of extermination against my colleagues made me decide to survive outside my country. I know now that the existence of the present army is incompatible with the existence of freedom of thought.

Testimony of
Rolando Castillo Montalvo

Former dean of the medical school, University of San Carlos

My name is Rolando Castillo Montalvo. I am a Guatemalan, 42 years old, and I presently live in Mexico, where I arrived 19 months ago after having been forced to leave my country, my home, and my responsibilities as dean of the School of Medical Sciences at the University of San Carlos in Guatemala.

As a physician, I know that the health of the Guatemalan people is in a precarious state, and is the product of misery and economic exploitation, as well as of oppression and social marginalization, conditions in which the immense majority of my fellow countrymen exist. To prove this, it suffices to point out that according to government statistics:

The average life expectancy is 56 years in the urban areas and only 41 years among the peasant population.

The general mortality rate is 12 per 1,000 inhabitants.

The infant mortality rate is 81 per 1,000 live births.

Of children under five years of age, 81% suffer some degree of malnutrition.

The 10 main causes of infant mortality and morbidity are entirely preventable.

There is only one doctor for each 4,000 inhabitants, and more than 60% of these doctors work in the capital city.

Less than one hospital bed exists for each 1,000 inhabitants.

In the light of such a poor state of health, and adding to these facts other analysis from the school of medicine itself, an important group of students and professors put together a "Workplan for the Dean's Office, 1978-1982, from the Democratic Coordinating Committee in Medicine." When this plan was proposed to the almost 8,000 members who elect the dean of the school, they voted in favor of the option we had chosen, and they elected me to be in charge of developing medical education in Guatemala from an entirely new perspective.

I took over on March 1, 1978, and after the Workplan was approved by the medical school's board of directors (the faculty body of highest authority) it became the program that the medical school was to implement over the next four years. In fact, it was launched during the first six months of academic work.

At the end of July 1978, a few days after the takeover by the government headed by General Romeo Lucas García, the recently appointed Minister of Health—an old contemporary of mine from medical studies—invited me and the board of directors to a work meeting with him and his group of ministerial advisers. As a result of this meeting, we agreed to a close inter-institutional cooperative project, through which students and professors would provide more medical care in government health facilities. The Ministry of Health would be able to increase the breadth of its services at no additional cost to itself. The direct beneficiaries would be the immense population marginalized from the advances of preventive and curative modern medicine.

The agreement would also allow about 500 students in their last year of school to be placed in an equal number of communities of fewer than 2,000 inhabitants, where no government health infrastructure exists. This would expand a program already carried out by 150 students of social welfare. It would be directed, monitored, and evaluated by the professors and authorities of the medical school and would constitute the last requirement for the title of doctor.

Given that the University of San Carlos does not have its own hospital facilities, and medical students have always done their practice in government hospitals, the agreement would formally establish the joint participation of both entities and their personnel.

The faculty was given responsibility to formulate a concrete program, which was then sent to the Ministry of Health for its input. According to the minister, the vice-minister, advisers, and ministerial authorities, the proposal was accepted completely and needed only to be ratified with signatures. But this never took place. At a later time, Dr. Roquelino Recinos, the celebrated minister himself, told me that this resulted from the absolute opposition of General Lucas, because "his government should not support nor get involved with the leftists from the University."

In the next three years, our students and professors continued to develop assistance to hospitals and rural communities. But this became increasingly difficult and, in the last stages, it meant the risk of losing one's life. Approximately 20 *compañeros* disappeared or were cruelly assassinated in their homes, in the streets or in the health centers themselves. Yet we continued our work because to withhold our presence would have meant a decrease of 40-50% in medical care delivered. Each day, 2,000 students and professors cared for the people who use government health facilities.

However, the lack of a signed agreement meant that the broadened coverage and improvement in the quality of care that we had wanted did not take place. Rather, University authorities had to act as "firemen," putting out fires instigated by several hospital directors and minor authorities. In this way those people could ingratiate themselves with "Mr. President" — not the President in the book by Nobel Prize winner Miguel Angel Asturias, but rather the assassin, Romeo Lucas García.

In addition, it became impossible to carry out the development of the medical school, given that harassment and repression against the University increased in the following fiscal year. The 1979 state appropriation to the University was not increased, as had been the norm over the previous four years, even though the student body, including that of the medical school, had increased in size.

The lack of financial resources necessitated the application of budget policies to prioritize the different tasks. This required an efficient administration that could facilitate the best development of teaching, research, and service. However, given the external budgetary strangulation, this regimen of austerity and readjustment which we established was insufficient to allow other improvements. As a final result, we were unable to: 1) develop research policy; 2) increase the processes of institutional research that would assist our understanding of the country's health problems; 3) disseminate the results of completed research within the national medical community; 4) edit the magazine *Ciencia y Medicina* (Science and Medicine); 5) increase teaching supervision, and evaluation within the hospital; 6) increase community work and preventive medical activities in rural areas; and 7) improve the academic level of post-graduate studies. . . .

At the beginning of 1981, the medical school was the victim of a new attack, this time on its physical plant. Early one morning, two vehicles with a dozen men armed with machine-guns shot the University guards at one entrance, and later the guards at two "N" Buildings on the University campus. They proceeded to burn files and student qualifications, and burned the terrarium, where for two years we had been collecting materials from two centuries before. They destroyed 75% of the collection, along with a substantial amount of office equipment and furniture.

This entire anti-University scenario evolved within the framework of the most cruel war of extermination against various sectors of the citizenry. We know that the army, the police, and paramilitary organizations had assassinated many University students. We learned from experience that the assassination of a distinguished professor in one of the schools, for example, in the School of Economics or the School of Law, would be followed by daily assassinations of two or three students, professors, or administrators. Thus, after the kidnapping of Dr. Arturo Soto Avendaño, a high-ranking medical school professor, whose body bearing signs of torture appeared three days later at the entrance of the University, at least 50 professors either resigned, separated themselves, or asked for leave. Finally, amid a series of indirect threats, I left my post six months before finishing the term of office for which I had been democratically and popularly elected.

I believe that my testimony about state terrorism perpetrated by the regime of Lucas García against the University is complemented by four experiences that I consider necessary to bring to the attention of this Tribunal.

1. On February 1, 1980, by agreement of the Superior University Council, the supreme authority of our alma mater, I was one

of three of its members who went to the morgue at the general hospital San Juan de Dios to claim the bodies of workers, peasants, citizens, Christians, and students who the day before had been burned alive by the police inside the Spanish embassy.

The sight was frankly something out of Dante: 26 bodies were lying one next to the other, thrown on the floor. What shocked me the most was to see the body of a peasant woman 7 months pregnant.

The most chilling task was to verify that, along with bodies that were totally charred and burned into the bone, there were others with burns on their hands and face and severe third degree burns on their thorax and abdomen—yet their clothes were practically intact. Though I am not an expert on these matters, those findings made me think that the material utilized in the collective assassination was a chemical that selectively incinerates live tissue. This is an extreme that I cannot prove, but my doubt begins to turn to certainty, or at least I think there is something that the government wishes to hide, since it did not allow the medical-legal autopsy that Guatemalan law requires in all cases of accidental or violent death.

2. At the end of June of the same year, also with the consent of the Superior University Council, we went to the private hospital "Centro Médico" to handle the transfer of Br. Víctor Valverth to the embassy of the Republic of Costa Rica, whose government had given him political asylum. Br. Valverth had been wounded as he left his class at the School of Engineering; he had resisted being kidnapped by unknown people who were subsequently identified by school authorities as members of G-2, the intelligence section of the army.

In Guatemala, it is widely known that those wounded by the security forces of the state and hospitalized are subsequently "finished off" or kidnapped by "unknown people" as soon as they recuperate. For this reason, to safeguard Br. Valveth's life, his family had sought asylum. When it was granted, they had asked the Council if we would guarantee his survival until he arrived at the embassy.

After three more hours of waiting at the hospital under the

authorization which, just the day before, had been given by the Minister of Governance, an army officer came up to us and told the University and diplomatic personnel: "I have instructions from superiors to advise you that it is preferable that he not be transferred, because the road is very long and something could happen to him. And what is more, I am sure that he is not going to arrive at the embassy."

Víctor Valverth was finally able to go into exile through an additional series of transactions involving various governments which intervened again so that he could go into exile alive.

3. On July 14 of that same year, at 8:35 a.m., an indeterminate number of University people, primarily students, were machine-gunned as they got off collective transport vehicles on the University campus. The attack came from heavily armed men in two moving vehicles: a red panel truck and a white Bronco, similar to the ones used by the secret police (the judicial guard). These vehicles came through the northern walkway that gives access to the University. The men fired into the crowd of people who were going to their classes and to work. Then they fled, leaving the white Bronco at the entrance to a peripheral road, where at approximately 9:15 a.m. it attacked a pickup that was leaving the University. The result was 7 dead and about 40 wounded.

In spite of the fact that the national police had surrounded the walkways of Petapa and Guilar Batres (which were two and five blocks away), they did not even come over to investigate what was going on. We can presume that information was given to them instantaneously by a third vehicle, a black pickup with a transmission antenna which, from barely 50 meters away, directed the entire massacre of new University martyrs.

4. After more than 10 requests for a hearing with the President of the Republic, and after more than two years of waiting for an answer, the University authorities had lost hope of any dialogue about the motivations, justness, and scope of the marginalization and persecution of University personnel.

It was not until after almost a hundred people were dead and disappeared, and after the democratically elected rector was no longer leading the University, that Lucas García consented to have an interview with University personnel. And so the Council decided that the deans would attend as representatives elected by the academic community of the alma mater.

At this meeting, the President, his ministers, and advisers presented no possibility for dialogue. Rather, we simply heard repetitions of their dogmatic, anti-academic and anti-University views that, when not entirely fascist, were of a caveman mentality.

For our part, we put out arguments on the proper role of the University, its reason to exist, and its critical activities as guaranteed in the Constitution and other explicative laws.

Again, the response was the same. The stereotypical "if you are not with me then you are against me" underlay the Presidential intervention, which was then capped off with: "The University is subversive—just look at *the supervised professional practice of medicine which is a nucleus of guerrillas and only serves to indoctrinate the peasants in exotic ideologies of international communism.*"

Thus it was very clear and out in the open why the Ministry of Health would not allow our medical students to practice preventive and curative medicine in communities where the government itself does not even manage to care for people, in settlements that may never have known a doctor, not even as a tourist or a transient.

It also became clear why the agreement that they refused to sign with our medical school was signed with the school of medicine at the most elitist private university in the country. This school had been open for only three years, as contrasted with the autonomous state University of San Carlos of Guatemala, which has existed for three centuries.

Only in the unbalanced mind of a Hitler, a Mussolini, . . . and a Lucas García could the idea be conceived that the entire membership of a medical school could be communists, that 100% of the members of our program were teaching "exotic ideologies," and that the entire population would be willing to join with us, even the sick, the undernourished, or the people about to die. . . .

I do not have personal and concrete experiences to relate regarding the government of General Efraín Ríos Montt. However, I have no doubts when I state that the governments of Lucas García and Ríos Montt, although with different shadings, are equally repressive, sly and dictatorial. They are the same regime with a different face in the Presidency. . . .

In essence, the functionaries of both governments are the same, though they change jobs and posts. There are many examples, and I will point out only one. Eduardo Castillo Arriola, during the previous government, occupied the post of Ambassador to the Organization of American States and later to the United Nations; now, after the overthrow of Lucas García, he is the Minister of Foreign Relations under Ríos Montt. Previously a soloist at a distance—he is my father—and now director of an orchestra, he has set in motion the foreign policy of both governments and is also a participant in the totality of state actions. . . .

The following are excerpts from a letter written by Rolando Castillo Montalvo, the person who just testified, to his father, Eduardo Castillo Arriola.

January 9, 1983

Dear Father,

This is not the first time I write you a letter that I never send. In fact, even as I begin this one I do not know for sure whether I will mail it or not. This stems from the anger, the sadness, the impotence, the distaste, and the frustration that I feel in knowing that we are in diametrically opposed camps. . . .

On March 23, the day of the military coup imposed by Ríos Montt, I telephoned to find out what was happening with you. I was very happy and satisfied when you said, "I am returning to Guatemala. I am still a man who can hold a hoe to feed my family." Do you remember that?

My happiness and satisfaction were based first on your spirit and your desire for personal struggle and secondly, but no less importantly, because this decision pulled you away from the governing circle responsible for the national deterioration and the indiscriminate and unjustifiable killing of people by the state, from which the University itself did not escape. It was this government that had forced part of your family—your son, your daughter-in-law, your grandchildren—to leave our country, our homes, our studies, our work in order to save our lives.

My disappointment and frustration in learning soon after that you occupied the post of Minister of Foreign Relations in the self-styled "New Regime" were immeasurable. . . . From that moment, you have shared responsibility for, among thousands of other things, the pseudo-legal scaffolding of the so-called "Military Tribunals of Special Jurisdiction," which are known internationally and among our people as a juridical monstrosity. As a lawyer, father, you have renounced the principles and the very essence of your profession. Or is it that the Minister of Foreign Relations only sees and directs foreign policy and does not make any other types of decisions?

The qualitative change lies in the fact that for the more than 10 years that you served as ambassador outside the country, it is assumed that because of distance you were never consulted on matters regarding the application of internal policy. But now you are immersed in all aspects of such policy. . . . General Lucas García publicly and repeatedly said: "The University is subversive." More than 300 University personnel dead or disappeared was the practical consequence of that phrase. The government of Ríos Montt, in which you are a first-line actor, offered to punish the corrupt and to prosecute the assassins. However, since May, the few second- and third-class functionaries who were arrested for the corruption that the coup d'état was directed against are beginning to go free for "lack of proof." A strange, double-standard application of justice. Not finding proof, you let thieves and hired thugs go free; yet not having proof, you execute your opposition after condemning them in the Tribunals of Special Jurisdiction, where they have no recourse to appeal.

And where is the trial of those who tortured and assassinated no less than 50 medical students and professionals? I shall answer for you. To date, no functionary of the civilian or military hierarchy has been arrested for crimes against the life and personal integrity of the thousands of murdered, kidnapped, and disappeared. Do you not find this curious?

Do you remember my classmate, Guillermo Muñiz? How many happy hours we spent while we were students. We were even fairly disorderly as young people. Did you know that his body appeared thrown in a field? There was no one like him in terms of his sense of medical service to the needy, to the people he loved so deeply. And as an example of the sadism and brutality of the regime, the famous surgeon, the specialist in hand surgery, was found without hands! . . .

The fact that only 16 countries failed to condemn the government of Ríos Montt in the recently concluded General Assembly of the United Nations demonstrates the absolute moral poverty of that government. Furthermore, those 16 countries have military governments, or militarist governments, or governments imposed by force. They represent despotism and, in some cases, Hitlerite anti-democracy. Only South Africa failed to join your defenders, and only because that country does not vote in the highest international organization.

To what depths has the Reagan administration sunk, not only by its association with the other 15 countries who voted against that resolution, but also because it cynically states that, "Human rights have improved in Guatemala," as if genocide were only a numerical and quantitative issue. The truth is that human rights in our torn country have improved only to the degree that Mr. Reagan and Mr. Ríos Montt could state that, "In the last year of the Lucas García government, his security forces assassinated 12,000 Guatemalans, while we have killed only 7,000."

It is sad to recognize what you are now defending. . . . I cannot even say Happy New Year, nor can I wish you success or good fortune, because to the extent that you achieve them, the pain and the suffering of my people would increase and be more indescribable. I will see you on the day of the victory of the Guatemalan majority; I will see you on the day when peace and tranquility are born in the new Guatemala.

Your son

Testimony of
Sandra Judith de Medina

Assistant professor,
Women's Institute for Higher Education

My name is Sandra de Medina, and I am an assistant professor of mathematics at the Women's Institute for Higher Education; I am also an engineering student. Every day I used to meet my husband, Rolando Medina Cuéllar, after he finished teaching his classes in the School of History [at the University of San Carlos — Eds.] and we would go home together.

On September 28, 1982, as usual, at 6:15 p.m., I met him at his classroom and we went down the steps in front of his department on our way to the parking lot where our car was parked. Suddenly, as I was putting on my sweater, I saw and heard one of his students calling to us. Rolando didn't pay attention and continued to walk toward the car. I stopped and began to talk with the student about some slides she was going to lend us. She said, "Look—what is happening?" At that moment a Colt bus with license plate P-111030 swung across the parking lot. Three people in civilian dress with long hair and with two machine-guns and a pistol jumped out.

My husband had already reached our car and was trying to start it. They pointed their guns at him and made him get out. He didn't resist, naturally; he was a peaceful person who dedicated himself to his academic career, and because he had chronic asthma and bronchitis, he didn't do any physical exercise. He was rather fat and managed to overcome this psychologically by studying. He was fairly well known in his field. He was an intellectual of high quality, and he even taught postgraduate courses at the Research Institute for Educational Improvement, when Saúl

Osorio was rector of the University. As his friends can testify, he was an excellent art critic and also a poet. He was a professor of logic and philosophy, with a degree in Latin American literature.

When all this happened, these men aiming their guns at him forced him out of the car and shoved him into the bus that was waiting, its motor running, with a man and a woman in the cab. I was about five meters away and started to walk toward our car when I saw the look of terror on Rolando's face. He pretended he didn't know me so his captors wouldn't realize that I was there. I managed to hide by the parking lot in a place where there were a lot of trees. Then another car with license plate P-212273 followed the bus as a sort of escort. This car had three armed civilians in it; you could see the barrels of the machine-guns they carried. The car was also a Colt like the bus. The car and bus disappeared without any apparent planned destination. I managed to jot down the license plates. After they left I got in our car and drove around the city for awhile, confused and lost, without knowing what to do. I finally decided to look up a friend, who let me stay at this house.

Testimony of
Luis Felipe Irías

Former General Secretary,
University Students Association

The University of San Carlos in Guatemala was the third university founded in Latin America, by royal decree of Charles V in 1676. The University became autonomous within the framework of the revolution of October 20, 1944, in the heat of popular struggles and as a result of those struggles.

Since that time, its principal authorities, such as the rector and the deans of different schools, have been elected by groups composed in equal numbers of professors, students, and various professional associations. The leading organization of the University, the Higher University Council, is composed proportionately of the deans of each of the schools, representatives of the professional associations, the professors' assembly, and representatives of the student sector. Similarly, students have the right to participate with parity in the contests to elect titled professors along with the administrators of each school and academic unit.

Student associations also exist in each of the academic units, and then there is the highest student entity, the Association of University Students (AEU), to which all of the individual student associations belong.

Since 1944, the national and autonomous University of San Carlos has played an important role in the defense of national interests, as well as in the struggle for the defense and promotion of human rights. It has also played an important role as a voice and channel of expression for the people's desires and demands. This role is all the more important in Guatemala, where opportunities for the exercise of democracy have been traditionally closed.

As we shall see, these circumstances compelled and continue to compel the military dictatorship to repress and attack the highest cultural institution of the country.

The tasks of the University of San Carlos are organizing, directing, and imparting higher education in the country. It is also charged with collaborating on the definition, study, and solution of national problems, in addition to bringing knowledge to all strata of the population by means of its university extension programs.

In fulfilling its tasks, the University participated in the study of a series of agreements that the different governments planned to sign with various foreign companies. The University had also conducted studies of the oil policies developed by various governments after the counterrevolution of 1954; agreements for the exploitation of nickel, which turned over our mineral wealth to foreign capital; the purchase of the company Eléctrica de Guatemala, Inc., a subsidiary of Bond and Share, and the purchase of the assets of the U.S. railroad company, IRCA. The University considered that national interests were harmed in all these instances, and presented viable alternatives in accordance with the necessities of the country. In response, the government accused the University of halting the country's progress; it refused to hear the University's opinion and proceeded to mount a publicity campaign against it.

Moreover, the University of San Carlos has played an important role regarding the defense of human rights. It has struggled to extend education to broader sectors of the population and, on its own, developed a program of scholarships that enabled young students from the most dispossessed strata of the population to have some degree of access to higher education. It conducted studies on the increase in the cost of living, and promoted the defense of workers' wages. With students in the health sciences, it created a program that carried medical attention to far corners of the interior of the country.

It is known that the people of Guatemala have been victims

of a campaign of violence which, from 1954 to the present, has left a toll of more than 80,000 dead and disappeared. In light of the daily harm to the most elemental rights of man, such as the right to life, the University constantly worked to denounce and condemn these deeds. It criticized the totalitarian system of political persecution, which is imposed for the smallest disagreement with official opinions. Evidently the University became a serious obstacle to the development of anti-popular and terrorist policies by the military dictatorship.

Similarly the university student movement, headed by the AEU, of which I was general secretary in 1977-1978, was developing at the same rate as the popular and democratic movement, maintaining a constant struggle for the people's interests. One can state that the whole of the student movement supported the University administration when it joined the people's struggles.

In mid-1978, the military dictatorship, then headed by Lucas García, decided to intervene in the University. . . . Since 1954, all sectors of the University had been persecuted by reactionary forces of state power. Such was the case in the assassination of University professor and deputy to the National Congress, Dr. Adolfo Mijangos López, who was shot in his wheelchair; the assassination of professor Julio Camey Herrera; the vile assassination of professor and member of the superior University Council and distinguished labor lawyer, Mario López Larrave; and the assassination and disappearance of dozens of students. But what happened in 1978 surpassed all previous experiences.

On October 20, 1978, Oliverio Castañeda de León, general secretary of the Association of University Students, was assassinated with impunity. His replacement, Antonio Ciani García, was kidnapped 16 days later, and never reappeared. Subsequently, the following persons were assassinated: Manolo Andreade Roca, adjunct general secretary of the University; Hugo Rolando Melgar, legal adviser to the University; Felipe de Jesús Mendizábal, director of registration; Dr. Jorge Romero Imeri, dean of the law school; Alejandro Cotí, eminent student leader and member of the Superior University Council; Alfonso Figueroa, director of the Institute of Economic and Social

Research; Dr. Alberto Fuentes Mohr, leader of the Democratic Socialist Party (Partido Socialista Democrático); Manuel Colom Argueta, a professor and leader of the United Front of the Revolution (Frente Unido de la Revolución), which is a social-democratic tendency. This is to mention only a few of the most notable victims of a criminal wave which, in the course of two years, left a toll of about 200 professionals, students, and workers dead or disappeared.

At the same time these events were taking place, lists of students, workers, peasants, and other people threatened with death were being circulated, signed by the Secret Anticommunist Army (ESA). The ESA kept the population in fear, creating a climate of such uncertainty and terror that many students were forced to leave Guatemala in order to save their lives and the lives of their relatives.

As if this were not enough, the budget of the University was cut back and the possibility of dialogue with the University administration was flatly denied by the government, which publicly accused the University of being a center of subversion.

The situation reached such an extreme that the rector of the University, Saúl Osorio Paz, lived almost underground in order to protect his life during his two years in office. He personally was one of the objects of terrorist repression against the University of San Carlos. His term should have lasted four years, but he finally had to leave the country when his situation became totally unbearable.

On June 14, 1980, the day that engineer Raúl Molina was assuming the position of rector, well-armed men in several vehicles indiscriminately machine-gunned a group of students in front of the bus stop on campus. They left 14 students dead and more than 60 wounded. This event nearly provoked the closing of the University; although such extreme measures were not taken, many students did not return to classes.

When Molina found himself forced to leave the country because of the repeated threats against him, those sectors within the University that were in league with the dictatorship mounted a vicious electoral campaign for a new rector. This election barely drew the participation of the necessary 50% of the electoral body.

The new administration immediately began to retreat from the advances that had been made in the last few years. The program for training faculty disappeared, with a consequent reduction in academic quality. The new authorities made public their desire to collaborate with the dictatorship. The medical school's program, which had brought health care to the interior, had been disappearing slowly. In addition, as a result of the exile of hundreds of professors, the overall quality of higher education declined. The result of all this is an occupied University, without it having been occupied militarily.

At present the campus is full of police dressed as civilians, who maintain constant surveillance. The student movement has managed to stay alive, but under very difficult conditions, and its leaders are constantly threatened by the brutal repression of the dictatorship which today is headed by General Ríos Montt.

Ríos Montt found a university that was occupied. He took advantage of the criminal deeds of Lucas García and, despite the fact that he continues promoting terror against the University, he acts as if he is free from guilt.

Some events which speak to the attacks of the Ríos Montt dictatorship against the University and against culture are the following:

— The recent kidnapping of a professor at the University, the esteemed contemporary Guatemalan writer and critic, Rolando Medina Cuéllar.

— The case of a professor in the School of Economics, Graciela Morales de Samayoa, who was kidnapped along with her family, including two young daughters.

— The kidnapping in mid-November of Tania Aracely Ardón, director of the library of the School of Medicine, and the young man Fiallos, student of library science and reference librarian of that same library, when they left work.

— The kidnapping of seven students whose names are: Marvin Iván Pérez, Alba Noemí Pérez, Lesbia Pérez, Sandra Solórzano, Milton Méndez, Edwin Reynaldo Guzmán, and Edwin Catalán, on June 3, 1982.

—The kidnapping on September 19, 1982 in the city of Quezaltenango of the students Ziomara Emilia Méndez, Rosa Josefa de León, and Luis Fernando Quan, whose bodies appeared burnt.

—The unjustified seizure of pediatrician Dr. Gustavo Castañeda Palacios, father of the assassinated Oliverio Castañeda de León, and the kidnapping of pediatrician and anthropologist Dr. Juan José Hurtado, both prestigious University professors who were set free only thanks to intense international pressure and the enormous national repugnance that these acts generated.

To conclude, honorable members of the jury, I would like to tell you about my own case. I was general secretary of the Association of the University Students from 1977 to 1978. In May 1978 I turned over this responsibility to Oliverio Castañeda de León, who was assassinated five months later. From that moment I suffered persecution and was forced to hide, even forced to leave my county. On October 17, 1981, my father, the dentist Luis Felipe Irías García, was kidnapped; his body appeared four days later on October 21, causing me and my family profound grief and an enormous sense of uncertainty and insecurity. The photograph of my father, with a report on his case, has been submitted for examination by this Tribunal.

I, Luis Felipe Irías, give my word that the facts given here are real and true.

The Complicity of the U.S. Government and U.S. Capital in the Violation of Human Rights in Guatemala

Susanne Jonas
Institute for the Study of Labor and Economic Crisis

This presentation was prepared with my colleagues at the Institute for the Study of Labor and Economic Crisis (ISLEC) in San Francisco, California. ISLEC has done extensive research and publications on Guatemala and Central America generally, with a view to educating and informing the American public. As the Institute's specialist on Guatemala, I am making the presentation on behalf of the Institute.

* * *

The Permanent People's Tribunal hearings on Guatemala are taking place at a critical juncture, as the threat to human rights in Guatemala and U.S. complicity in human rights violations there are greater today than ever. The Ríos Montt regime in Guatemala has been identified by such human rights organizations as the Council on Hemispheric Affairs in Washington, D.C., as the worst violator of human rights in Latin America, having surpassed even the Salvadoran regime in the killing of innocent civilians. The number of such killings since Ríos Montt took power in March

1982 is, moreover, greater than during any comparable period under the universally condemned regime of Lucas García.

And it is precisely at this moment that the Reagan administration is insisting that the human rights picture in Guatemala is improving, a lie proportionate to claiming that black is white. More serious, the Reagan administration is promoting this lie in order to justify resuming arms sales to Guatemala, despite significant opposition in the U.S. Congress and despite American public opinion. These events portend a further escalation in U.S. intervention in Guatemala, raising the spectre that within a short time, U.S. involvement there will reach the level of current U.S. involvement in El Salvador.

In our presentation, we shall focus upon the nature of the Ríos Montt regime as the epitome and culmination of the U.S.-created counterinsurgency state in Guatemala—and upon the particular forms of U.S. intervention in Guatemala today. First, however, we shall outline briefly the framework for the situation today by highlighting the points that are presented in substantive detail in the written document which we have submitted to this Tribunal.

THE CREATION OF THE GUATEMALAN COUNTERINSURGENCY STATE BY THE U.S. GOVERNMENT AND U.S. CAPITAL

1. The violations of the rights of the Guatemalan people today are a product of Guatemalan history since the 1954 U.S. intervention, which closed off the road of democratic revolution.

2. Since the 1954 intervention, the U.S. government has been committed to a permanent course of intervention in Guatemalan life. This has taken the form of the establishment and maintenance of the counterinsurgency state as an institutionalized apparatus for controlling the population and physically eliminating all opposition forces. Through its programs of military aid to the Guatemalan army and police and its collaboration with paramilitary "death squads," the U.S. government has provided the training, the equipment, and the hardware needed to maintain the Guatemalan counterinsurgency state. This includes nearly 4,000 police and military forces directly trained, approximately $30 million in military aid from the U.S. government, and $40

million in U.S. military sales through 1981, with an additional $600 million in direct U.S. economic asistance, and more than $800 million in aid through U.S.-controlled international institutions from 1953 through 1982.

3. The observance of human rights is incompatible with the institutionalization of the counterinsurgency state and its prosecution of a full-scale war against ever-broadening sectors of the Guatemalan population.

4. As will be seen, the current regime of Efraín Ríos Montt, rather than representing any break in this pattern, is the product and the epitome of the counterinsurgency state. It therefore *cannot* make, and in reality has not made, any "improvements" in the human rights situation.

5. Because the counterinsurgency state was designed, imposed, and maintained by the U.S. government in an attempt to prevent the emergence of any independent government in Guatemala, its existence implies the negation of Guatemalan national sovereignty in even the most limited terms.

6. The determination not to permit an independent and sovereign state in Guatemala has been a constant of U.S. policy since 1954, and has been reflected in the actions of every administration since that time.

7. U.S. government officials have justified continuing U.S. interventionism in Guatemala in terms of the country's "strategic importance to the U.S." An independent state there would "threaten U.S. interests," given that the dominant sectors of the U.S. capitalist class have defined in these terms any government in Central America that they cannot control and dominate. But the "interests" which the U.S. government is protecting in Guatemala are not the interests of the working class majority of the American people. It is protecting the interests of significant sectors of U.S. capital and in particular the interests of more than 300 U.S.-based corporations which over the years have invested hundreds of millions of dollars in Guatemala.

Although they are neither as visible nor as vocal as the Reagan administration, these corporate interests have been lobbying for the maintenance of the counterinsurgency state in Guatemala, and in a number of cases have been directly collaborating with the repressive agencies (the Guatemalan army and the right-wing death squads). Thus, U.S.-based capital is the invisible accomplice in the massive human rights violations in Guatemala.

8. In evaluating the options of the U.S. government today, we must take into account certain basic changes in the international context—in particular the decline and loss of U.S. political hegemony within the capitalist world—and changes within the U.S. domestically. Unlike the situation in 1954, the Reagan administration today is politically isolated in its aggressive stance towards Guatemala and Central America generally. The traditional allies of the U.S. government in Western Europe and in Latin America, as well as the Socialist International, are no longer willing to follow dictates from Washington, and have developed an independent stance in regard to Central America. Within the U.S. as well, since the late 1970s, public opinion polls have consistently shown that over two thirds of the American public oppose U.S. intervention in Central America; anti-interventionist pressure is also coming from important sectors of the religious community, and from some sectors of labor and the U.S. Congress.

9. This situation has redefined the options for U.S. intervention in Guatemala. Politically (in terms of the "hearts and minds" of the people in Guatemala, and in terms of international and domestic public opinion), the U.S. government has lost the battle. Militarily, in the post-Vietnam era, sending massive combat troops or intervening directly as in 1954 are less immediately viable options. Thus, as will be seen, the Reagan administration has been forced to continue its indirect intervention through a series of mechanisms ranging from the use of "proxies" like Israel, to military aid in indirect forms and increasingly in covert and even illegal forms. These constitute the prelude to more direct forms of intervention which are becoming more evident today.

THE RIOS MONTT REGIME:
EPITOME OF THE U.S.-CREATED COUNTERINSURGENCY STATE

The most significant advance in the Guatemalan popular resistance movement in the late 1970s and early 1980s has been its extension to large sections of the countryside. Militarily this forced the Guatemalan army to expand and generalize the war against the rural population, particularly in the Indian highlands. This in turn created a political problem for the brutal Lucas García regime: Guatemala's human rights atrocities were so blatant that even a massive lobby campaign by the Reagan administration in 1981-82 failed to convince the U.S. Congress to approve a renewal of vital military aid, cut off in 1977.

Politically Washington responded to the necessity of maintaining the counterinsurgency state by attempting to give it a new image: hence the Ríos Montt coup of March 1982, which Washington knew about for months, if it did not directly engineer. Even before the Ríos Montt regime asked for it, the U.S. was pushing for a renewal of U.S. military aid.

The U.S. mass media initially played up Ríos Montt as a "born-again Christian." In fact, however, the most salient aspects of Ríos Montt's background are not his new-found fundamentalist commitments (which in any case, as will be seen, are much more reactionary than progressive), but the following:

— He is part of a "modernized," technologized sector of the Guatemalan army, trained in "special warfare" using the techniques of civic action, psychological warfare, etc., which are essential components of counterinsurgency.

— In the early 1970s, under the brutal Arana regime, he was Chief of Staff of the Guatemalan army, and in that capacity he presided over a massive peasant massacre.

— In 1973 he became the head of the Department of Studies of the Interamerican Defense College in Washington, D.C., developing close ties with the U.S. counterinsurgency establishment.

In short, the most significant factors shaping Ríos Montt are his army career and in particular his U.S. counterinsurgency training. As a consequence, it is not surprising that in prosecuting the war against the guerrilla movement, his government has resorted to techniques that are best known to the world from the U.S. war in Vietnam: "scorched earth" policies; indiscriminate, village-wide massacres of children, women, and men; forced relocation of populations into controllable towns (similar to Vietnam's "strategic hamlets") in order to clear out guerrilla areas, and so on.

The appearance of Vietnam-type techniques in the Ríos Montt pacification campaign is no coincidence; in fact, it corresponds to a specific U.S. plan, the "Program of Pacification and Eradication of Communism" developed in the mid-1970s according to direct testimony by Elías Barahona, who read the project while press secretary for the Ministry of the Interior from 1976 to 1980. According to Barahona, the Lucas regime was unable to implement the plan effectively, and this was a reason for the coup that brought Ríos Montt to power. The current regime is applying this plan, which details lessons and tactics from the Vietnam war. For example:

— Forced recruitment of thousands of Indians and peasants in the guerrilla areas into pro-government "civil defense" (paramilitary) units or civilian patrols designed to perform the functions of right-wing death squads against guerrilla sympathizers.

— Stepped-up psychological warfare, sending in official forces dressed as guerrillas in order to blame the guerrillas for army massacres, combined with a U.S.-advised propaganda offensive about guerrilla "abuses."

— The use of fundamentalist preachers who double as counterinsurgency aides to the army in mobilizing villagers into the anti-guerrilla militias.

In the urban areas, the government has prosecuted its war with the aid of sophisticated computer technology and the centralization of all counterinsurgency functions.

In sum, the Ríos Montt regime represents the institutionalization of U.S.-developed counterinsurgency war against the Guatemalan people.

FORMS OF U.S. INTERVENTION IN GUATEMALA TODAY

Without presenting verbally the details that are laid out in our full presentation, we start from the well-known and uncontestable reality that the U.S. government is isolated in its Central

American policies, both internationally and at home, and has lost *political* legitimacy for a direct military intervention in Guatemala on all fronts. It is for this reason that the Reagan administration has until now been playing out other options for covert and indirect military intervention in Guatemala. These are as dangerous for Guatemala as sending the Marines, both in themselves and as a prelude to more direct intervention, and therefore must be fully exposed and denounced.

Given the constraints on direct military intervention, the issue for the Reagan administration today is *how* to intervene through maintenance of the counterinsurgency state in Guatemala.

In 1966-68, there was no widespread challenge to Washington's authority to sustain the counterinsurgency efforts of the Guatemalan government. But in 1982-83, broad sectors of the American people recognize this as the first stage of another Vietnam in the making, and U.S. military aid has become an issue of intense debate in the U.S. Congress.

To the extent that it is operating in the political arena at all, the Reagan administration has pulled out all the stops to gain congressional authorization for the resumption of military aid, working for two years with a combination of right-wing and business interests, both Guatemalan- and U.S.-based, to lobby for the resumption of military aid; and now the administration has resumed such aid (through military arms sales) without congressional authorization, a move that is doubtlessly only the first step in opening the floodgates for resumption of full military aid in the coming months.

Upon closer examination, we see that, even prior to this move, the Reagan administration has actually been sending military aid through a series of mechanisms, ranging from indirect and disguised to covert and illegal (i.e., in defiance of a congressional ban).

1. Indirect Military Aid

This aid is distributed through U.S. allies (mainly Israel), proxies in Central America (mainly Honduras), and regional military alliances.

a. Israel. Although Israeli involvement did not begin with the Carter "military aid cutoff," it was fully developed after that time to the extent that, by 1982, Israel had become Guatemala's major source of arms. Both Lucas García and Ríos Montt have attested to the importance of Israeli aid. The scope of Israeli military assistance includes:

> ...arms, training, and military advisers in the field, together with sophisticated computerized systems for keeping files on suspected guerrillas and a computerized system that detects electricity consumption in suspicious locations across the capital city... (Benjamin Beit-Hallahmi, unpublished research).

All of the Israeli assistance is specifically designed for counterinsurgency operations—from the transport planes to the Israeli funded and technologically equipped Escuela de Transmisiones y Electrónica servicing Guatemala's military intelligence.

Particularly since the rift between the U.S. and Argentina in the wake of the Falklands War, Israel has fulfilled a vital function on behalf of the U.S. government in maintaining the Guatemalan counterinsurgency state.

b. Regional Aid to Central America and the role of Honduras. Since the 1960s, the U.S. has given great importance to regional alliances and coordination among the Central American armies.

The older CONDECA project has been revived in the form of the so-called "Central American Democratic Community," founded in January 1982, which includes all of the Central American military dictatorships and excludes the Sandinista government in Nicaragua. While the CDC is not explicitly a military alliance, military collaboration is one of its two stated objectives.

Since 1980, the U.S. has attempted to consolidate an "Iron Triangle" in the region (El Salvador-Guatemala-Honduras). The linchpin in current U.S. "regional security assistance" is Honduras.

The involvement of Honduran troops against the Salvadoran resistance and in support of the Nicaraguan *contras* has already begun: and such a role will no doubt emerge as needed with respect to Guatemala. It is no coincidence that Reagan chose Honduras as the site for his meeting with Ríos Montt in December 1982, which was followed by the decision to resume U.S. arms sales to Guatemala.

    c. International Financial Institutions. There has developed a pattern of U.S. military aid that is not only *indirect* (i.e., avoiding congressionally scrutinized and approved bilateral aid from the U.S. to Guatemala) but also *disguised*—military aid in the form of economic assistance. Such aid is channeled in part through the international financial agencies, such as the Inter-American Development Bank and the World Bank, which presumably exist to finance economic development. But in the case of Guatemala, recent loans have virtually nothing to do with "economic development," and are clearly military in orientation. As a legacy of Carter's "human rights" policy, the U.S. government was supposed to vote against loans through the international banks to governments identified as consistent human rights violators, unless those loans fulfilled "basic human needs." However, this stipulation is honored more in the breach than in the fulfillment.

    The clearest example is the IDB loan for funding a rural telecommunications system, which under no interpretation is oriented toward meeting basic human needs. According to Amnesty International:

> The selection of targets for torture and murder and the deployment of security forces to carry out these acts is coordinated from an annex of the National Palace of Guatemala under the direct control of the President of the Republic. . . . the presidential agency which runs the governmental program of murder was known until recently as the Regional Telecommunications Center.

This telecommunications facility was built by the U.S. in 1964. At this late date, it is absurd to deny that "telecommunications" is part of the military infrastructure. This loan has been approved, a decision which will doubtless affect numerous other IDB and World Bank loans totaling hundreds of millions of dollars.

2. Direct (Bilateral) U.S. Aid

    This aid is sent through government-licensed commercial military sales, and through official government aid by way of loopholes and reclassifications in which military aid is disguised in nonmilitary terms:

a. *Commercial Sales.* The most obvious way to get around the congressional prohibition on official U.S. military aid to Guatemala has been through private (but State Department-licensed) commercial sales of military hardware, including police weapons. To take one example: Guatemala purchased $750,000 worth of police arms and equipment in this manner in 1982.

b. *The Foreign Military Sales Program.* This program, including official U.S. government sales and credits, was partially covered by the 1977 congressional ban; nevertheless, deliveries of military aid under this program never ceased (even under the Carter administration).

c. *Loopholes and Reclassifications.* Military equipment has flowed into Guatemala under various loopholes and technical reclassifications amount to bending legal restrictions. For example: paratroop carriers and helicopters were sold as "nonmilitary" items in 1980 and 1981; in 1981, the Commerce Department issued a license for the export of $3.2 million worth of trucks, jeeps, and spare parts to Guatemala by reclassifying these obviously military items.

One source estimates that, through the above mechanisms, the U.S. has permitted the flow of more than $35 million in military equipment to Guatemala from 1978 through 1981.

d. *"Economic Assistance."* Direct military aid to Guatemala has also been continued under the disguise of various economic assistance programs, as can be seen in the "Economic Support Fund" assistance approved in 1982 under Reagan's Caribbean Basin Program.

3. Covert and Illegal Aid.

As emerges clearly from the above, the Reagan administration (and the Carter administration before it) has bent every regulation that would have really stopped the flow of U.S. military assistance to Guatemala. The above is an accepted part of political manipulation in Washington. In the last few months of 1982, however, evidence has begun to emerge that the U.S. is engaged in far more dangerous forms of aid.

a. *Green Berets.* Under the congressional ban in effect since 1977,

U.S. military training and U.S. advisers in Guatemala have been flatly prohibited. However, the administration had already proceeded covertly to send military advisers. As was revealed in October 1982, at least one Green Beret, Jesse García, is functioning in Guatemala as a counterinsurgency adviser, both in the Guatemalan army officers' training school and in the field. Furthermore, he replaced another Green Beret who had been serving in the same functions. García predicted that within one to two years, up to 1,000 U.S. combat troops would be needed to wipe out the insurgency in Guatemala; but in the meantime, despite official assurances to the contrary, there is no guarantee that more Green Berets have not *already* been sent covertly to Guatemala.

b. Helicopter Spare Parts and Communications Equipment. A focus of public debate has been the authorization of spare parts for U.S.-bought helicopters and communications equipment, which are truly essential for the Guatemalan government's prosecution of the counterinsurgency war. To circumvent opposition in the U.S. Congress, the Reagan administration has been selling Guatemala civilian helicopters, which are then equipped for military use; in addition, for most of 1982 (and particularly since the Ríos Montt coup), the administration has been threatening to send spare parts for the idled military helicopters with or without congressional consent, and has now proceeded to do so. Moreover, evidence found in a helicopter shot down by one of the organizations of the resistance showed that essential aircraft communications equipment is already being shipped to Guatemala covertly; and there are reports that Guatemalan pilots were being trained at Bell Helicopter's U.S. headquarters in early 1982.

* * *

The fact that the Reagan administration has already proceeded so far down the path of covert military intervention in Guatemala indicates how dangerous the situation is, not only for the Guatemalan people but also for the American people and the peoples of the world. In his determination to maintain the counterinsurgency state in Guatemala, Reagan is in fact engaged in the early stages of another Vietnam—but this time without congressional authorization, and over massive public opposition. This open defiance of the will of the American people exposes the contradictions and the sham of political democracy within the U.S. that go hand in hand with the administration's lies about "improvements in human rights" in Guatemala.

More generally, this perilous situation is of concern to progressive people throughout the world. If the U.S. government—despite all the considerations to the contrary—should continue upon a course of direct intervention in Guatemala, introduced gradually (as in Vietnam), which is the logical course of its current policy, the consequences will be not only national for Guatemala (untold destruction) and regional for Central America, but international. The Reagan administration has, in word and deed, defined the conflict in Guatemala today as a focal point of global U.S. Cold War policy. In today's transnational world, such an interventionist posture, if continued (whether directly or indirectly), will have international repercussions that are not predictable or necessarily controllable. In this respect, ending the 30-year history of bestial violations of human rights in Guatemala and securing the sovereignty and independence of the Guatemalan people are imperatives of world peace.

U.S. Penetration and Intervention in Guatemala

Jenny Pearce
Latin American Bureau

1. The government of the United States of America is supporting a bloody battle in Central America, whose main objective is to pacify the entire region. The consequences, however, reach far beyond this region and point to the re-establishment of U.S. hegemony in the Third World, which has been seriously weakened since the Vietnam War. El Salvador today is a real test case for U.S. foreign policy, which, according to ex-Secretary of State Haig, would offer the possibility of a confrontation with "communist subversion." The real test case, however, is an unprecedented military effort to suppress these people's right to self-determination and to suppress their attempts to build a more just, more democratic society based on the will of the people. The importance of this struggle has reached a worldwide scale, and the intent to suppress it should not be underestimated.

2. I do not speak lightly when I affirm that the U.S. is supporting a policy of war and that it is committed to a military solution to the conflicts in Central America, a solution with the following objectives:

—The overthrow of the Sandinista government in Nicaragua;

—The military defeat of revolutionary struggle in El Salvador and Guatemala.

3. In order to understand Reagan's policies in Guatemala, it is necessary to understand his policies toward the region as a whole. The general outline of his program is as follows:

—Operation "Destabilization" in Nicaragua, which, according to evidence gathered in the last few months, is being coordinated by the CIA and includes training and logistical support and arms to counterrevolutionaries based in Honduras;

—Re-establishment of a counterinsurgency strategy of a regional nature, based on the "Iron" (northern) Triangle of Honduras, El Salvador, and Guatemala.

With these goals, the U.S. has gradually increased the sale of arms and military aid to the regimes of El Salvador and Honduras as part of a growing militarism in Central America.

4. There are now approximately 100 U.S. military advisers in Honduras, and at least 50 in El Salvador. It is estimated that there are approximately 200 CIA agents in the Central American region, which, according to the *New York Times,* constitutes "the CIA's most ambitious political and paramilitary operation in a decade." It is already possible to observe a gradual regionalization of the Central American conflict: Honduran troops have participated in military operations in Salvadoran territory, and their participation in counterrevolutionary actions against Nicaragua has been well documented.

5. Guatemala is the only country that so far has not played the role it should in this regional strategy. This country has a great deal of experience in counterinsurgency warfare, beginning in the 1960s, and it has, in addition, the most powerful army in the region. In my opinion, Guatemala is the most important country for the U.S. in terms of investment and geopolitical location.

6. The third element of Reagan's strategy is political in nature. While military strategy is based in Honduras, political strategy is centered in Costa Rica. The object of this strategy is the political and diplomatic isolation of Nicaragua: there is an attempt to persuade U.S. and international public opinion that the Reagan administration is really promoting peace, freedom, and democracy in Central America, and that Nicaragua is impeding the actualization of these objectives. Thus, in January of 1982, under the auspices of the U.S. government, the Central American Democratic Community was established, with the participation of Costa Rica, Honduras, and El Salvador. It is interesting to note that the day that Guatemala announced its participation in

the Community (July of 1982), Ríos Montt had been President of the country just one month. In October of 1982, another political initiative took place: the Forum for Peace and Liberty, once again launched from San José. The important thing about these political initiatives is the relatively secondary character they have within Reagan's basic strategy.

7. I would like to refer more specifically to Reagan's policies toward Guatemala. These policies have, in my opinion, two basic objectives:

—The defeat of revolutionary movements;

—Guatemala's participation in the campaign for pacification of the Central American region.

I have addressed the second point above, and will turn my attention to the first point, the defeat of Guatemalan revolutionary movements. The key to my analysis is the strategic alliance between Reagan and Ríos Montt, and the importance of this alliance for Guatemala's present and future. In order to fully understand this alliance's importance, we must refer to the historical legacy of U.S. intervention in Guatemala and the series of problems that it created for the U.S. up to the arrival of Ríos Montt.

8. It is impossible to discuss modern Guatemalan history without mentioning on the one hand the role the U.S. has played and the close ties between the Guatemalan oligarchy and sectors of U.S. capital, and on the other hand the relationship between the Pentagon and the Guatemalan army. One cannot forget that 1954 is a crucial date not only in Guatemalan history but also in the history of all of Central America: the United States cemented its alliance with the Guatemalan oligarchy through the coup d'état organized by the CIA. In the years that followed, the U.S. supported this oligarchy by helping to form a repressive apparatus that was soon to transform itself into the support system sustaining all of the regimes thereafter. During the 1960s, the U.S. played a leading role in the elaboration of a counterinsurgency strategy based on the Vietnam experience, whose importance for Guatemala and the current situation cannot be ignored or underestimated.

9. The strategy of the Carter administration in Central America revolved around the prevention or restriction of the development of revolutionary movements, through reforms or gradual change. But the base necessary for such a strategy to work did not exist any more. The oligarchy, strengthened through U.S. aid, was not willing to accept a policy that implied a threat to its monopolistic domination of the country's economy and wealth. In addition, the oligarchy itself accepted the fact that gradual changes were no longer possible. Electoral fraud and the apparatus of violence and institutionalized terror had already destroyed all popular illusions of the possibility of democratic change in Guatemala. The people's support was gradually being swayed to those who proposed the need for structural change through armed struggle.

10. This was the great dilemma of U.S. policy in Central America: if the United States abandoned the oligarchy, this would imply recognition of the fact that popular movements were growing. Faced with the option of accepting a popular or democratic government or supporting an inflexible and repressive oligarchy, the United States will always opt for the latter. It is important to emphasize that the oligarchies in Central America know that this is the only viable alternative for the United States. Even during the Carter administration, according to testimony given by the journalist Elías Barahona, two American advisers, Jim Dumeb and Julian Kilhamer, stayed on in Guatemala in order to maintain contact between the Pentagon and the Guatemalan armed forces. In this way, the capacity of the U.S. to manipulate the oligarchies in Central America has diminished. These oligarchies pursue only one objective: the destruction of the popular movements, without bothering themselves with such subtleties as human rights or the implementation of reforms.

11. The problem is that these "subtleties" are necessary for the United States. A U.S. President in the 1980s cannot carry out a foreign policy with the same independence that he would have had in the 1960s; he must take into account national public opinion. The U.S. government has to maintain at least the semblance of concern for the respect of human rights in order to justify

military aid programs in the post-Vietnam era. Central American
oligarchies do not appear to be willing to understand this need.

12. The consequences of this dilemma are evident today in
El Salvador. Since the triumph of the Sandinista revolution in
Nicaragua in 1979, U.S. policy has aimed at preventing the occurrence of similar events in the rest of Central America. This strategy
in El Salvador has included a policy of repression combined with
limited reforms; but the facts show that the United States could
not convince the oligarchies that reforms were necessary. This
was true even when these reforms were more cosmetic in nature
and when their objectives clearly supported the military strategy,
e.g., creating a support base in a sector of the peasantry. Reagan
tried to utilize José Napoleón Duarte and later General García,
in addition to military support, to create the political space
necessary to negotiate with the oligarchy and implement his
counterinsurgency strategy.

13. In my opinion, this policy has been a failure. The guerrilla movement in El Salvador grows stronger every day. The army
has not adopted the military strategies suggested by the United
States, nor their political corollaries. It appears that the Reagan
administration is learning to apply in Guatemala what it learned
by trial and error in El Salvador. Under the Lucas García regime,
the situation in Guatemala was similar to that of El Salvador today:
a growing revolutionary movement, along with a massive and
open wave of repression, made it difficult for Reagan to give the
support that was really needed. We must observe, however, that
this support existed anyway. There is ample evidence that illegal
indirect aid was provided by the Reagan administration to the
Guatemalan government before the official reinstatement of aid
was announced in January of 1983.

14. In order to re-establish his influence in the counterinsurgency campaign in Guatemala, Reagan had to find a political
space that would permit him to counteract the intransigence of
the oligarchy. A similar situation existed in the 1960s, when Peralta
Azurdia refused to adopt the policy suggested by the United States
to defeat the guerrilla movement. The problem was solved with
the arrival of Méndez Montenegro as President: in exchange for

U.S. economic aid, Méndez Montenegro gave the U.S. and the Guatemalan army broad freedom of action in their counter-insurgency campaign.

15. Ríos Montt's importance lies here: he is creating precisely the political space that the United States requires. The most coherent counterinsurgency strategy of the last decade has been worked out and is being implemented under Ríos Montt. "Beans and Guns" is not a new strategy—it is classic. It is the formula that was put into practice in Vietnam: repression and terror used against the peasants suspected of aiding the guerrilla effort (this is called "counter-terrorism"), combined with a program of civic action— "Beans" —to gain the support of the peasants and at least give the appearance of socioeconomic reform to what is essentially a military strategy. Ríos Montt came into office at a moment that was critical for Reagan, and—what is more important—he has succeeded in promoting his image as a born-again Christian and is trying to create his own social and political power base around popular evangelism.

16. If one examines the trajectory of U.S. policy since Ríos Montt took power, especially since July of 1982, one can clearly observe the consolidation of a very important alliance. After the coup in March of 1982, the Reagan administration began a propaganda campaign designed to convince the American public that Ríos Montt represented something new and positive, and that he was making a significant effort to improve the human rights situation in Guatemala. This campaign has been carried out at a very high level. I would like to mention just one example: in July of 1982, Amnesty International published a report concerning the 69 massacres perpetrated since Ríos Montt took power. Thomas Enders himself, U.S. Secretary for Interamerican Affairs, wrote a widely distributed letter in which he severely criticized Amnesty's report. He based his arguments on data released through the U.S. embassy in Guatemala. However, in October of 1982, the Americas Watch Committee sent a delegation to Guatemala and produced a report confirming Amnesty International's conclusions and showing that Enders's criticisms lacked substance.

17. The government of the United States also launched a

campaign to demonstrate that Ríos Montt was a good democrat. The campaign ended with a meeting between Reagan and Ríos Montt in Honduras in December of 1982. The purpose of the meeting was twofold: to strengthen Ríos Montt's position with one fraction of the oligarchy and the army, and to re-establish normal diplomatic relations between the United States and Guatemala. In my opinion, this was the most significant event of Reagan's tour of Latin America. The decision to resume military aid and the sale of arms, although not formally announced until January of 1983, was really adopted long before this date, showing absolute disregard for U.S. and international public opinion by ignoring the evidence that there was widespread violation of human rights by the Ríos Montt government.

18. We must include the United States when we seek to establish who is responsible for the terror in Guatemala today. The United States is responsible not only for supplying a counterinsurgency strategy prepared by U.S. advisers, but also for the widespread use of terror as a key element in this program. Beyond this, the Reagan-Ríos Montt alliance and the application of counterinsurgency strategies are key aspects of U.S. foreign policy in Central America.

19. Contrary to what is carried in the U.S. press, the guerrilla movement in Guatemala is not defeated—far from it. The guerrilla movement represents, in my opinion, the legitimate aspirations of an oppressed and exploited people, and it could win. It is U.S. intervention in Guatemala, like U.S. intervention in El Salvador, that will prolong the struggle, suffering, and misery of the Guatemalan people.

20. If the United States maintains its position of military solutions for the problems of Central America, it is possible, in my opinion, that we will witness a regional war with international repercussions. During his visit to Mexico in August 1981, Claude Cheysson told the Mexican public that he believed that Central America would become as explosive an area as the Middle East, with the same danger of conflict among the superpowers. One month later, France and Mexico recognized the FMLN/FDR as a representative political force. This is the road to peace.

Report on Guatemala in the Light of International Law

Fernando Mariño Menéndez

This is a synopsis of the report by Mariño, Professor of International Public Law at the Autonomous University of Madrid.

The report establishes that the main responsibility for violations of international law lies with the government of Guatemala, which must answer to *"international crimes" against fundamental human rights*. The violations are serious, massive, systematic, and structural. The indiscriminate massacres of civilians, indigenous peasants, or opponents of the regime are acts of genocide, in the light of both the 1948 Convention and previous decisions by the Permanent People's Tribunal.

The government must also answer to *crimes against the right of free self-determination* by the people of Guatemala. The law of March 27, 1982, promulgated by Ríos Montt's regime, which annulled the 1965 Constitution; the mass elimination of civilians opposed to the regime; and other actions can only be intended to prevent the people from exercising their right of self-determination, which is illegal under international law.

The government is also committing *other internationally illegal acts* that, although they may not qualify as "crimes," underscore the repression: indefinite suspension of major civil and political rights, as well as economic, social, and cultural rights. With regard to the latter, it is important to point out that maintenance of the masses of the Indian population in a constant condition of misery and poverty constitutes racial discrimination, which is prohibited by international law.

Circumstances make it possible to affirm the existence in Guatemala of an *internal, armed conflict,* to which are applicable the fundamental norms of human rights in time of war. Their violation makes the individuals responsible "war criminals."

Third-party states are responsible for *complicity in the international crimes* of the Guatemalan government. It is important to point out the complicity of Israel, which sells Guatemala equipment for use in unlawful repression. Likewise, the nations of Argentina and the United States cooperate in the repression by training personnel for this purpose. The United States also provides economic aid without guarantees that it will not be used for repression (in any case, it strengthens the regime).

The Permanent People's Tribunal should reaffirm that the correct meaning, in the case of Guatemala, of the right to nonintervention in the internal affairs of this country in no way prohibits Third States from demanding from the Guatemalan state respect for human rights and self-determination.

The international responsibility of the Guatemalan government consists of three main obligations: *to re-establish a nation based on law; to punish individuals* responsible for the violations; *to provide reparations,* wherever possible, for the illegal harm done to individuals.

The international responsibility of Third States consists above all in: *ceasing all aid* that strengthens illegal repression and *providing reparations* for the harm done by their actions.

This report reaffirms the right of the Guatemalan people to fight for human rights and free self-determination, including by the use of arms, as established in Article 78 of the 1965 Constitution.

Third States should *refrain from granting asylum* to individuals responsible for international crimes; they should be tried or extradited. The duty of not returning innocent victims of repression to Guatemala *(non-return)* is in force for those states.

Third States *should demand that Guatemala fulfill its obligations* under international agreements.

International organizations (such as the U.N. or the OAS) competent in matters of human rights should *intensify their measures of international control* to compel fulfillment with international law in Guatemala.

Finally, the duty of the Central American states to find *peaceful solutions to the conflicts* in that region has acquired enormous importance. This should be of relevance to the Tribunal's Judgment.

III

THE
TRIBUNAL'S
JUDGMENT

Judgment of the
Permanent People's Tribunal

The Permanent People's Tribunal Convened in Madrid January 21-31, 1983, Taking into consideration

- the Charter of the United Nations of June 26, 1945,
- the Statute of the International Military Tribunal at Nuremberg, of August 8, 1945,
- the Universal Declaration of Human Rights of December 10, 1948,
- the Declaration concerning the protection of all peoples against torture and other cruel, inhuman, or degrading treatment or punishment contained in Resolution 3452 (XXX), adopted by the General Assembly of the United Nations, December 9, 1975,
- the Charter of the Organization of American States of 1948,
- the American Declaration of the Rights and Duties of Man of 1948,
- the American Convention on Human Rights of November 22, 1969 (at San José, Costa Rica), ratified by Guatemala May 26, 1978,
- the Convention on the Prevention and Punishment of the Crime of Genocide of December 9, 1948,
- the International Convention on the Elimination of All Forms of Racial Discrimination of December 21, 1965, signed by Guatemala,
- the Convention Regarding the Responsibility for War Crimes and Crimes Against Humanity, November 26, 1968,
- the Principles of International Cooperation in the Identification, Detention, Extradition and Punishment of Those Guilty of War Crimes and Crimes Against Humanity, contained in Resolution

3074 (XXVIII) of the General Assembly of the United Nations
of December 3, 1973,

— the Hague Conventions of 1899 and 1907, on the Uses and
  Customs of War,

— the Geneva Accords of August 12, 1949,

— Additional Protocols I and II of 1977, to the Geneva Accords
  of 1949,

— Convention No. 87 of the International Labor Organization on
  Freedom of Association and Protection of the Right to Organize,
  July 9, 1948, ratified by Guatemala,

— Convention No. 98 of the International Labor Organization on
  the Right to Organize and Collective Bargaining, July 1, 1948,
  ratified by Guatemala,

— the Equal Remuneration Convention of 1952, ratified by
  Guatemala,

— the Convention on the Political Rights of Women, of December 20, 1952, ratified by Guatemala,

— Resolution 2625 (XXV) of the General Assembly of the United
  Nations: Declaration of Principles of International Law Concerning Friendly Relations and Cooperation Among States in Accordance with the Charter of the United Nations, of October 24,
  1970,

— Resolution 34/169 of the General Assembly of the United
  Nations, which establishes the Code of Conduct for functionaries
  who are in charge of law enforcement, of December 17, 1979,

— Resolution 34/178 of the General Assembly of the United Nations
  concerning the rights to protection, habeas corpus, and other
  juridical recourse of December 17, 1979,

— specific resolutions pertinent to the situation in Guatemala, and
  particularly the resolution of the General Assembly of the United
  Nations of December 17, 1982,

— specific resolutions pertinent to the situation in Guatemala
  adopted by the European Parliament, and particularly the one
  adopted during the last session in December 1982,

— the Constitution of the Republic of Guatemala, September
  15, 1965,

— the project to elaborate draft Articles on the International

Responsibility of States, of the Commission on International Law of the United Nations (C.D.I. yearly, 1979, II, second part),

— the Code of Crimes Against the Peace and Security of Humanity (Document A/36/535 U.N., October 16, 1981),

— the Universal Declaration of the Rights of the Peoples, approved on July 4, 1976 in Algiers,

— the Statute of the Permanent People's Tribunal, adopted June 24, 1979,

— the judgments handed down by the Russell Tribunal on Latin America in sessions held in 1964, 1965, and 1966,

— the sentences handed down by the Permanent People's Tribunal in sessions on:

—the Western Sahara (Brussels, November 11, 1979),

—Argentina (Geneva, May 4, 1980),

—Eritrea (Milan, October 3, 1980),

—the Philippines and the Bangsa Moro people (Anvers, November 3, 1980),

—El Salvador (Mexico City, February 11, 1981),

—Afghanistan (first session, Stockholm, May 3, 1981),

—East Timor (Lisbon, June 21, 1981),

—Zaire (Rotterdam, September 20, 1982),

—Afghanistan (second session, Paris, December 20, 1982).

Having heard on January 27, 1983 the reports and testimony* that are listed as follows:

— the opening speech, given by George Wald, President of the Tribunal,

— information provided by Gianni Tognoni, Secretary General of the Permanent People's Tribunal, on procedures adopted to guarantee the exercise of the right of defense and particularly the notification to the government of Guatemala that this session was being held,

— the report, "Analysis of the Economic Structure," by Rafael Piedrasanta Arandi, economist,

---

*The presentations referred to here were the full-length versions rather than the synopsized versions published in this volume. Since the titles of long and short versions sometimes differed, titles of presentations listed here may vary from the published ones. Some titles have also been shortened by the editors.

— the report, "Social Analysis of Guatemala," by Miguel Angel Reyes, sociologist,

— the testimony of Miguel Angel Albizures, union leader,

— the testimony of Israel Márquez, union leader.

Having heard on January 28, 1983, the reports and testimony listed as follows:

— the "Report on the Guatemalan Army," by Gabriel Aguilera Peralta, of the Central American Institute for Social Research and Documentation (ICADIS), Costa Rica,

— the testimony of Elías Barahona, journalist and ex-press secretary of the Ministry of the Interior,

— the testimony of Pedro Luis Ruiz, ex-sergeant in the Guatemalan army, from Quiché,

— the report, "Political Analysis," by Raúl Molina Mejía, ex-president of the University of San Carlos in Guatemala,

— the testimony of Juan Velázquez Jiménez, a Mam peasant and refugee,

— the communication of Carolina van den Heuvel, deputy of the European Parliament, vice president of the socialist group,

— the testimony of Philippe Texier, magistrate, member of the commission of investigation organized by Pax Christi International, which visited Guatemala June 22-29, 1981 to obtain information about the human rights situation there in general,

— the testimony of Harald Edelstam, ex-Ambassador of Sweden to Guatemala and Chile,

— the report, "Historical Analysis of Guatemala," by Guillermo Toriello, ex-Foreign Minister of Guatemala,

— the report, "Popular Culture, Indigenous Cultures, Genocide and Ethnocide in Guatemala," by Arturo Arias, of the Alaide Foppa Association of Guatemalan Cultural Workers (Costa Rica),

— the testimony of Manuel José Arce, writer,

— the testimony of Luis Felipe Irías, ex-general secretary of the Association of University Students,

— the testimony of Rolando Castillo Montalvo, physician, ex-dean of the medical school of the University of San Carlos,

— the report, "Analysis of the Indigenous Question," by Fr. Ricardo Falla, anthropologist,

— the testimony of Pablo Ceto, peasant leader, Ixil.

Having heard, on January 29, 1983, the reports and testimony listed as follows:

— the testimony of José Efraín Rosales, peasant, Quiché,

— the testimony of Rigoberta Menchú, peasant, Quiché,

— the testimony of Gabriel Ixmatá, peasant, Mam,

— the testimony of Juan José Mendoza, peasant from Atitlán,

— the report, "The Persecution of Christians and the Church in Guatemala," by Julia Esquivel, Guatemalan Committee for Justice and Peace, Mexico,

— the report, "On Human Rights in Guatemala," by Marco Antonio Sagastume, Guatemalan Human Rights Commission, Spain,

— the testimony of Carmelita Santos, peasant, Quiché,

— the testimony of Irma Consuelo de Azmitia, housewife,

— the testimony of Guillermo Morales Pérez, peasant and refugee, Mam,

— the testimony of Regina Hernández, teacher of religion,

— the testimony of Sandra Judith de Medina, professor of mathematics,

— the report, "The Complicity of the U.S. Government and U.S. Capital in the Violation of Human Rights in Guatemala," by Susanne Jonas of ISLEC (Institute for the Study of Labor and Economic Crisis), United States,

— the report, "U.S. Penetration and Intervention in Guatemala," by Jenny Pearce of the Latin American Bureau, Great Britain,

— the "International Juridical Report Concerning the Situation in the Republic of Guatemala," by Fernando Mariño, professor of public international law at the Autonomous University of Madrid.

Having seen:

— the written testimony dated January 25, 1983, sent by the Secretary-General of Roman Peace, Geneva,

— the written testimony, dated December 25, 1982, of a witness 35 years old from Bullaj,

— the written testimony of Verny Aníbal Samayos López, Honduras, dated January 14, 1983,

— the written testimony of a professor of law of the University of San Carlos,

— testimony gathered by the Guatemalan Human Rights Commission from Guatemalan refugees in Mexico during November and December, 1982,

— written testimony contained in the document "Other Testimony."

Having seen:

— the report of the Commission on Human Rights of the United Nations on "The Situation of Human Rights in Guatemala," 38th period of sessions (1982),

— the report of the Organization of American States on the human rights situation in the Republic of Guatemala, 1981,

— the report of the mission of Pax Christi International about the human rights situation in Guatemala, 1982,

— numerous reports from Amnesty International, primarily the July 1982 report, "Guatemala, Extrajudicial Executions on a Large Scale in the Rural Zones Under the Government of General Efraín Ríos Montt"; the 1981 Annual Report dated October 26, 1981; the report, "Disappearances, a Work Book" (1981); and the report of 1981, "Guatemala: A Government Program of Political Murder,"

— the report of the International Commission of Jurists, June 1982, Geneva, and the report of its visit to Guatemala in June 1979,

— the report of an investigation carried out by the North American Commission on Guatemala organized by the National Council of Churches, November 7-12, 1982,

— the report presented at the 37th session of the United Nations General Assembly by the Unitary Delegation of the Opposition in Guatemala: "Guatemala: a Case of Constant and Systematic Violation of Human Rights,"

— the report of the Guatemalan Human Rights Commission to the first World Congress on Human Rights, December 6, 1982,

— the report of Oxfam America, "Witnesses to Political Violence in Guatemala: The Suppression of a Rural Development Movement," 1982,

— the report of Americas Watch, "Human Rights in Guatemala: No Neutrals Allowed," November 23, 1982,

— the report of Survival International USA, "Testimonies of Refugees in Mexico, August 1982, and a Report on the Present Situation of Indians in Guatemala,"

— the dossier sent by the Secretary General of the World Federation of Trade Unions on the violation of human rights in Guatemala, December 1982,

— the report, "We, the Guatemalan Women Denounce Before the Permanent People's Tribunal the Constant and Systematic Violation of Human Rights in Guatemala," January 1983.

Taking into account the abundant documentation, written and photographic, which has been given to the members of the Tribunal.

This concludes the first section of the Tribunal's Judgment. On the next page, the Judgment goes on to address Historical Antecedents, the Facts, the Economic, Political and Social Context, the Law, and the Rights of the People — the Struggle for Liberation and Peace. It concludes with its findings, or Disposition.

I. HISTORICAL ANTECEDENTS

Guatemala is a country of about 110,000 square kilometers with a population that may now reach about 7.5 million. Ethnically, this population is divided into indigenous and non-indigenous peoples, the latter ordinarily called "ladinos." Although the census undercounts the indigenous population (in 1973 it was 43%), the majority of the rural population of the republic is certainly indigenous.

These people are descended from the creators of the Mayan civilization, which was comparable in its historical development to that of the Incas and Egyptians. The invasion by Toltecan groups pushed these peaceful and contemplative inhabitants away from the flat jungle lands to the high plains, where they were able to situate themselves in easily defensible areas. The new habitat of hills and canyons contributed to the internal differentiation of languages and customs. That is why there presently exist about 20 different language groups. The majority speak Quiché, Kekchí, Mam, and Cakchiquel.

The "ladino" population comes from the Spanish invasion of 1524. After a ferocious and technologically unequal war, a government dependent on the Spanish crown was imposed on the indigenous people. They were obliged, under various forms of servitude, to give the surplus of their production both to Spain and to the Creole society that was established in Guatemala. In its lower echelons the Creole society became mixed with the indigenous to form the "ladino" or "mestizo" population. The war left numerous victims but not as many as the plague that decimated the native inhabitants, who had no immunity to it. Although there were frequent attempts at indigenous rebellion, exploitation was established and became the structural cause of famine as well as racial and ethnic discrimination against the indigenous people and the mestizos.

In the beginning of the 19th century there were indigenous uprisings against the payment of tribute, but political independence from Spain (September 15, 1821) did not entail structural change for the indigenous people, particularly the peasants. In 1871, the "liberal reform" brought a change in the economic orientation of Guatemala. Measures were decreed that favored the export of coffee and broke down the property of the indigenous communities, imposing forced labor upon them so that they had to send able workers to the coastal zone where coffee was grown. The introduction of capitalism reinforced the domination of the exploiting classes and the subjugation of the Indians, whose "ladinization" increased with the formation of settlements on the plantations.

The opening up to the world market of agricultural exports attracted a German population to Guatemala. At the same time, it offered North American capital the opportunity to initiate the cultivation of bananas on a large scale. In 1904 the United Fruit Company was established. A subsidiary of this company, the International Railways of Central America, dominated the railways used for the transportation of fruit. Finally, Electric Bond and Share came to control 80% of the electrical energy of the country. A power above the state was established, which owned, besides *latifundios* (very large estates), the railroads, the ports, maritime transportation, telegraphic communication, and the international telephone system. This power supported the tyrant Estrada Cabrera from 1898 to 1920 and placed Guatemala among the "banana republics" of Central America.

The main liberation effort against this structure of domination arose when the approaching end of World War II permitted a realignment of the domestic power structure. The revolution of October 1944 ended the era of lifetime tyrants and initiated such democratic reforms as the popular vote, the legal existence of political parties, legalization of unions and strikes, the elimination of forced labor by indigenous people, a social security system, etc. From 1945 to 1951, the government of Dr. Juan José Arévalo gradually expanded its base of support, which initially was primarily urban, to the countryside. On the southern coast and the northeastern coast—the zones of the United Fruit Company—the main struggles of peasant workers, particularly strikes, had government support. The anti-imperialist character of the workers' movement was deepened in 1952, under the government of Col. Jacobo Arbenz, through an agrarian reform decree.

In an alliance with the landed oligarchy, the lawyers of the United Fruit Company, among them John Foster Dulles and his brother Allen Dulles, (Secretary of State and chief of the CIA of the United States respectively) prepared an invasion from Honduras that would end these liberation efforts in 1954.

In response to the violation of the rights of labor, political, student, and cultural organizations, and to the murder of hundreds of leaders and peasants by the anticommunist regime of Castillo Armas, there gradually arose a new liberation movement. It was fueled by an attempt to reconstitute the labor union, student, and political movements, by support from the Catholic Church in the rural areas, and particularly by the birth of a guerrilla movement in the capital city and in the northeastern region of the country. In March 1963, this movement precipitated a new coup d'état, and in the second half of the 1960s it was brutally repressed. About 12,000 civilians were murdered under the pretext of combating 300 guerrillas.

The repression conducted by General Arana Osorio in accordance with counterinsurgency plans eradicated the guerrillas from the rural areas. They regrouped, however, and insurgent activity began again in some indigenous zones. At the same time, the movement of students and workers was being strengthened in the capital and gradually became linked with the open peasant movement, culminating in demonstrations like none ever seen before in Guatemala, such as the miners' march from Ixtahuacán to Guatemala City in 1977.

The guerrilla movement expanded its bases when the possibility of genuine elections was repeatedly negated (especially by the frauds of 1974 and 1978), and when the repression of mass organizations forced those in struggle to change their methods and strategies. The massacre at Panzós in May of 1978 and the burning of the Spanish embassy (1980) were two historical milestones that strengthened the unity of all sectors—workers and peasants, indigenous and ladinos, men and women, students and professionals, Christians and non-Christians—in a common struggle.

II. THE FACTS

The Tribunal has corroborated the following widely reported facts, not only through reports from governmental and nongovernmental organizations, but also through the direct testimony of the affected persons.

1. Political and Juridical Institutions

The democratic process, which had been instigated by the people for such a long time and then set in motion by Presidents Arévalo and Arbenz, was suffocated in 1954 with massive help from the United States. From that time on, only a "restricted democracy" was allowed.

The Constitution of Guatemala of September 15, 1965 can be called "liberal"; it recognizes the equality of people and such traditional freedoms as individual freedom, freedom of association, freedom of expression, freedom of the press and teaching, religious freedom, and above all the freedom of property and the freedom of commerce and industry. It also instituted a series of legal guarantees such as the recourse to habeas corpus.

But this Constitution carries with it indications of the social repression that characterized the previous period. Thus the freedom of labor to organize is limited to "economic self-defense and social advancement" (Article 114, 12). Strikes are permitted only after the process of conciliation has failed and political strikes are excluded.

The most obvious sign of reduction in the space allowed for political activity is manifested in Articles 27ff concerning political parties. Their founding and functioning remain necessarily linked to legal registration, which is denied to "all parties and entities that support communist ideology or, because of their doctrines, actions or international connections, threaten the sovereignty of the state or the foundations of the democratic organization of Guatemala" (Article 27, paragraph 2 and Article 64, paragraph 2, which concerns the right of association and has an analogous provision). Legal registration is granted only to organizations that have a minimum of 50,000 followers, all of whom must be inscribed in the electoral registers, and of these at least 20% must know how to read and write (Article 28). This last provision tends to prevent the formation of new parties that would be authentic expressions of the poor people, particularly the indigenous people, even though their program may not fall under the restrictions of Article 27.

It is evident that this Constitution sanctions a move backward in relation to the opening that made the 1945 Constitution possible. It sets a narrow framework for political action; the established social order is committed to a process of capitalist development. In a society that shows such great social divergencies, these limits also restrict respect for fundamental freedoms and political and constitutional guarantees.

Opposition forces that do not respect the limits of the established socioeconomic system are not protected, either by fundamental rights or by juridical guarantees. Thus in May 1966, not long after the Constitution took effect, 28 communists were detained, tortured, and murdered, even though the Constitution forbids torture (Article 55, paragraph 2), guarantees due process of law and rights of defense (Articles 51 and 79ff), and limits capital punishment to extremely serious acts and to situations where there are no doubts of any kind.

Constitutional provisions have not sufficed to contain the political mobilization of the masses within the framework of the so-called liberal democratic system. To complete the juridical modifications, it was necessary to use clearly illegal manipulations and at the same time growing brutality and systematic mass murders, which totally negated the validity of recognized, fundamental rights and political freedoms.

Within this context we can cite the following facts:

Fraudulent elections. Every time an election has threatened to produce unwanted results, it has been manipulated or falsified. That was the case in 1974 (the election of General Laugerud García instead of Ríos Montt) and in 1978, when General Lucas García came to power through electoral fraud involving all political parties, up to the elections of 1982. The military coup d'état of General Ríos Montt on March 23, 1982 put an end to such complications by abolishing the Constitution. In so doing, he confirmed the process which had started long ago: the seizure of power by the army. The Constitution is only a facade.

The seizure of the state by the army. The overthrow of President Arbenz, suffocating radical bourgeois democracy for the benefit of foreign interests and the oligarchy, and setting aside the interests of the people, unleashed a process of political dissolution. The bourgeois fractions were incapable of controlling the armed resistance to which the people resorted; this conferred on the army a growing, central role. When popular demonstrations against counterrevolutionary policies, especially the protests of 1962, endangered the government of General Ydígoras Fuentes, they were repressed by the army, whose leading role thus increased. The army, after getting rid of its own progressive sector, and through an internal restructuring, became the main political decision-maker. In the face of the political parties' incapacity to use "restricted democracy," the army imposed itself as the arbiter of the situation, ready to take over power each time the constitutional process ran the risk of breaking down.

Thus, in 1963, power was usurped in the face of the risk of an electoral victory by former democratic President Arévalo (1945-1950). In 1954, the army had made possible the expulsion of President Arbenz by refusing to support him, and in 1982 it ended the fighting between the political parties with a coup d'état by General Ríos Montt. The latter immediately replaced the Constitution with a Fundamental Statute of Government that concentrated all political power in the hands of the junta.

In spite of the fact that the Statute of Government of March 27, 1982 adopted almost word for word the fundamental freedoms and the legal and political guarantees of the abolished Constitution, its provisions are in reality only a facade:

—The Statute transfers all legislative and executive power to the military junta (Articles 3 and 4).

—Secret Tribunals and Tribunals of Special Jurisdiction are created whose functioning is outside the procedural guarantees as set by Decree 46/82.

—Repression continues, and petitions to General Ríos Montt

by the parents of disappeared people go unanswered.

—The "amnesty" conceded after the coup d'état by Decree-Law 33/82 in practice has not benefited anyone except the authors of the previous repression. To the knowledge of this Tribunal, no penal sanction has ever been instituted against them, nor a single punishment.

—The State of Siege promulgated by Decree-Law 45/82 of July 1, 1982 has been regularly prolonged.

—The creation of an army with unlimited powers corresponds to the militarization of the entire society, that is, its forced integration into the repressive structure.

—The "civilian patrols," created by the regime of Ríos Montt under the pretext of protecting the population against subversion in fact serve to control the population through the army and to pit the different ethnic groups against each other (the various indigenous peoples against each other and town against town), thus destroying awareness of the people's fundamental unity vis-à-vis the repressive state apparatus.

—The "strategic hamlets" and the institution of the "military commissions" are part of the same penetration of society by the repressive apparatus.

—The development of the state structures as elaborated above and the very function of the state clearly show that the violation of fundamental rights, which will be addressed in the following chapters, is a necessary and logical consequence of the established sytem and of the will to maintain this system.

2. Cultural Repression

Among the Indigenous Peasants. In a deliberate attempt to root out indigenous culture, the army of Ríos Montt attacks the population. In addition to killing people, it forces them to be displaced, and thus obliges them to leave their sacred places: the cemeteries, the ceremonial centers, "the centers of power." At the same time, the army destroys the looms where the women weave their *huipiles* (blouses); it destroys the raw materials for making *huipiles*; it destroys all the old *huipiles* that it finds in the villages, which represent tradition. (Before dying, grandparents give these *huipiles* to their grandchildren and explain the significance of the embroidery to keep that tradition going.) Communion with the land, with the corn, is broken. Corn is the sacred, life-giving element whose planting signifies the reaffirmation of faith and the people's eternal gratefulness for creation.

When the army of Ríos Montt concentrates the indigenous population in strategic hamlets, it imposes upon them "Western" clothing, thus depriving them of their last valued possessions. For indigenous women, to stop wearing one's native dress constitutes betrayal of one's ancestors.

In addition, their hair is cut, which is another sacrilege in indigenous culture. Finally, they are given a minimum of food and are not allowed to go outside of the strategic hamlets to plant corn or to celebrate their sacred rites at the places and on the dates established for centuries.

In this way the army seeks to destroy in a systematic and conscious way the most sacred values of the indigenous people in order to subvert the people's values and identity, annihilating them from within and thus destroying their consciousness and their readiness to defend their ethnic identity.

At the University and in the Sphere of Education. Policemen and members of the military intelligence dressed in civilian clothing carry out kidnappings and murders, in homes and workplaces or even on the street. Repression at the University [of San Carlos—Eds.] and in the educational field has been aimed at about 250 University-connected people, students, professors, professionals, labor unionists, University and student leaders. That is, against persons from almost every sector of the University.

It is possible to mention individual cases, such as that of Víctor Valverth, or collective cases such as the machine-gunning of the speakers and the audience attending a round table at the University cultural center at the end of 1980. There have also been thefts, and bombs have been placed, for example, in the University Center of the North and the University Center of the East. Places such as the headquarters of the Association of Economics Students and the school of medicine's Documentation Center have been set on fire.

The most flagrant, recent instance of repression against the University, whose autonomy is guaranteed by Article 99 of the Constitution, took place when machine-gun fire from private vehicles was opened up against students descending from buses at the bus terminal in front of the university rectory. Dr. Rolando Castillo Montalvo, dean of the medical school, was witness to this event.

Practically all cultural sectors have suffered persecution. It is enough to cite the following examples:

In July 1979, there was the murder of Rita Navarro, lawyer and director of the University cultural center, which brought together all the artistic groups subsidized by the University, such as the arts theater.

In the same year, ferocious repression began against the popular neighborhood art movement of loosely organized theater and musical groups, which had emerged from various marginal neighborhoods of the capital and generally had a Christian orientation.

At the level of primary and secondary education, the policy followed by the Lucas García and Ríos Montt governments has been one of economic strangulation of all institutions of public education with a view to liquidating them, and favoring only the existence of private institutions. According to the very words of former Minister of Education Colonel Clementino Castillo, "The public schools are the focus of subversion, and therefore the state does not have to subsidize them." Needless to say, only the middle and upper sectors have access to the private institutions, which exist only in the capital and some of the main cities. If this gradual liquidation of public education continues, it will—by means of a conscious and deliberate effort—condemn all popular sectors in the country to illiteracy and ignorance.

It is also important to take note of the harassment and psychological repression aimed at quieting the "critical consciousness of the nation" by diverse means. Examples: anonymous messages and public threats from the authorities and civilian and military functionaries at all levels, including President Romeo Lucas García himself.

In Other Cultural Spheres. On a different level, in July 1980, the group "Teatro Vivo" (Living Theater) of Guatemala, perhaps the most brilliant of the theater groups, was forced into exile as a whole when two of its more prominent actors miraculously escaped an attempt on their lives in Chinautla, Guatemala. In response to their escape, police occupied the cultural center of La Galera, an autonomous center where writers and artists gathered. All who worked there or came together there had to go underground.

In September of 1980 a theatrical director was kidnapped— Carlos Obregón, veteran of Teatro del Sol of Paris, France. He was saved from death by the prompt intervention of the French authorities, who demanded his return, but he did not escape being savagely tortured, and lost an eardrum as a consequence of torture.

On September 19, 1980, the writer Alaide Foppa was kidnapped in the downtown area of the capital. She was 67 years old and had returned to the country only to visit her elderly mother who was sick. The first feminist of Guatemala and perhaps its most brilliant writer in this century, Alaide also lost her son, the journalist Mario Solórzano Foppa, founder of the first television news program, who was assassinated in June 1981. Alaide Foppa was not seen again in spite of an international campaign demanding her reappearance.

In February 1981, a G-2 group arrived at the offices of the Department of Archeology, where the writer Franz Galich was working. Luckily the doorman was able to warn him and Franz hid on the roof of the building, avoiding capture. Later the same worker took him secretly to the embassy of Costa Rica.

In June of that year the musician Tito Medina had to leave the country suddenly after escaping an attempt on his life.

In the same month, the writer Adolfo Méndez Vides left the country following his kidnapping by a group of the judicial [secret—Eds.] police; he was freed after having witnessed the execution of a friend and colleague who had accompanied him.

In November of the same year, the sculptor Edgar Guzmán managed to leave the country after he learned confidentially that he was about to be kidnapped.

In September 1982, Rolando Medina, the most brilliant literary critic in the history of Guatemala, also a novelist and poet, was kidnapped. His kidnapping took place in the parking lot of the School of History of the University of San Carlos and was witnessed by his wife Sandra Judith, who noted the license plate of the vehicle and has testified about the sequence of events.

Finally, among the cases that we have fully corroborated, the playwright Otto Gaytán escaped from kidnappers in November 1982 by jumping into the patio of the house in back of his home when they came to kidnap him.

In the Press. There is self-censorship instigated by government terror, and direct censorship imposed upon the directors and journalists of the various newspapers.

In the last three years as many as 23 journalists have been kidnapped; to this date they have not appeared and no one knows anything about them. Another 23 have been machine-gunned and killed in the street. Among those kidnapped we can mention Sonia Calderón de Martell, Abner Recinos Alfaro and Irma Flaquer. Among those machine-gunned were Marco Antonio Cacao Muñoz, Jesús Marroquín Castañeda, and Jorge Marroquín Mejía.

According to the Interamerican Press Society (SIP) in a 1980 report, Guatemala is one of the countries where it is most dangerous to be a journalist. About 100 journalists have had to leave the country because of attempts on their lives or death threats.

On July 5 the journalist Marco Antonio Cacao Muñoz, a member of the Democratic Socialist Party, was machine-gunned by the G-2 of the army. He was accused of traveling frequently to Mexico and Costa Rica, according to what the Minister of the Interior, Donaldo Alvarez Ruiz, told his press secretary, Elías Barahona. The killing was attributed to the Secret Anticommunist Army (ESA). Alvarez Ruiz confidentially told Barahona that Cacao Muñoz was "a good guy, but he didn't control his tongue when he was bad-mouthing the government."

As a consequence of all that has been described above, journalists are forced to work in secret in order to report objectively about what is going on in their own country.

3. Religious Repression

In spite of diplomatic relations with the Vatican, the first repressive act against Christians in this period took place after the violence was denounced by the Bishops on May 9, 1967.

In 1968, the Melville brothers, priests from the United States, were expelled from the country. Later, as popular opposition to the government grew, clergymen and pastors became aware of what was going on. They gave voice to those without a voice in confronting the poverty and the discrimination against poor people, particularly against the profoundly religious indigenous people.

In December 1971, a group of pastors called for lifting the State of Siege. Those who were foreign were expelled and those who were Guatemalan were threatened.

The Christians became more involved in popular struggle at the time of the earthquake of February 4, 1976, and through the Pastoral Letter of July 1976 entitled "United in Hope." The Bishop of El Quiché defended the persecuted Christian leaders, who were students. During Lent of 1977, the Federation of Guatemalan Priests (Confederación de Sacerdotes de Guatemala, COSDEGUA) was founded, and the Guatemalan Committee for Justice and Peace was established in November 1977.

All this culminated at the time of the massacre of 130 peasants in Panzós on May 29, 1978. The Bishop of the Verapaz provinces and the pastors protested; the Spanish sister Raimunda Alonso Queralt was expelled from Guatemala, and the police began an investigation of the priests of the region.

On June 30, the priest Hermógenes López Coarchita was murdered because of his identification with the social struggles of his community and his opposition to the army.

Repression under the Romeo Lucas García regime increased; on August 4, Mario Mujía Córdoba, a Christian leader, and other leaders were assassinated.

Fr. Carlos Stetter from the Diocese of Huehuetenango, who was working on social advancement, was expelled in 1979.

The Jesuits in particular were accused of being communists; they answered, on January 11, 1979, with a profession of faith and service.

In 1980, two sets of events stand out: the repression and closure of the Diocese of El Quiché and similar repression in Esquintla.

1. On January 31, 1980, 27 indigenous peasants, workers, students, and residents of El Quiché were machine-gunned and burned in the Spanish embassy by order of the President and the Minister of Security. Several religious teachers died there.

On June 4, Fr. José María Gran Cirera, M.S.C.M., a Spaniard and the priest of Chajul, was murdered along with his sexton. On July 10, Fr. Faustino Villanueva, M.S.C.M., priest of Joyabaj, was murdered. On July 19, murder was attempted against Bishop Juan Gerardi of El Quiché, President of the Bishops' Conference of Guatemala. The Diocese of El Quiché was closed down in protest. On November 1, the Pope addressed a letter of encouragement and support to the Bishops, but still Bishop Gerardi was not allowed to enter Guatemala when he returned from Rome.

2. The Diocese of Esquintla also suffered persecution after Bishop Ríos Montt, the brother of President Ríos Montt, acted as advocate for the peasants on March 1, 1980. The Center of Emaús, used for meetings, was raided. Fr. Conrado de la Cruz, I.C.M., a Filipino and priest of Tiquisate, was kidnapped. E.P. Walter Voordeckers, J.C.M., a Belgian priest in the parish of Santa Lucía Cotzumalguapá, was assassinated.

4. Labor Union Freedoms

The attacks against union rights and the repression of unions began in the 1960s and have become increasingly serious. All the testimony gathered by the Tribunal and the reports gathered by the International Labor Organization are proof of the repeated violations of union rights, of restrictive legislation regarding the right to strike, of death or detention of union leaders, and the raiding of union offices (for example, see the report given by the International Labor Organization on September 17, 1981 to the Secretary General of the United Nations).

After 1970, the murder of union leaders intensified. Between October 1978 and April 1979, violence became acute at the Coca-Cola bottling plant, where the collective bargaining laws were violated and union members were threatened and finally attacked by 80 armed men in the plant itself. Among the attackers were members of the judicial police's "model platoon." The strikers were beaten and some of the workers were kidnapped. On August 24, 1980, the security forces detained and tortured 17 union leaders on the "Emaús" plantation in the department of Esquintla. In the same year, the elimination of union leaders reached its peak with the assassination or kidnapping of more than 80. On June 21, 1980, the Workers Central of the CNT was raided and surrounded by the army: 27 union leaders, the majority of them general secretaries, were kidnapped and have disappeared. In two months, 44 leaders disappeared.

Since then, union organizations have been unable to exist publicly because of the impossibility of speaking out and the kidnapping of their leaders, many of whom have been assassinated. Any attempted strike has been repressed. Lawyers cannot defend the rights of workers, who have no organization.

On July 1, 1982, a State of Siege was established, suppressing all intellectual and collective rights and "prohibiting the functioning of labor organizations and political parties." The offices of workers' organizations were closed and in practice union rights ceased to exist in Guatemala.

5. Personal Liberties

The problem of forced and involuntary disappearances began in Guatemala in 1966 and has continued with varying intensity (see reports of task forces of the United Nations Commission on Human Rights and testimony gathered by the Tribunal). The victims of the disappearances come from diverse social backgrounds, but the majority are labor leaders, peasants, indigenous people, and responsibles in the Christian communities. In the great majority of cases, there is no legal detention; rather victims are kidnapped in their homes, workplaces, during meetings, and even on the street.

The kidnappings were carried out by groups of individuals who are almost always members of the security forces, who act openly, driving vehicles ordinarily used by the police.

In the majority of cases, we have assumed that the person who has disappeared is in fact dead, without ever knowing for certain. Only the discovery of sites where killings have taken place or of clandestine cemeteries confirms this hypothesis. For example, in the cemetery of Comalapa, 30 bodies were found in 1980, and 23 bodies were found buried in a common grave in 1981.

The extent of the phenomenon is extremely difficult to evaluate. Legal recourse for survivors, and particularly the "Recourse of Personal Exhibition" [the right to demand to see the physical evidence — Eds.] contained in Article 79 of the 1965 Constitution, practically cannot be used. In 20 years, only once has it been possible through legal recourse to obtain the reappearance of someone who disappeared. The threat of violent reprisal explains the lack of effective investigation.

There are no complete lists of the forced disappearances. The Tribunal has sufficient information to affirm that the disappearances have been uninterrupted from 1966 to 1982, and that they have been systematic. For example, the task force of the United Nations Commission on Human Rights concerned with forced and involuntary disappearances gave us a list of 615 persons who disappeared from June 1978 to October 1981, with names, dates of disappearance, place of detention, etc.

Torture is also used in a systematic manner. Reports given to the Tribunal reveal that it has continued to be used since 1954; it takes the most diverse and also the most cruel forms. There are very few who survive, and above all, the state of mutilation of the corpses gives us some idea: men and women torn apart by machetes, corpses without heads, burned, beaten, pregnant women whose bodies have been opened and the fetus placed in their hands.

Torture is the seal of the army, of the security forces, and particularly of the elite troops called "Kaibiles."

The Tribunal has received numerous written testimonies, and has listened to many indigenous people who were eyewitnesses to these acts of barbarism.

Many members of the family of one of the witnesses died under torture: his mother, his father, the members of his community. The descriptions revealed the horror: women who had been raped and their breasts cut off before they were killed, little by little with the machete; fingernails torn off one by one, destroyed bodies thrown down a well.

Elías Barahona, who was press secretary to the Minister of the Interior for four years, has told the Tribunal the location of clandestine centers of torture in the capital. He has also stated that in a counterinsurgency project suggested by the United States to General Lucas García and the Guatemalan military, there were instructors from Israel and Argentina.

A February 1981 report of Amnesty International concludes its observations with this statement: "Torture and death are part of a deliberate long-term program of the government of Guatemala."

It is recognized that Guatemala is the first country where the forced and involuntary disappearance of people was practiced as a form of repression, inspiring various other Latin American governments, particularly those of Chile, Uruguay, and above all, Argentina.

6. Murders and Massacres

Repression in Guatemala started a long time ago, but the present situation of permanent and systematic violence dates from the beginning of the 1960s, at the time of the military uprising against the government of General Ydígoras Fuentes.

During that time, the paramilitary forces were organized— the Organized Anticommunist National Movement (MANO, the White Hand), the Death Squad, and many others—which contributed to the elimination of all forms of political opposition through threats, torture, and assassination. The victims were not only guerrillas but also, increasingly, groups that formed part of the political opposition, and the entire populations of specific rural areas like Quiché, Huehuetenango, Chimaltenango—mainly those presumed to support the guerrilla forces.

The numerous testimonies that have been given to the Tribunal, the numerous reports that have been received and the study of abundant reports of missions sent by the Organization of American States, Amnesty International, and the International

Commission of Jurists clearly accuse the military authorities, the government authorities, and the security forces of acts of extrajudicial execution against the civilian population. The murders often are targeted in towns and in the capital city, as in the case of ex-Minister of Foreign Affairs Alberto Fuentes Mohr, killed January 25, 1979, political leaders such as ex-mayor Manuel Colón Argueta, or numerous professors at the University of San Carlos (27 of them between March and September, 1980).

But when we speak of peasants and indigenous people, the crime is much more massive. The examples are abundant and the Tribunal has been able to obtain considerable documentation; we cite the most recent cases to illustrate their massive character. In Panzós, Department of Alta Verapaz, on May 29, 1978, about 700 peasants were gathered in a plaza; the army machine-gunned them, killing 130. On January 31, 1980, 27 indigenous people of Quiché peacefully occupied the embassy of Spain. The embassy was rapidly surrounded by 400 policemen. In spite of the Spanish ambassador, the police invaded the place and it was set on fire. Only two people escaped alive, the ambassador and one peasant. The following day the peasant was kidnapped from the Herrera Hospital where he was being treated, and his body appeared some days later in front of the University of San Carlos. In the fire at the embassy, 39 died, among them eight members of the embassy staff.

Elías Barahona has told the Tribunal that the order to attack the embassy came from the President of the Republic, General Lucas García, and that the majority of the officials and police who participated in the action still hold their jobs.

Another example subsequent to the coup d'état of 1982 is the massacre of San Francisco, perpetrated by the army on July 17, 1982, which caused the death of 352 people. The Tribunal has in its possession a list of 302 names and the testimony of the survivors (living as refugees in Mexico) brought by Ricardo Falla, a priest who came to give his testimony to the Tribunal.

The Tribunal knows of a great number of killings of entire populations: they cover the recent years up to the end of 1982. These killings provide evidence that the situation has become more serious since the coup d'état of 1982.

The documents in the hands of the Tribunal do not allow a precise evaluation of the number of murders from 1954 to this date, but one cannot think in terms of a figure under 50,000. They may exceed 100,000.

7. Generalized Terror

Since the coup d'état of March 1982, a phase of terror has begun which affects a great proportion of the population, near and far; between March and November of 1982, the killings add up to more than 8,000.

The forms of terror consist of public torture and massacre, with the goal of intimidating the population as a whole. Thus, for example, from March 23 to September 30, 1982, 4,044 peasants have been massacred in groups of up to 500 persons.

The description of the massacre of San Francisco illustrates the procedure utilized consistently, in this and other cases, of separating the men and making them believe that a meeting is taking place, and locking them up in a building of the village. Then the soldiers gather the women and children of all ages in the church. The army begins to shoot the women in the church. The survivors are separated from their children and taken in groups to their homes where they are murdered with machetes. Later on the soldiers kill the children. A witness has seen how they slice open the stomachs of children with knives and then throw them against big sticks to break their heads. The soldiers take a brief break and then start executing the men. They make them go out, tie their hands, throw them to the ground and shoot them in that position. The massacre continues for an hour, and then it is ended by throwing grenades at the houses. Those responsible for the San Francisco massacre were 600 soldiers, headed by six officers.

Parallel to this, the "scorched earth" policy consists of systematically destroying the villages to force the indigenous population to leave and regroup in "model villages" that have been set up since the coup d'état of March 1982. It is also since that date that the army has tried to forcefully incorporate the peasants in "civilian patrols." The Tribunal heard a great deal of testimony about recent incidents (August 18, 1982; October 5, 1982) in which this was done. The officers refer to "orders from the government of Efraín Ríos Montt...to protect the population." If the peasants refuse to organize civilian patrols, they are threatened with "destruction of the village at one fell swoop"; if they persist in refusing, the officers burn down the houses in which there are young children.

The forced displacement of entire populations involves the construction by the army of "model villages" copied from the strategic hamlets of the Vietnam War.

In October 1982, for example, 5,000 peasants from 15 villages in the Department of Chimaltenango, which had been destroyed by army attacks, fled to the mountains. They have been concentrated under the control of the army in the zone of Chuatalum, in San Martín Silotipeque, where a "model village" has been set up. Some have died. As access to the zone is forbidden, one cannot be definite about numbers.

The reign of terror imposes the forced migration of populations, on a massive scale. It is impossible to furnish precise figures. There is no census; but such Guatemalan human rights organizations as the Guatemalan Human Rights Commission, the Episcopate, etc., estimate that one million people have been displaced, of whom 200,000 have taken refuge in foreign countries, particularly Mexico.

8. The Armed Forces, the Paralegal Forces, and the Creation of the Dehumanized Man

The Armed and Security Forces have developed immensely, exercising an influence that surpasses the area of military action. This process has occurred on two levels. Collectively, the army has begun to engage in economic activities, such as the creation of a munitions factory and participation in creating a cement factory, the establishment of its own bank and the so-called "parking tower" in the capital. In the generation of ideology, it broadcasts on TV Channel 5 and has a project to create a military university. Individually, officers of higher rank have been incorporated into factions of the ruling groups, whose social interests come to be reflected in their social behavior.

In addition, militarization is reflected in the decisive influence exercised by the military over the political life of the country: determining electoral processes and controlling, by means of political forces that have no life of their own, the very government of the country. This militarization of both political society and civil society explains the continual use of terror as a state policy, for which army and police units are directly utilized, or groups that appear to be "paramilitary" but in reality are dependent on the army.

This also explains the absence of any real democratic life or alternatives, which has characterized the political system of Guatemala to date.

Military behavior can be partially explained by officer training techniques and the peculiar process of socialization that tends to separate officers from the rest of society, beginning in adolescence. This even includes living in their own exclusive neighborhoods, such as the "military colony" of "Santa Rosita" in Guatemala City, as well as developing in them habits of cruelty and insensitivity to human suffering.

The Tribunal also finds itself facing the development of another phenomenon: the training of whole armies so that they rape, assassinate, torture, and mutilate women, men, children, and elderly people of the civilian population in a deliberate way. These acts are carried out publicly, without any secrecy whatsoever, and with the victims shown off openly, in order to terrorize the civilian population and thus prevent them from organizing themselves politically or economically. We first encountered this phenomenon in the Tribunal on El Salvador. Since then, we have asked ourselves: how can a government succeed in getting peasants to put on uniforms (as happens in the armies of El Salvador and Guatemala) so that they commit such acts against other, non-uniformed peasants? In fact, we have sufficient proof that these atrocities are carried out by soldiers of peasant origin, not only in their own towns and villages, but also against their own relatives.

How can a policy like this be implemented on such a huge scale, involving tens of thousands of people in the Guatemalan police and army?

There exists a constant process of brutalization and aliena-
tion that begins when soldiers are recruited and continues
systematically throughout their entire training. A typical example that we have been given is as follows: a young peasant 17 years
of age, doing his military service, has shoes and good clothing
for the first time in his life. What follows is somewhat strange:
he is locked up in jail for two days. Later, together with 60 fellow
soldiers, he is transferred and beaten hard on a frequent, regular
basis. The beatings continue throughout the first phase of their
training, accompanied by constant insults and invective regarding their origins (particularly if they are Indians), their families,
their villages, all aspects of civilian life. It is as if they are totally
destroyed in order to be reborn as Guatemalan soldiers.

In the words of one of our informants[verbal testimony—Eds.],
an ex-sergeant major: "Every day they would say the same thing to
us, how a soldier must defend his country, how powerful and
respected he is. And the training was to beat us until we bled.
This practice leaves you ready to kill your own *compañeros*. A certain
Lt. Morales disliked the Indians and our customs. He demanded
that we trade in our relatives for machine-guns and our girlfriends
for prostitutes. He taught us how to rape women. When he asked
it, we would grab women and take them to him, and after he raped
them he would turn them over to the soldiers. In this way I came
to be first a soldier, later a corporal, and then a sergeant. They
promoted me because I had the courage to beat my own *compañeros*
and I had the stomach to watch anything that was done."

Moreover, there are proven cases of threats of, gestures
towards, and the actual practice of cannibalism, especially among
lieutenants and captains, to set an example to their troops and
to provoke terror in the civilian population. A lieutenant
announced in the public plaza that for him "blood is sweet";
another officer yanked out the heart from the warm body of one
of the people massacred at San Francisco and put it in his mouth;
a captain or lieutenant in Todos Santos, Huehuetenango, ate the
raw liver of a man who had been judged subversive. Cannibalism
is a practice for which soldiers and officers are trained at the
military bases, using the blood of the kidnapped.

All of these barbarous acts obviously generate hatred and violence. It is through these methods that the Guatemalan army is capable of transforming thousands of Indian peasants into brainwashed instruments, tools of terror ready to carry out any atrocity, completely subordinated to their officers, completely disconnected from their people, even from their families, literally an army of psychopaths and dehumanized, brutalized zombies, until they are totally unable to live as civilians among civilians, even to reunite with their groups and ethnic communities.

9. Ethnocide and Genocide

The reduction of the Indian to the category of subhuman is referred to, for example, in frequent expressions by officers of middle and high rank who proclaim they will exterminate whole populations that, according to them, support the guerrillas, until "we do not leave a single seed."

The idea that guilt and crime are transmitted biologically underlies the leveling of entire villages—to the extreme of killing small children too young to reason. It is as if they were part of an infected fabric, a cancer or some kind of bad weed that must be eradicated.

A perfectly documented example of the leveling of a whole population unit at the base level (village or farm, or a combination of both) is the massacre at San Francisco. The survivors have been interviewed separately on different dates by different people; their stories always coincide. It cannot be an invention, fabricated by an international conspiracy. The informants are immediate eyewitnesses of the massacre, who survived only because three of them escaped while the soldiers were killing the men and setting fire to the building. The smoke and the heat facilitated their escape without being seen when they jumped out a window. There was one other survivor, who was not wounded by the soldiers' last grenades. He threw himself to the ground, and as it was night, the soldiers thought he was dead. The intention of the soldiers and officials was to exterminate the entire village.

During the period of Ríos Montt we can mention other similar cases at different times and in different parts of the country. For example, in April before Holy Week, La Unión, Ixcán, 390 murders; June 14, in Pambach, San Cristóbal, Alta Verapaz, 96 murders; July 18, in Plan de Sánchez, Rabinal, Baja Verapaz, 200 to 250 murders; September 13, in Agua Fría, Uspantán, Quiché, about 350 murders; September 26 in Las Rosas and Chijocón, San Martín Jilotepeque, Chimaltenango, about 275 murders.

The villages or cantons, that is, the social units at the lowest level of organization except for the home, are ethnic microgroups which enjoy their own identity as such. They are distinct from— although not opposed to—the larger identity of the township, of the linguistic area, and of the indigenous sector in general. In this way, for example, an inhabitant of the village of Paxjut has a cultural identity that links him to his village, to the township of Rabinal, and more broadly to the group that speaks the language Achí and to the indigenous people in general.

Therefore, to eliminate an ethnic microgroup with the intention of totally destroying it, including the very small children, is an action that has not only political motives but also racist motives. It is believed that crime is biologically transmittable. We are talking about genocide in the strict sense of the word.

III. THE ECONOMIC, POLITICAL, AND SOCIAL CONTEXT

All the facts gathered by the Tribunal cannot be correctly interpreted unless they are seen in a more global context, which integrates the elements of the economic, social, political, and cultural structure of Guatemalan society, and addresses the fundamental motives for the kinds of behavior that have been described here.

1. Main Charactcristics of the Coup d'état of 1954

The coup d'état of 1954 completely changed the orientation of Guatemalan society. The principal actor was the government of the United States, and particularly the CIA, as has been documented in recent studies. The military coup, defending the interests of big U.S. corporations, and supported by the

Guatemalan landowners, resulted in the permanent exclusion of the masses from political power and the loss of any popular consensus. A veritable state of war was established, expressed in the organization of a strategy of counterinsurgency whose genesis and roots are found in the existing socioeconomic structures and in the phenomena of international domination.

2. Regional Differences of the Economic System and Social Heterogeneity: Its Progressive Hierarchization

The predominance of agriculture in the economy (70% of the active labor force works in the agricultural sector, 12.5% in the industrial sector, and 17.5% in the service sector), together with the importance attained by the petroleum industry, result in the fact that land ownership continues to be a decisive factor in the social structure.

Inequality in the productive value of the soil has led to different forms of land appropriation. This historical-colonial phenomenon has been maintained, and is even accentuated today by technological development. This explains the concentration of land in the hands of large agricultural enterprises (for instance, in 1979, 2.6% of the agricultural proprietors had more than 45 hectares each and used more than 65.1% of the cultivated land), and also the increase in the number of *minifundios*—small farms— under the pressure of fast population growth (an annual rate of 2.82%). In 1950, there were 74,300 farms of less than .7 hectares; in 1979 there were 166,700, while 88.1% of the landowners occupied 16.1% of the land. In addition, there were 174,900 peasants without land in 1970.

This differential appropriation of the land and the difficulties of communication in a country with very rough terrain have created a society where one region is strongly separated from another. At present this social segmentation tends to be reduced on the one hand because of the economic mobility of the agrarian bourgeoisie, and on the other hand by the geographic mobility imposed on the rural labor force, and particularly on the indigenous groups because of economic conditions.

We can observe two kinds of regions:

a) *The Regions of an Expanding Capitalist Economy.*

The South Coast has large agricultural enterprises whose products are oriented toward export (cotton, sugar, citrus). These are owned by a modern bourgeoisie. The labor force is made up of resident ladino workers and unattached temporary workers.

The North Coast is the region of banana enterprises, with foreign capital directed by local intermediaries. They are a point of attraction for peasants without land.

The High North is a region of high plains, which the local bourgeoisie converted into a cattle zone for the export of meat, and from which foreign companies extract oil. Large numbers of ladino and indigenous peasants are coming to this zone.

The East, with an exclusively ladino population, is the region of medium-sized enterprises belonging to rich peasants who seek to concentrate ownership by expelling the small peasants.

b) *The Economically and Socially Traditional Regions.*

La Boca is the region of coffee plantations owned by an oligarchy whose labor force consists of a nucleus of permanent wage workers (ladinos) and temporary indigenous workers.

The Altiplano (High Plateau) and the Low North, both mountainous regions, are totally Indian. Because of demographic growth, the population is forced to emigrate either temporarily or permanently. The Low North was formerly characterized by the alternating presence of large farms of the *colonos* and small farms of the Indian communities. The possibility of oil and nickel production here has practically expelled the indigenous population.

Because of its slow development, industry cannot absorb the surplus of rural labor. This is the reason why, in 1979, 20% of the available labor force was unemployed and subcontracting reached 54%. In the final analysis, it is necessary to examine the growing foreign dependency, which will be dealt with later.

From the social standpoint, rural society continues to be a dual society: an agrarian bourgeoisie, which is often industrial as well, in opposition to a wage labor force largely composed of temporary indigenous workers. The bourgeoisie is not homogeneous. There exists the coffee oligarchy, the modern bourgeoisie of agribusiness, and the rich peasantry. Within the peasant class, the ethnic factor is not only an aspect of social status but has consequences that affect how the class is employed and how stable it is.

3. Economic Domination

After the intervention of 1954, the permanent alliance of the United States with those sectors of the dominant classes willing to accept subordination facilitated an increased penetration of foreign capital in the Guatemalan economy. This phenomenon constitutes a determinant factor in structural dependency and the growing insertion of Guatemala into the sphere of North American domination.

In the 1960s a process of change began in the composition of foreign investment, which had traditionally been in the banana sector, transportation, and communications. The new investments, primarily North American, were directed toward industries linked to the Central American Common Market as the key element in the developmentalist strategy put forward by the United States. Beginning in the 1970s, monopoly interests became oriented toward tourism and such strategic products as nickel ($250 million) and oil ($300 million). In 1980, private North American investment controlled 34 of the 40 most important enterprises in the country.

We should also point out the significant role played during these last years by big finance capital. In June 1981, the assets of the eight major U.S. banks in Guatemala reached $331.9 million. As the movement of business, of currency in circulation, was stimulated, the margin of profit also increased.

The dependency of Guatemala's economy on foreign capital is reflected in the foreign debt, which was more than $45 million in 1961, $130 million in 1971, and $864 million in 1980. This situation has produced an irreversible dynamic of indebtedness to alleviate the permanent disequilibrium in the balance of payments (-$50.3 million in 1979, -$322.1 million in 1980, and -$336 million in 1981). For this reason, the bilateral or multilateral programs that allow an increase in the flow of capital become very important.

During the period between 1953 and 1979, the United States has provided, through direct financial aid or through international financial institutions, the sum of $1,119 million to Guatemala.

The subjection of the Guatemalan economy to the orientation and objectives of transnational capital, with trade oriented primarily toward the United States, has sharpened the traditional distortions of the economy. Some enterprises, because they employ a relatively small labor force and evade tax and duty payments, provide very few benefits to the country (as is the case of the nickel and oil industries).

The consequences of the international capitalist crisis, and the impossibility of maintaining a climate of security for foreign capital through counterinsurgency, have led recently to a decrease in foreign investment. Since September 1980, EXMIBAL (nickel) has cut back its activities, and about 100 businesses linked to tourism have closed down.

Economic dependency has sharpened the antagonisms within Guatemalan society to an extreme degree, and at the same time has strengthened the will of foreign investors to defend their interests at any price. In this sense, dependency constitutes one of the major barriers to any structural change in the country's economy.

4. Religious and Cultural Conflict

The economic and political relations of domination tend to spill over onto the cultural and religious terrain. The dominant sectors of Guatemalan society have not been able to consolidate a national identity. Instead they have developed a culture which is a reflection, a series of imitations of the various hegemonic centers, from Spain to the United States, that have controlled the country politically and economically since the Conquest.

It is from the standpoint of this dependent culture that the dominant sectors attempt to impose their hegemony over the popular sectors, and particularly over the Indians, through a major effort at cultural destruction. At the same time, they deny those sectors access to the fruits of so-called Western culture when these do not serve the goals of domination.

Ideological domination begins through the myth of Spanish

superiority and through the Catholic religion, considered as the fundamental sign of this superiority: the fraudulent notion of a submission presumably decided by God has been imposed upon the indigenous people. However, the indigenous population has never forgotten that preserving its culture is essential to preserving its identity. In the face of the dominant groups, indigenous defense of ethnic specificity becomes a subversive element and contains ideological elements that lay the basis for transformation of the social system.

In recent years the cultural and religious dialectic has intensified greatly. On one hand, the process of cultural destruction has reached gigantic dimensions, and has been translated into a policy of literal annihilation. On the other hand, the defense of cultural identity has become central to the struggle for liberation, and the Christian faith itself has come to play a positive role in transforming the consciousness of the people.

Today, President Ríos Montt is trying to manipulate the Protestant churches to legitimate his government and even to convert it into a virtual theocracy. He has said of himself that he governs "not by vote, nor by arms, but by the will of God." Some fundamentalist sects (in contradiction with the majority of evangelicals) have come to see the coup d'état and the government as a miracle of God and the defeat of Satan.

However, in the 1960s a process of transformation characterized by a clear identification with the oppressed of the country began in ever-broadening sectors of the Catholic Church and the Protestant churches. That is how the Peasant Unity Committee (CUC), the Coordinating Committee of Settlers [i.e., Squatters— Eds.] (CDP), the Robin García Student Front (University and Secondary, FERG-U and FERG-S), the Guatemalan Committee for Justice and Peace, and the Guatemalan Church in Exile came to exist. Particularly deserving attention is the emergence of the "revolutionary Christians," who take their name from D. Vicente Menchú, an indigenous religious teacher from Quiché who was murdered in the massacre at the Spanish embassy. This massacre symbolized a blood marriage between workers and peasants, Indians and ladinos, believers and nonbelievers, and it gave new life to the popular revolutionary struggle.

In this struggle, the Christian faith, which had been used as a means of repression against the Mayan cultural identity, has become a stimulus to defend it. This has provoked brutal repression against so many lay Christians, priests, pastors, and even bishops.

5. Guatemala in the Central American Geopolitical Region

a) Today, the countries of Central America, and Guatemala in particular, continue providing raw materials and benefits to U.S. corporations. Their geopolitical strategy has acquired a particular importance. Guatemala is the key country for U.S. control of the entire Caribbean area, including the northern part of South America. The government of the United States believes that a democratic revolution in Guatemala would be the fall of a "domino" that would provoke very profound change in the entire region.

b) The U.S. government subordinates the sovereignty of all the governments of Central America, and the government of Guatemala in particular, to its policies of global confrontation with the Soviet Union. It is essential, in this sense, that the regimes of this area can be mobilized to support U.S. positions unconditionally in international forums.

c) Guatemala has served the geopolitical interests of the United States in a variety of ways:

The military coup of 1954, supported and directed by the United States, has served as a model and reference point to stifle future revolutions in Latin America. This was evident in the Bay of Pigs invasion of Cuba in 1961, according to Richard Immerman. In his book *U.S. Intervention in Guatemala* (quoting secret and confidential information from the U.S. government), Immerman points out that many agents of the CIA who had actively intervened in the military coup in Guatemala in 1954 also participated in organizing the Bay of Pigs invasion.

Guatemala has also served as a point of support for North American interventions in the Caribbean and Central American area. In the most recent period, the regimes of Lucas García and

Ríos Montt have offered sanctuary and support to the Somocista terrorists who are attempting to overthrow the Sandinista government.

Finally, the Guatemalan military regimes, together with that of Somoza, were the major instruments in the creation of the regional military organization CONDECA, established by the United States to act as a "regional police force" against local revolutions, without the need to send American troops directly. After the Nicaraguan Revolution, CONDECA was superseded by the strategy of the "Iron Triangle," which coordinates the armed forces of Guatemala, Honduras, and El Salvador in its repression against popular movements and its attempt to overthrow the Sandinista government of Nicaragua.

It must also be remembered that at the end of the 1960s the government of the United States chose Guatemala as its laboratory to test techniques of conterrrevolutionary repression. These techniques and methods were later applied to other regions of Latin America.

d) Other states are also intervening in Guatemala, with even more force, since the 1977 suspension of military aid from the United States. We are in particular talking about Israel, which from that date has assumed the role of principal arms supplier to the army. It provided, among other things, ARAVA airplanes, REY-MK armored vehicles, 81 mm. mortars, bazookas, grenade launchers, "Galil" rifles, and tons of munitions. Israel also provided training for the air force and contributed to the training of the police.

The governments of Chile and Argentina have also collaborated in training the army and the police in counterinsurgency methods, thus establishing a new dimension, the Latin American dimension, in the Guatemalan situation.

6. Socioeconomic Consequences

An economic, social, political, and cultural structure of the type described above entails a variety of consequences.

Sudden Social Transformation and a New Configuration of Social Opposition.

One of the main characteristics of this process is the dissolution of the traditional peasantry without the emergence of a new
social structure that could open the way to cultural and economic
development. The mechanisms of this process are varied: displacement of rural populations, primarily of Indian origin, through
economic expropriation, political terror, or the establishment of
"strategic hamlets"; the emigration of workers, which transforms
hundreds of thousands of peasants into agricultural workers with
barely sufficient means to survive; the growth of marginal groups
in the economic system, which swell the ranks of the urban
"squatters."

On the other hand, the dominant groups are being rapidly
transformed, and the contradictions which exist among them are
a fundamental cause of their inability to establish authentic power.
These contradictions also lead them to unite with the army to
ensure their economic interests, in turn sacrificing to a certain
extent their political interests. The military hierarchy also uses
its power in the political arena to become the protagonist of the
economy, taking over land, primarily plantations.

*The Growing Impoverishment of the Peasant and Working-Class
Population.*

This political and economic situation generates the growing
impoverishment of the peasant and working-class groups (70%
of the population has an annual income of $42), whose most vital
necessities of subsistence, health care, and education are not being
met.

Infant mortality (88.8 per 1,000 babies under one year old);
malnutrition (75% of the children under 5 years old); illiteracy
(60% of the population over 7 years old and 82% of the rural
population); endemic diseases, aggravated by the lack of potable
water and sanitation systems in almost 60% of the houses, are
constantly increasing among the poor classes and reaching alarm-
ing proportions.

Expropriation of the Wealth of the Country.

It must be emphasized that Guatemala has suffered a veritable
expropriation of its natural resources. Mining and oil production

are in the hands of foreign companies. Moreover, agro-industrial production is oriented essentially toward exports, while the population suffers from hunger and malnutrition.

Establishment of a Totalitarian State.

The permanent political crisis existing since the overthrow of democracy in 1954 has become manifest in the use of military force and the illegitimate character of the country's political leadership. The coup d'état of March 1982 simply added one more episode to this history.

The army has become increasingly indistinguishable from the state apparatus, leading to an intense military occupation of the countryside and consequently ever more massive massacres of the peasants. The well-known doctrine of national security has constituted the ideological basis of the state, but in 1982 a new aspect appeared: the use of religion as an ideological factor. Its function is, on the one hand, to legitimate military action by identifying the internal enemy with Absolute Evil; and on the other hand, to improve the image of the government abroad, giving it the appearance of respectability, honesty, and a spirit of anti-communist crusade.

Special Repression of the Indigenous Population.

The Indian population has been the object of a particularly cruel policy of repression, as part of the economic program. In effect this program demands, by its own logic, not only the dissolution of precapitalist social formations in order to facilitate the establishment of a labor market adequate to the development of agrarian capitalism, but also the prevention of any sociocultural form of popular resistance. This explains in part the brutality of the repression against the indigenous population.

It must be added that contempt for Indians, who are almost not considered human beings, is today being revived among the repressive forces, thus legitimating the brutality and the killings. For a century the coffee oligarchy built its profits not upon liberal ideology but upon an anti-indigenous ideology that facilitated racist exploitation and denied the natural inhabitants of the land their conditions of citizenship, thus reinstating colonial practices in all institutions of civil society. Destroying the Indians in their ethnic identity becomes an objective in the service of economic interests.

7. Popular Resistance

Faced with this situation of blatant injustice, popular resistance developed progressively. While in the 1960s the groups of organized resistance were composed of people from the middle class and the urban working class, today they are rooted in the rural areas, with strong social bases in the peasant or indigenous population, flowing from the new modalities of their economic exploitation and cultural destruction.

The four principal movements of armed struggle, coordinated in the Guatemalan National Revolutionary Unity (URNG), are: the Guerrilla Army of the Poor (Ejército Guerrillero de los Pobres, EGP), the Rebel Armed Forces (Fuerzas Armadas Rebeldes, FAR), the Organization of the People in Arms (Organización del Pueblo en Armas, ORPA), and the Guatemalan Labor Party (Partido Guatemalteco del Trabajo, PGT). In the respective regions where they have a base, these movements—each with its own characteristics—bring together peasants, intellectuals, workers, Indians, ladinos, Christians, and non-Christians. They give continuity to the social struggle, above all through labor union organizations, workers' parties and the new prospect of broadened peasant bases. In certain aspects, their development resembles the movements of resistance against the Nazis in Europe during the Second World War.

In addition, the broad front formed by the Guatemalan Committee of Patriotic Unity (CGUP) organizes broad sectors of political parties opposed to the totalitarianism of the regime, and cultural, humanitarian, and religious organizations. The Guatemalan Human Rights Commission and the Committee for Justice and Peace must also be added.

However, in Guatemala the resistance has fundamental cultural aspects because of the indigenous populations. For several centuries these populations mainly developed a passive, cultural resistance. Today this resistance manifests itself in a growing level of organization that is developing more fully through the local communities.

On the other hand, the pastoral decentralization begun by the Catholic Church with the development of the base communities, the increase in the number of religious teachers and Delegates of the Word, and a more intense utilization of the Bible have caused, along with the development of political consciousness, the opening up of religious conscience to social dimensions. This same dynamic can be seen in several Protestant churches.

We are dealing with a conflict between, on the one hand, a military power that guarantees the interests of a local minority and some foreign enterprises, and on the other hand, various components of a people denied their elemental rights. It is not a case of confrontation between the extreme right and the extreme left with the army as the arbiter—much less a conflict between East and West, as it is usually presented.

IV. THE LAW

1. The Illegitimacy of the Regime and the Government of Guatemala

Considering the proven facts of the second part of this judgment and specifically those relative to institutionalized repression in the Guatemalan state, the political regime in this country since 1954, including the present government of General Ríos Montt, is illegitimate according to the judicial principles that inspire all democratic states and according to the norms of international penal law.

With Relationship to the Principles of Democratic States.

a) Although the Constitution of Guatemala of September 15, 1965 was still in effect up to March 22, 1982, the political practice of those in power has established a regime whose functioning has necessarily entailed the violation of the principles of democratic representation, the separation of powers, and the guarantee of and respect for the fundamental rights of man.

b) Since the coup d'état of March 23, 1982, and the annulment of the Constitution, the basic legislation of the Ríos Montt government has been in direct contradiction to the very notion of the democratic state. Decree-Law 24-82, which contains the Fundamental Statute of Government, Decree-Law 46-82, which established the Law of Tribunals of Special Jurisdiction and Decree-Law 45-82, which established the State of Siege, all presuppose:

— Negation of the principle of democratic representation and the free exercise of political rights, by the suppression of political parties and the annulment of electoral legislation (Article 112 D.24-82).

— Violation of the principle of separation of powers, with the army assuming both legislative and executive functions, the appointment and removal of the president of the Judicial Court or Institutions and Supreme Court of Justice, of all the magistrates of the other collegiate tribunals, and of the attorney general of the nation; as well as "the exercise of any public function or attribution not established in the Statute of Government or in the legislation in effect in the nation" (Articles 4-26-108 of D.24-82).

— Violation of the principles of independence and of the permanent tenure of judicial power, of the principle of penal law and of minimum guarantees of due process (the phases of indictment, decision, and appeal) in the penal process (Articles 3, 4, 5, 8, 33, 37, and 39 D.46/82).

— The permanent State of Siege, which remains in effect up to this time.

According to General International Law.
a) Implementation of the counterinsurgency plan, as central to the internal policies of the regime and the present Ríos Montt government, generates institutionalized violation of the norms of international law, and the perpetration of acts that qualify as international crimes.

At the same time, "It has created an endemic climate of total alarm, and even terror, that has subverted the state of law and in practice has compromised the majority of the rights established in the American Convention on the Rights of Man" (report from the Organization of American States, October 14, 1981, transmitted to the Commission on Human Rights of the United Nations, Document E/CN.4/1501).

b) The decomposition and dysfunction of the institutions that make up the state render the government in power incapable of ensuring the fulfillment of international commitments or guaranteeing the stability of civil society, which are minimum conditions for effectiveness required under international law. Symptoms of this situation are the assault on the Spanish embassy on January 31, 1980 by the security forces of the state itself; the growth of the repressive apparatus, including the official acknowledgment that "adequate conditions of security do not exist" in order to receive the representative of the Secretary General of the United Nations or the International Commission on Human Rights of the Organization of American States (letters from the Permanent Representative of Guatemala in the United Nations to the Secretary General and to the Commission on Human Rights of the U.N., Official Documents E/CN.4/1438).

As a result, the regime of Guatemala and the government of General Ríos Montt not only fail to fulfill the prerequisites of a state of formal democracy; they also place themselves outside all legality and in clear contradiction to the prevailing norms of General International Law. In this situation, it can be affirmed that, according to General International Law, the people of Guatemala have a right to insurrection.

2. Internal Armed Struggle

a) The struggle in which the armed forces of Guatemala confront the organizations that make up the Guatemalan National Revolutionary Unity (URNG) constitutes an internal armed conflict, according to Article 1 of the 1977 Additional Protocol II of the Geneva Accords of August 12, 1949, whose norms are applicable. Consequently, the government of Guatemala is obliged to comply with those resolutions which:

— Prohibit assassination, torture, collective punishment, the taking of hostages, and terrorist acts (Article 4).

—Establish the protection of civilian populations, who cannot be the object of attacks, and prohibit all acts or threats of violence whose principal goal is to spread terror among the civilian population, as well as orders to displace those populations (Articles 13 and 17).

—Ensure the protection of prisoners of war, particularly their right not to be condemned without due process in an impartial and independent tribunal.

b) To the degree that the regime and the government of Guatemala are organized around the serious and systematic violation of the fundamental human rights of the people of Guatemala, it is possible to state (according to a progressive evaluation of International Law) that this situation constitutes a violation of the Right to Self-Determination of the Peoples.

According to Resolution 2625 (XXV) of the General Assembly, this means that:

—The diverse forms of resistance of the people of Guatemala, including the armed struggle of the guerrilla organizations that represent the people, are legitimate; and that

—The use of armed force by the army and security bodies of Guatemala is illegitimate to the degree that these entities deprive the people of their right to self-determination, freedom, and independence.

c) Given the very real involvement of the URNG in the armed struggle in Guatemala, as indicated in Sections 1 and 2 above, it would be possible under International Law to recognize it formally as a belligerent party.

3. The Violation of Human Rights

a) The facts proven in Part II of this Judgment constitute a violation of fundamental human rights recognized and guaranteed by the international judicial or legal order (general and conventional) and specifically by the Charter of the United Nations, the Charter of the Organization of American States, the Universal Declaration of Human Rights of the United Nations, the American Declaration of the Rights and Duties of Man, the American

Convention on Human Rights, the Equal Remuneration Convention, Convention No. 87 of the International Labor Organization on Freedom of Association and Protection of the Right to Organize, ILO Convention No. 98, on the Right to Organize and Collective Bargaining, and the Convention on the Political Rights of Women, all of these documents accepted or ratified by Guatemala.

b) These violations of fundamental human rights are characterized as "serious" because they affect such fundamental rights as the right to life, physical and moral integrity, and judicial security; they are "systematic" because they correspond to concrete plans or policies of repressive action directed against specific rights of the population; they are "massive" because they harm a very large number of Guatemalans and extensive sectors of the population, such as the indigenous peasants; they are "structural" because criminal action or complicity extends to the main institutions of the state of Guatemala as a whole.

These features characterize a situation that can be regarded as an "international crime" of the violation of fundamental human rights in the terms of Article 19 of the project to elaborate draft Articles on the International Responsibility of States, which is an expression of general principles incorporated into contemporary international law and such other international legal instruments as the International Convention concerning the crime of "apartheid" and the resolutions of the General Assembly of the United Nations regarding torture.

c) As a whole, and to the degree that such violations of fundamental human rights are barriers to the right of self-determination of the Guatemalan people, they also constitute an international crime in violation of the governing norm of the rights of the peoples to self-determination, which imposes on states the duty of respecting that right (in this regard, see Article 1 (2) of the Charter of the United Nations, Resolution 15,14 (XV) of 14-12-60; Resolution 2625 (XXV), Article 1 of the International Treaties of Human Rights, Resolution 22-20 (XXI); and Article 19 of the project of Articles cited above).

d) Furthermore, the consistent facts concerning the indiscriminate, collective killings of indigenous peasants, including women, elderly people, and children, and the form in which those actions have taken place, are evidence of the government's intention to destroy in whole or in part the Indian population of Guatemala. These are acts categorized as the crime of genocide, in accordance with Article 2 of the Convention on the Prevention and Punishment of the Crime of Genocide of 1948 (ratified by Guatemala), which states that genocide is to be understood as "acts perpetrated with the intention of totally or partially destroying a national, ethnic, racial, or religious group as such," and which consists of:

— killings of members of the group;

— grave injury to the physical or mental integrity of members of the group;

— the intentional subjection of the group to conditions of existence that could lead to their partial or total physical destruction;

— measures destined to prevent births within the group;

— displacement by force of children from the group to another group.

e) Similarly, within the framework of the progressive development of international law and according to the norms of the Statute of the Nuremburg Tribunal, of the Draft Code of Crimes Against Peace and the Security of Humanity, the violations of human rights perpetrated in Guatemala are to be characterized as crimes against humanity. They constitute "inhuman acts such as murder, extermination, deportation or persecution against any civilian population for any political, racial, religious or cultural motives, perpetrated by the authorities of the state or by individuals who act at the instigation of those authorities or with their permission" (Article 2, Project 11, Article DOC. A/36/535 U.N.).

f) Similarly, from an examination of the facts presented to this Tribunal, one sees a permanent violation of the economic rights of the great majority of the people of Guatemala, and particularly their right to development, in opposition to the American Convention on Human Rights ratified by Guatemala and also Articles 55 and 56 of the Charter of the United Nations, according to which states have the obligation to provide higher standards of living, permanent jobs for everyone, and conditions of progress and social development. As guarantees to make these rights effective, various resolutions of the United Nations and specifically Resolution 1803 (XVII) and the charter of the Rights and Economic Duties of the States enshrine the right to the people's permanent sovereignty over their country's wealth and resources. The exercise of this right is in great measure relegated by the government of Guatemala to the benefit of foreign economic interests.

4. International Responsibility

a) *International Responsibility of the State of Guatemala.*

The acts which constitute the violations of human rights summarized in Part III of this Judgment are attributable to the state of Guatemala, insofar as they have been carried out by organs of the state of Guatemala or by persons who in fact act on its behalf. This falls under the principles of General International Law as gathered in Articles 5 to 10 of the previously cited project to elaborate draft Articles on the International Responsibility of States. Consequently, the state of Guatemala, specifically the government of Ríos Montt, is responsible:

— For the violation of its obligations contracted in international agreements regarding human rights ratified by that state. That responsibility can be exacted by the other states which are party to such agreements.

— For the perpetration of international crimes against the people's fundamental rights and against their right of self-determination. That responsibility to the world community as a whole can be asserted by any state of the international community.

— For the commission of the crime of genocide, being responsible in terms established by the convention on the prevention and punishment of this crime.

— For the violation of humanitarian rights in time of war, in the terms indicated in the 1977 Additional Protocol II of the

Geneva Accords of August 12, 1949 (cited).

As a consequence, the state of Guatemala and the government in particular have the obligation:

— To re-establish a constitutional regime of public freedoms and respect for fundamental civil, political, economic, social, and cultural rights under the domestic judicial order.

— To fully realize, in the domestic judicial order, the norms contained in the treaties which it has signed, particularly those regarding human rights.

— To respect the right of the people of Guatemala to freely choose their own political, economic, and social system, and to seek their own road to development.

— To punish all individuals responsible for the illicit deeds, according to adequate domestic penal legislation;

— To provide reparations, on a case by case basis, in accordance with relevant legislation, for the damages which have been done illicitly, in violation of fundamental human rights, to persons under its jurisdiction.

b) *Responsibility of Individuals*

The members of the government, of the army, of the organs of state security, as well as of paramilitary organization which act on behalf of the public powers, are personally responsible for the crime of genocide and for crimes against humanity, to the degree to which they have participated directly or indirectly in committing acts that violate the fundamental human rights described above (III, 2, 3, 4, 5).

This means, in accordance with the Convention on the Prevention and Punishment of the Crime of Genocide and the Convention on War Crimes and Crimes Against Humanity of November 26, 1968, and Resolution 3074 (XXVIII) of the General Assembly regarding the Principles of International Cooperation in the Identification, Detention, Extradition, and Punishment of Those Guilty of War Crimes and Crimes Against Humanity:

— The obligation of states, and particularly of the state of Guatemala, to ensure, through domestic jurisdiction, the incarceration and punishment of those who are guilty.

—The unconditional character of the crime.

—The obligation of states not to refuse requests for extradition of the guilty parties by affirming the political character of the crime; and in addition not to give them political asylum.

c) *International Responsibility of Third States.*

The events taking place in Guatemala permit us to affirm that third-party states are accomplices to the "international crimes" perpetrated by the state of Guatemala.

This complicity, according to Article 27 of the project to elaborate draft Articles on State Responsibility (cited previously), can be established by the following facts:

—The sale of arms to the state of Guatemala, which are destined to be used in carrying out repressive actions that constitute crime, the principal provider being the state of Israel.

—The training of Guatemalan personnel in order to increase their repressive capacities. This activity is carried out by the United States of America and by the states of Argentina and Chile.

—Economic aid given to the state of Guatemala without the condition that it may not be used for acquiring the means of repression or reinforcing those already in existence. Recent economic aid from the United States to the Guatemalan regime can be viewed within this framework.

Similarly, the intervention of the United States in the internal affairs of Guatemala, to the extent that it contributes to the consolidation of the regime, determines U.S. responsibility for maintaining a situation in which the international crimes described above have been perpetrated.

Third States consequently have the obligation:

—To halt the flow of any aid that may serve to reinforce the mechanisms of illicit repression by the state of Guatemala; and also to refrain from giving such aid in the future.

—To answer, when the occasion arises, to the legitimate government of Guatemala for the damages that their illicit acts may have caused to the people or the citizens of that country.

—To refrain from any act of direct or indirect intervention in Guatemala.

V. THE RIGHTS OF THE PEOPLE—
THE STRUGGLE FOR LIBERATION AND PEACE

The situation in Guatemala irrefutably presents an armed conflict in which the opposing parties are, on the one hand, a limited fraction of the country that has taken over the state apparatus, militarized it completely, and, thanks to massive foreign aid, transformed it into a powerful machine of destruction; and on the other hand, the Guatemalan people in their diverse components, ethnic groups, and social strata.

This situation has the character of a local war, which, like almost all local conflicts in the postwar period, is linked to the systematic denial of the right of peoples to create their own history and find the difficult road of self-affirmation as subjects of the international community.

It has been observed that the matrix of these local wars leads fatally to a contradiction with the provisions of the laws of war: in effect, when a war takes place with the object of denying a people the right to self-determination, the logic of this objective causes its identification with the destruction of the people, thus transforming the conflict into a criminal war.

Examination of the case of Guatemala confirms all the points of this proposition. Not only are the armed forces of General Ríos Montt and all his predecessors seen as responsible in a continuous manner for a whole series of violations of the international conventions and protocols regarding the laws of war; in addition they have progressively engaged in genocidal conduct.

It may appear then as contradictory, if not absurd, to invoke the Geneva Accords and to claim Belligerent Status on behalf of the organizations of the resistance and the insurrection of the Guatemalan people. Because the right to wage a just war presupposes a type of neutrality in the international community towards both parties to the conflict, its goal is to prevent the belligerent parties from inflicting senseless suffering and destruction in relation to the only acknowledged objective: defeating the adversary. However, the international community cannot be permitted to remain neutral in regard to a party that voluntarily places itself outside the constitutive values of that community, committing the crime of genocide, as against the party that suffers the genocide. Further, the international community cannot concede that the adversary of one of the parties in conflict is an entire people and not a government or a state; but it also cannot remain indifferent in the face of the goal of depriving this people of its right to self-determination.

In reality the contradiction that we have just underlined is but the reflection of a deeper contradiction in the present system of international relations, which holds as fundamental values the respect for human beings and for peoples, and the relations among them which should be governed in a peaceful way. In spite of the status of these values in principle, international relations today are still dominated by processes and structures in which only states and the interests they represent have both voice and weight. The true subjects of the international community, the peoples and the individuals who constitute it, do not find in the international sphere either the forces or the means suitable to protect their rights.

The duty of this Tribunal is to denounce that contradiction and to indicate all the ways that exist in the present state of law and international relations to overcome that contradiction, though it be in stages.

To accord Belligerent Status to the organizations of the Guatemalan people is the most immediate of these ways.

This would allow the Guatemalan people to express themselves in the international arena and to denounce in the first person the criminal character and outlaw nature of the government of their country.

This can also contribute to breaking the abstraction by which a people is always and exclusively represented by the state, even when the state is an "alienated state," a simple instrument of domination, subjecting the people to foreign interests and when any homogeneity between the people and the government has become nonexistent.

A similar effort has accompanied the whole movement of decolonization and has strongly contributed to the development of international law and the rights of peoples, rejecting the mystification of the colonial powers which, under the guise of the principle of nonintervention, tried to treat the events that took place within their colonies as their own, internal affairs. The liberation movements have thus been recognized as subjects of international law.

Similarly, where even the smallest shred of homogeneity between government and population has disappeared, one has to confront a state which invokes the principle of nonintervention, with the right of the people to self-determination, and with its character as an expropriated state.

Even more: international law has admitted the total legitimacy of struggles of liberation against colonialism. Thus the recourse to insurrection, far from being in contradiction with the profound aspiration of humanity for peace, must be recognized in those cases where the most elemental rights are abused as the only instrument for affirming the values of peace and humanity to which the international community aspires.

The preamble of the Universal Declaration of Human Rights makes reference to this, and Article 28 of the Universal Declaration of the Rights of the Peoples develops this position:

> Any people whose fundamental rights are gravely ignored has the right to realize these rights, particularly through labor or political struggles, or even, in the last instance, by the use of force.

In this case, as happened before in the struggle against colonial oppression, the struggle for liberation allows the integration of important elements for the defense of human dignity into the patrimony of humanity and these can become a moving force for building peace.

Thus, in the Guatemalan insurrection we see new values emerging that can help humanity to overcome its anguish and the profound causes of conflict and destruction.

For the first time in this part of the world, we see the possibility of overcoming in concrete ways the rupture that occurred four centuries ago with the genocidal destruction of an entire culture, a civilization, and the populations which inhabited this zone of the planet: one of the most heinous crimes that the white man has ever perpetrated. The Guatemalan resistance today is rooted in the indigenous culture, in the values and elements of a new undertaking: this resistance movement is making as its own the demand for the redress of indigenous identity, culture, and needs. To these demands are added other specific ones, those of women, of the marginalized people, of the peasants, in a framework of reciprocal recognition, mutual respect, and harmonious co-existence with the values and necessities of Western man.

In this perspective, the indigenous man escapes the alternatives that industrial civilization has imposed on him—either he becomes integrated, renouncing his own identity, or he is destroyed (and integration frequently corresponds to a subtle and insidious form of destruction). A third way consists of valuing diversity, exalting the dignity of man, respecting his ethnic and cultural specificity, recognizing in this diversity a source of human enrichment and growth, and feeling profoundly that the negation of difference is not only an attack but an amputation of the human dimension of each individual.

From this flows the strength of the Guatemalan resistance. There are also valuable implications for the peoples of all the continents, a lesson for the societies of the "first world," where each day numerous human riches are destroyed in the exorcism of diversity, the homogenization of culture, the negation of that which is different. The Tribunal, faithful to its mission of advancing the construction of an authentic peace among men, has wanted to show at the end of this session that, above the crimes against the people of Guatemala, there is a ray of hope which their struggle gives to mankind.

VI. DISPOSITION

In consequence, the Tribunal

DECLARES that the successive Guatemalan governments since 1954, including the General Ríos Montt regime, are guilty of serious, repeated, and systematic violations of human rights, and thus of infringing the Universal Declaration of Human Rights, and the American Convention on Human Rights;

DECLARES that the successive Guatemalan governments since 1954, including the General Ríos Montt regime, are guilty, due to the totality of those violations, of attacking the inalienable right of the Guatemalan people to political and economic self-determination and the right of that people to exercise sovereignty over its own natural resources, as is established in the United Nations Charter and in numerous resolutions of the General Assembly of the United Nations;

DECLARES that the successive Guatemalan governments since 1954, including the General Ríos Montt regime, are guilty, in the armed conflict against the forces now grouped in the URNG (Guatemalan National Revolutionary Unity) of serious, repeated, and systematic violations of the provisions of the 1949 Geneva Accords, and of the Additional Protocols of 1977, with these violations constituting war crimes;

DECLARES that because of their breadth and extent, the tortures, killings, and forced disappearances of people constitute crimes against humanity in the sense of the Statute of the Nuremburg Tribunal;

DECLARES that the massacres and the terror unleashed against the indigenous peoples with the demonstrated purpose of partially destroying them, constitute genocide in the sense of the 1948 Convention;

DECLARES that the heads of the successive governments in Guatemala since 1954, including General Ríos Montt, are personally responsible for the international crimes specified above, which is not to exclude the responsibility of the other leading members of those governments as well as the principal higher officials and upper functionaries implicated in the above-mentioned crimes;

DECLARES that the authors of these crimes cannot invoke as an excuse the orders they received, except in the case of junior officers who can cite extenuating circumstances;

DECLARES that the government of the United States of America is guilty of the crimes listed above, because of its determinative interference in the affairs of Guatemala, and that the Israeli, Argentine, and Chilean governments are guilty of complicity because of their aid and assistance.

IN CONCLUSION

The Tribunal declares that, in the face of the perpetration of the above-mentioned crimes by the public powers of the Guatemalan government, the Guatemalan people, through their representative organizations, have the right to exercise all forms of resistance, including that of armed force, against tyrannical government powers; and that the use of armed force by the Guatemalan government to repress the resistance is illegitimate.

APPENDIX

The Tribunal's Letter to the Pope

This is the text of the letter sent to the Pope and signed by all 15 members of the Tribunal on Guatemala.

Madrid, January 31, 1983

Your Holiness:

The members of the Permanent People's Tribunal, who met in Madrid in a session on Guatemala, have heard about the dramatic situation of the people of this country, which you plan to visit in a few weeks. We have received countless testimonies about the massacres which have left tens of thousands of victims, above all among the Indian population, since 1954 and at a more rapid rate in recent years. We have also heard about the brutal and despicable manner in which the present military government wields repression.

What has caused the most consternation among the members of the Tribunal is the fact that this atrocious and inhuman violence is committed more and more against the Indian peasant communities. These communities, which are organized in a spirit of mutual solidarity, and are frequently under the leadership of religious teachers, try to confront the extreme poverty that they suffer and to resist the aggressions against them. Entire villages, including women, children, and the elderly, have been exterminated after having been tortured indescribably. It is the very image of man which is being abused in Guatemala. The astonishment and anguish which we have encountered in three days came from mothers who had their children yanked from them, from wives who had seen their husbands die, frequently by torture; from young girls who had been raped; from poor peasants persecuted as if they were predatory animals. Many of these witnesses were Christians, imbued with values from the Gospel, and some of them were connected to the activities of the Church. The Tribunal was also informed of the relentless exploitation of the people of Guatemala.

With complete trust in the spirit which inspires your Holiness in your visit to the martyred people of Guatemala, the members of the Tribunal wish to send you the text of the Judgment we have pronounced, with our greatest respect.

Full Listing of
Tribunal Members and Honor Committee

Officers of the Permanent People's Tribunal

President:	François Rigaux (Belgium)
Vice-Presidents:	Ruth First (South Africa)
	Makodo Oda (Japan)
	Armando Uribe (Chile)
	George Wald (U.S.)
Secretary General:	Gianni Tognoni (Italy)

**Session on Guatemala of the Permanent People's Tribunal
(Madrid, Jan. 27-31, 1983)**

President:

George Wald — Vice President of the Permanent People's Tribunal
Former Professor of Biology at Harvard University
Nobel Prize winner

Members:

Victoria Abellán
Spain — Professor of International Law, University of Barcelona
Ex-Vice-Rector of the University of Barcelona

Richard Baümlin
Switzerland — Constitutional Jurist and Deputy Professor of Constitutional Law at the University of Bern
Member of Parliament

Amar Bentoumi Algeria	Ex-Minister of Justice General Secretary of the International Association of Democratic Jurists
Susy Castor Haiti	Professor of Sociology at the National Autonomous University of Mexico
Harvey Cox United States	Theologian Writer Victor S. Thomas Professor of Divinity, Chair of the Department of Applied Theology, The Divinity School, Harvard University
Eduardo Galeano Uruguay	Writer, specialist on Latin America
Giulio Girardi Italy	Philosopher Theologian
François Houtart Belgium	Professor at the Catholic University of Louvain Doctor Honoris Causa from the University of Notre Dame in Indiana
Leo Matarasso France	President of the International League for the Rights and Liberation of the People Lawyer in the Court of Paris
Dom Sergio Méndez Arceo Mexico	Bishop of Cuernavaca
Vicente Navarro United States	Physician Professor of Social Policy at Johns Hopkins University in Baltimore
James Petras United States	Professor of Sociology at the State University of New York at Binghamton
Adolfo Pérez Esquivel Argentina	Nobel Prize winner

Salvatore Senesse   Magistrate
Italy   Member of the Higher Council of the
                          Magistracy

Honor Committee:

His Excellency, The Mayor of Madrid, Professor D. Enrique Tierno Galván

Alfonso Bauer País: Guatemalan, Writer, Social Scientist, Lawyer

Luis Cardoza y Aragón: Guatemalan, President of the Guatemalan Committee of Patriotic Unity

Ernesto Campuano: Guatemalan, Lawyer

Ana, Widow of Colom Argueta: Guatemalan, Lawyer

Shirley, Widow of Fuentes Mohr: Guatemalan

Manuel Galich: Guatemalan, Ex-Minister of Education

Carlos Gallardo: Guatemalan, Vice President of the Guatemalan Committee of Patriotic Unity, Member of the PSD, Physician, Surgeon

Juan Gerardi: Guatemalan, Bishop of El Quiché

Carlos Paz Tejada: Guatemalan, Engineer, Colonel in the Army

Juan Aguirre Alonso: President of the Group and of the Board of Directors of Young Lawyers, Illustrious Association of Lawyers of Madrid

Rafael Alberti: Poet, Painter

José Alcina: Director of the Department of American Anthropology, Vice-Rector of the Universidad Complutense de Madrid

Vicente Aleixandre: Writer, Poet, Nobel Prize Winner

Serafín Aliaga: Secretary of the Department of International Politics of the C.C.O.O.

Marcos Ana: Secretary of the Department of International Policy of the P.C.E.

Carlos Collado Mena: President of the Regional Assembly of the Autonomous Community of Murcia

Jesús Vicente Chamorro: Prosecutor of the Supreme Court

Rafael Estrella Pedrada: President of the Foreign Relations Commission of the Senate

Benjamín Forcano: Representative of the John XXIII Theologians Group

Juan Gomis: President of the Spanish Commission for Justice and Peace

Julio González Campos: Rector of the Autonomous University of Madrid

Angel Hernández Craqui: Member of the Council of Social and Neighborhood Relations of the Municipal Government of Madrid

Alberto Iniesta: Auxiliary Bishop of Madrid

José Luis Lassaletta: Mayor of Alicante

Félix Martí Ambel: President of the MIIC (International Movement of Catholic Intellectuals)

Juan Antonio Martín Pallín: Prosecutor

Roberto Mesa: Vice-Rector of the Universidad Complutense de Madrid

Manuel Molina: President of the Foreign Relations Commission of the Congress of Deputies

Antonio Ojeda Escobar: President of the Parliament of Andalucía

Carlos París Amador: Professor

Luis Poveda: Theologian, Evangelical Church of Spain

Nicolás Redondo: General Secretary of the UGT

Manuel Simón; Secretary of the Department of International Politics of the UGT

Leopoldo Torres Boursault: First Vice-President of the Congress of Deputies

Luis Yáñez Barnuevo: President of the Institute for Iberoamerican Cooperation

Fernando Alvarez de Miranda: President of the Spanish Federal Council of the European Movement, President of the Humanism and Democracy Foundation

Alberto Aza: Coordinator of International Relations of the CDS

Marcelino Camacho: General Secretary of the C.C.O.O

Gabriel Celaya: Poet

Enrique Miret Magdalena: President of the Higher Council for the Protection of Minors

Raúl Morodo: Rector of the Menéndez Pelayo International University

Joaquín Nadal y Ferrara: President of the Federation of Municipalities of Catalonia

Mateu Sanclimes: Representative of the Capuchin Fathers of Catalonia

Luis Rosales: Poet

Complete Program*

Thursday, January 27

Welcome by the Mayor of Madrid, Professor Tierno Galván

Opening of the Session by the President of the Tribunal

Reading of the Permanent People's Tribunal's Invitation to the President of the Republic of Guatemala, Efraín Ríos Montt

Presentation of the Prosecutor, Edelberto Torres-Rivas

Presentation of the Guatemalan Human Rights Commission and the Reading of the Petition to the Tribunal for the Session on Guatemala

Presentation:	*Social Analysis of Guatemala* by Miguel Angel Reyes Illescas
Slide Show	
Presentation:	*Analysis of the Economic Structure* by Rafael Piedrasanta Arandi
Testimony:	Israel Márquez
Testimony:	Miguel Angel Albizures

Friday, January 28

Presentation:	*Historical Analysis of Guatemala* by Guillermo Toriello Garrido
Presentation:	*Report on the Guatemalan Army* by Gabriel Aguilera Peralta
Testimony:	Elías Barahona

---

*The presentations listed here were the full-length versions, not the synopses used in this volume. Presenters sometimes gave different titles to their short and long versions; as a result, titles of presentations as given below may vary from those used elsewhere in this book. We have also shortened some titles for reasons of length. —Eds.

Testimony:	Pedro Luis Ruiz
Presentation:	*Political Analysis of Guatemala* by Raúl Molina Mejía
Testimony:	Juan Velázquez Jiménez
Testimony:	Carolina van den Heuvel
Testimony:	Philippe Texier
Interrogatory	
Testimony:	Harald Edelstam
Presentation:	*Popular Culture, Indigenous Cultures, Genocide and Ethnocide in Guatemala* by Arturo Arias
Testimony:	Luis Felipe Irías
Testimony:	Rolando Castillo Montalvo
Testimony:	Pablo Ceto
Testimony:	Manuel José Arce
Presentation:	*We Charge Genocide: An Analysis of the Indigenous Question* by Ricardo Falla

Saturday, January 29

Presentation:	Tape Recording of General Efraín Ríos Montt's Speech at the Time of the Seizure of Power
Testimony:	José Efraín Rosales
Testimony:	Rigoberta Menchú
Testimony:	Gabriel Ixmatá
Testimony:	Juan José Mendoza
Interrogatory	
Presentation:	*On the Persecution of Christians and the Church in Guatemala* by Julia Esquivel
Testimony:	Carmelita Santos
Testimony:	Irma Consuelo de Azmitia
Presentation:	*On Human Rights in Guatemala* by Marco Antonio Sagastume
Testimony:	Guillermo Morales Pérez

Testimony: Miguel Morales Ordóñez
Interrogatory
Testimony: Regina Hernández
Testimony: Sandra Judith de Medina
Presentation: *The Complicity of the U.S. Government and U.S.*
                  Capital in the Violation of Human Rights
                  by Susanne Jonas
Presentation: *U.S. Penetration and Intervention in Guatemala*
                  by Jenny Pearce
Presentation: *International Legal Report on the Situation*
                  in the Republic of Guatemala
                  by Fernando Mariño Menéndez
Interrogatory
Closing of the Tribunal

Chronology of Guatemalan History

300–900 A.D.	Classical Mayan period centered in Tikal, El Petén. Theocratic society governed by priests; free federation of semi-autonomous states.
900–1524	Tribal rebellion, main cities abandoned. Arrival of Qukiché and Cakchiquel tribes from Mexico. During the 14th century, the Quichés establish their political hegemony in the area, build their capital in Utatlán. Intensive period of war and trade.
1524	Spanish conquest headed by Pedro de Alvarado. Two thirds of the native population die. Indians are deprived of their land. Guatemala becomes a Spanish colony. Principal export: cacao.
17th century	The Spanish transfer cacao production to Venezuela; indigo becomes the main export product. Indians are subjected to different types of forced labor (*encomienda, repartimiento*).
1784	Abolition of *encomienda* through new laws; the natives become direct subjects of the Spanish Crown. Strong tensions between Spain and local landowners.
1820	Indian uprising in Totonicapán.
Sept. 15, 1821	Independence from Spain.
1823	Creation of the Central American Federation.

1826-1829	Central American war between liberals and conservatives, factions of the upper class.
1831–1838	Mariano Gálvez (liberal) becomes President. British economic influence replaces Spanish hegemony. Important land concessions to British interests in El Petén.
1838	Gálvez is overthrown by a conservative armed movement. Dissolution of the Central American Federation.
1839–1871	Rafael Carrera (conservative) becomes President. Beginning of 40 years of conservative government.
1850	The discovery of cheap dyes in Europe ruins the cochineal industry.
1856	Dallas-Clarendon Treaty between England and the United States; the English give up their rights in Central America.
1871	The "liberal period" starts under the Presidency of Justo Rufino Barrios. Coffee becomes the main export product. The lands owned by the church and the Indians are confiscated and given to the owners of large land estates for coffee production. German economic influence begins.
1883	Foundation of the Polytechnic (Cadet Training School). Forced conscription of the Indians.
1901	First shipping agreement of the United Fruit Co. (UFC) in Guatemala.
1904	Minor Keith builds a railway; the banana railway empire starts.
1912	International Railways of Central America (IRCA, dominated by the UFC) takes over all the railways.
1914–1917	World War I. German economic influence decreases; U.S. economic influence grows.

1920	A "democratic" uprising overthrows the dictatorship of Estrada Cabrera. The U.S. company Electric Bond and Share takes over the German installations of the EEG (Electrical Enterprise in Guatemala), establishing a U.S. monopoly over energy supply.
1924	Formal land concession to the UFC for banana growing.
1929	The world economic depression affects coffee prices, hurting the economy of Guatemala.
1931	Jorge Ubico takes over the Presidency. The vagrancy laws take the place of other methods of forced labor for the Indians.
1933	One hundred people, including worker and student leaders and members of the opposition, are executed.
1940	During World War II, the U.S. government forces Ubico to nationalize German coffee interests.
June 1944	Popular pressure forces Ubico to resign. A military triumvirate takes over.
October 20, 1944	The October Revolution: a coalition of the urban petty bourgeoisie, students, intellectuals, and dissident army oficers overthrow the military junta.
October 1944	Indian uprising in Patzicía.
1945	Juan José Arévalo is elected President. The new Constitution abolishes the laws against vagrancy, establishes freedom of the press, and gives the vote to all adults except illiterate women. Autonomy from governmental power is guaranteed to the University.
1947	The Labor Code anticipates the organization of workers, allows the right to strike and other important workers' rights.

1949	The Forced Renting Law compels land-owners to rent their uncultivated lands to peasants.
1950	Jacobo Arbenz is elected President, with 63% of the votes.
1951	The PGT (Communist Party) is legalized.
1952	The Agrarian Reform Law is approved.
1953	The Arbenz government confiscates IRCA (railroad company) capital because IRCA did not pay taxes. The government takes 162,000 hectares of uncultivated land and distributes it to 100,000 families by the middle of 1954.
March 1954	OAS Conference in Caracas; the U.S. succeeds in getting approved a resolution against Guatemala, concerning hemispheric protection against "communist aggression."
June 18–27, 1954	The mercenary forces of Castillo Armas invade Guatemala from Honduras. Bombings by the CIA. Arbenz resigns.
July 8, 1954	Counterrevolution starts: the land distributed during the Agrarian Reform is given back to the landowners; labor unions and peasant movements are dissolved (labor groups' membership is reduced from 100,000 to 27,000); the National Defense Committee is established to carry out witch hunts against communism.
August 1954	The cadets' uprising in Guatemala City is crushed by official forces.
1955	New Oil Code gives subsoil rights to foreign oil companies.
May–June 1956	Large protest demonstrations against the Castillo Armas government by workers and students.

1957	Castillo Armas is assassinated by a right-wing sympathizer.
1958	Miguel Ydígoras Fuentes is elected President.
1959	The Industrial Promotion Law gives exemptions from income taxes and import duties to new industrial investments. Cuban Revolution.
1960	Ydígoras breaks relations with Cuba. He allows the U.S. to train Cuban refugees in Guatemala for the Bay of Pigs invasion.
November 13, 1960	Important uprising against Ydígoras with participation by one third of the army. When the government puts down the uprising, Luis Augusto Turcios Lima, Marco Antonio Yon Sosa, and Alejandro de Léon are forced to hide in the mountains of Izabal and Honduras.
1960	U.S. military advisers start the first "civic action" program. EXMÍBAL is established as a subsidiary to International Nickel and Hanna Mining Co. The Central American Common Market is formed.
1961	The PGT approves a resolution supporting armed struggle.
September 1961	Military leaders from five Central American countries meet and recommend the formation of a united defense council (which afterwards becomes CONDECA).
March–April 1962	Huge, very important demonstrations to overthrow Ydígoras by students and workers in Guatemala City.
December 1962	The guerrilla organization Rebel Armed Forces (FAR) is born from an alliance between the PGT and the army officers who took part in the November 13 uprising.

March 1963	Ydígoras is overthrown by a military coup d'état headed by Colonel Enrique Peralta Azurdia. The military government abolishes the Constitution.
June 1964	The FAR divides into the MR-13 and the PGT.
1964	CONDECA is established to coordinate alliances between all the Central American armies.
1965	EXMIBAL gets a 40-year mining concession. Colonel Houser, chief of the U.S. military mission, is assassinated. State of Siege is declared. A new Constitution is adopted and new elections planned.
March 1965	The FAR reappears from the merger of the PGT and the Edgar Ibarra Guerrilla Front. The MR-13 remains a separate organization.
March 1966	Julio César Méndez Montenegro is elected President. The U.S. intervenes with increased military and financial aid and a well-planned counterinsurgency campaign.
May 1966	Twenty-eight communists are arrested, tortured, and murdered.
October 1966	Turcios Lima dies in a car accident. Headed by Arana, the army starts an important counterinsurgency campaign in the northeast. A new right-wing terrorist group called MANO (the White Hand) is born in the northeast. Strong repression all over the country.
1967	The main guerrilla strongholds are seriously weakened by the government's counterinsurgency campaigns.
1968	Rogelia Cruz (Miss Guatemala 1959) is tortured and murdered by MANO. Two U.S. military advisers and the U.S. ambassador in Guatemala are killed by the guerrillas.

1969 | War between El Salvador and Honduras. Crisis in the Central American Common Market. The German ambassador is kidnapped and executed by FAR when the government refuses to meet their demands. OJO POR OJO (An Eye for an Eye), a new right-wing terrorist group, appears.

March 1970 | Carlos Arana Osorio is elected President.

November 1970 | A State of Siege is established (until November 1971). A new wave of terror starts; many assassinations are committed by rightists; curfew is imposed; press censorship, etc. The army occupies the University; Guatemala City is submitted to house-to-house searches. Julio Camey Herrera and Adolfo Mijangos are assassinated while Alfonso Bauer Paiz is wounded after protesting against the EXMIBAL contract and denouncing the terror.

February 1971 | The EXMIBAL contract is signed.

1971 | International campaign against Arana's terrorist government.

1972 | In spite of public protests, the Guatemalan government acquires the Electrical Enterprise of Guatemala for $18 million.

May–October 1972 | A very severe drought brings near-starvation to Guatemala's peasant farmers. The international monetary crisis affects Guatemala; serious inflation starts.

March–August 1973 | A teachers' strike spreads all over the country. The government is obliged to accede to the strikers' demands. A new period of strikes in the public sector starts. Popular demonstrations against the high cost of living.

March 1974 | General Ríos Montt, the opposition candidate, wins the election, but the government imposes the official candidate,

	General Kjell Laugerud García, by blatant fraud. Huge protest demonstration.
May 1, 1974	On International Workers' Day, demonstrators protest against the government's intimidation of the opposition and against the high cost of living.
July 1974	General Laugerud García takes over the Presidency.
1975	Guerrilla activities resume: the Guerrilla Army of the Poor (EGP). Paramilitary and police groups start up their violence again.
February 4, 1976	Earthquake: 25,000 persons die, 70,000 are injured, and more than a million become homeless.
April 1976	The National Committee of Labor Union Unity is created (CNUS).
1977	Repression extends to the workers' and students' movements.
March 1978	With 65% abstention, General Romeo Lucas García becomes President of the Republic. In spite of electoral fraud, the army is constituted as the guarantor of clean elections. The counterinsurgency strategy continues.
May 29, 1978	Panzós massacre of Indians. More than a hundred Kekchis are massacred by the army after having their lands divided among the officers in charge.
October 1978	General strike against the increase in urban bus fares.
February 1979	The Democratic Front Against Repression is established (FDCR). The popular and revolutionary struggle intensifies.
September 1979	A new guerrilla organization appears: the Organization of the People in Arms (ORPA).

January 31, 1980	The police set fire to the Spanish embassy: 39 peasants from Quiché, Spanish diplomats, and other Guatemalans are assassinated. Spain breaks diplomatic relations.
1980	The January 31 Popular Front is constituted (FP 31). Twenty-seven labor union leaders are kidnapped.
April 9, 1981	Massacre of Indian peasants in Quiché. General repression.
June 1981	The U.S. reinstates military aid to Guatemala.
January 1982	The Guerrilla Army of the Poor (EGP), the Rebel Armed Forces (FAR), the Organization of the People in Arms (ORPA), and the Guatemalan Labor Party (PGT) join together to form the Guatemalan National Revolutionary Unity (URNG).
February 1982	The Guatemalan Committee of Patriotic Unity (CGUP) is formed.
March 1982	The official candidate, General Aníbal Guevara, is fraudulently elected President of the Republic.
March 23, 1982	A coup d'état sets up a military junta of General Efraín Ríos Montt, General Horacio Maldonado Schaad, Colonel Francisco Luis Gordillo. The "scorched earth" strategy and new massacres start.
May 31, 1982	The Constitution is repealed. The military junta grants amnesty for political and common crimes together, for 30 days.
June 9, 1982	The military junta is dissolved. The army appoints General Ríos Montt as President of the Republic.
July 1, 1982	State of Siege is established. All individual and social guarantees are abolished for 30

	days. The "scorched earth" strategy is intensified.
August 1, 1982	State of Siege is extended for another 30 days. Secret tribunals are created. 100,000 people seek refuge in Mexico and Honduras. 500,000 are relocated.
September 1, 1982	State of Siege is extended again.
September 17, 1982	The first executions by the secret courts of the army.
October 1, 1982	State of Siege is extended.

Initials Used:

OAS	Organization of American States
EXMIBAL	Exploration and Exploitation of Izabal Mines, Inc.
CONDECA	Central American Defense Council (Consejo de Defensa Centroamericano)
MR-13	November 13 Revolutionary Movement
MANO	Movement for Nationalist Action (Movimiento de Acción Nacionalista)

References to Persons:

Carlos Arana Osorio, military man (Right)
Jacobo Arbenz, military man (Center-Left)
Juan José Arévalo, professor (Center-Left)
Carlos Castillo Armas, military man (Right)
Aníbal Guevara, military man (Right)
Romeo Lucas García, military man (Right)
Julio César Méndez Montenegro, lawyer (Center-Right)
Efraín Ríos Montt, military man (Right)
Jorge Ubico, military man (Right)
Miguel Ydígoras Fuentes, military man (Right)

INDEX

About the Editors

Susanne Jonas, Ed McCaughan, and Elizabeth Sutherland Martínez are all with the Institute for the Study of Labor and Economic Crisis (ISLEC) and on its editorial board.

Susanne Jonas, a noted Latin Americanist, has done research and writing on Guatemala since 1967. She co-edited the book *Guatemala* (with David Tobis) and wrote the book *Guatemala: Plan Piloto para el Continente.* She has published numerous articles on Latin America, especially Central America, in *Ramparts*, *Caribbean Studies*, *New Chile*, and other journals, and co-edited with Marlene Dixon the books *Revolution and Intervention in Central America* and *Nicaragua Under Siege.* A staff member of NACLA from 1971 to 1976, she is currently an associate editor of ISLEC's journal *Contemporary Marxism.*

Ed McCaughan has taught, lectured, and written extensively on Latin American affairs for more than 10 years. He co-authored the book *Beyond the Border: Mexico and the U.S. Today* and was formerly on the staff of NACLA. He is currently an associate editor of ISLEC's journal *Contemporary Marxism.*

Elizabeth Sutherland Martínez is the author or editor of numerous articles and books on political and social issues, including *The Youngest Revolution: A Personal Report on Cuba, Letters from Mississippi*, and *450 Years of Chicano History.* More recently, she has provided editorial assistance on publications of ISLEC concerning Latin America and Central America in particular.

Other Titles from Synthesis Publications

Nicaragua Under Siege
Marlene Dixon and Susanne Jonas (eds.)   036-4 $ 8.95

Revolution and Intervention
in Central America   029-1 cloth $19.95
Marlene Dixon and Susanne Jonas (eds.)   027-5 $10.95

The New Black Vote: A Look at Four
American Cities
Rod Bush (ed.)   038-0 $ 9.95

Black Socialist Preacher: The Teachings of
Reverend George Washington Woodbey   026-7 cloth $19.95
Philip S. Foner (ed.)   025-9 $ 8.95

The Future of Women   031-3 cloth $14.95
Marlene Dixon   021-6 $ 7.95

Grassroots Politics in the 1980s: A Case Study
*Institute for the Study of Labor and
Economic Crisis*   017-8 $ 6.95

Contradictions of Socialist Construction
Marlene Dixon and Susanne Jonas (eds.)   008-9 $ 4.95

Karl Marx Remembered:
Comments at the Time of His Death
Philip S. Foner (ed.)   020-8 $ 9.95

The New Nomads: From Immigrant Labor to
Transnational Working Class
Marlene Dixon and Susanne Jonas (eds.)   018-6 $ 8.95

Proletarianization and Class Struggle in Africa
*Bernard Magubane and
Nzongola Ntalaja (eds.)*   019-4 $ 8.95

World Capitalist Crisis
and the Rise of the Right
*Marlene Dixon, Susanne Jonas and
Tony Platt (eds.)*   016-X $ 8.95

ISBN Prefix: 0-89935
Order from your local bookstore or directly from the publisher. Send payment plus $1.50 for the first book, 50¢ for each additional book to **Synthesis Publications**, Dept. 140, 2703 Folsom St., San Francisco, CA 94110